Jhingran, Saral,
1939-

Aspects of Hindu
morality.

$26.00

DATE			

[redacted]

ASPECTS OF HINDU MORALITY

ASPECTS OF
HINDU MORALITY

SARAL JHINGRAN

MOTILAL BANARSIDASS PUBLISHERS
PRIVATE LIMITED
Delhi

First Edition: 1989

MOTILAL BANARSIDASS
Bungalow Road, Jawahar Nagar, Delhi 110 007

Branches
Chowk, Varanasi 221 001
Ashok Rajpath, Patna 800 004
24 Race Course Road, Bangalore 560 001
120 Royapettah High Road, Mylapore, Madras 600 004

ISBN: 81–208–0574–7

PRINTED IN INDIA

BY JAINENDRA PRAKASH JAIN AT SHRI JAINENDRA PRESS, A-45 NARAINA INDUSTRIAL AREA, PHASE I, NEW DELHI 110 028 AND PUBLISHED BY NARENDRA PRAKASH JAIN FOR MOTILAL BANARSIDASS PUBLISHERS PVT. LTD., DELHI 110 007.

TO MY HUSBAND

with love and gratitude

FOREWORD

The study of Hindu ethics is a recent phenomenon even though the literary sources are as vast as they are ancient. The approach adopted by most Indian writers in this field has been normative and apologetic, chiefly because of the bad press given the subject by early Western exponents, such as John McKenzie (1922) who concluded that "Hindu philosophy furnishes no satisfactory basis for an ethic," and Albert Schweitzer (1936) who dubbed the Hindu ethical system as "world and life negating". Regrettably, echoes of these voices are heard today through the international news media and also through formal studies, as India's population explosion, terroristic communalism and inveterate casteism are high on a long list of social evils which westerners attribute to a culture whose values are deemed fundamentally ascetical, illogical and anti-social. The defensive posture of Indian writers on ethics is therefore understandable, especially because of the widespread correlation in the Western world between economic underdevelopment and moral impoverishment.

Saral Jhingran, author of *Aspects of Hindu Morality*, breaks ranks with her colleagues and advances the study of Hindu ethics beyond the apologetic stage. She writes with the authority of one who knows the tradition from the inside, both in terms of its strengths and weaknesses, and for the most part succeeds in maintaining the objectivity of an impartial researcher.

The sources of her research are expanded beyond the classic philosophic texts to include materials dealing with such unconventional subjects as ritualism and polytheism. The inclusion of these data sets Hindu ethics in a lived context, and underscores the rich cumulative tradition which still lies waiting to be explored.

A major procedural problem in the discipline has been that of defining Hindu ethics. Jhingran adopts an ecological motif, demonstrating an organic relationship between ethics, on the one hand, and religion, philosophy and social culture, on the other. The relationship is both one of autonomy and dependence. The final picture that emerges of Hindu ethics is that of a discipline which is intellectually systematic, socially comprehensive, and yet always struggling with internal contradictions which are tackled in ingenious ways.

Saral Jhingran has earned the appreciation of her fellow ethicists for breaking ground in several places, and in a style and spirit that is as critical as it is sympathetic. And so, from these Hawaiian islands where East meets West, it is my hope that this book receives its due of warm aloha both in India and the West.

Department of Religion *Cromwell Crawford*
University of Hawaii

PREFACE

The present work aims at a critical evaluation of Hindu ethics in all its diversity, richness and profundity. It also seeks to understand Hindu ethics in the wider framework of entire Hindu 'religio-culture'. Very early in the course of this study I was forced to acknowledge certain basic truths about Hindu thought, both philosophical and ethical, which have not always been properly appreciated. They are: (i) The holistic nature of Hinduism in which ethical norms and values are integrally related to and naturally influenced by both Hindu religion and philosophy; (ii) The diversity and complexity of Hindu 'religio-culture' (including Hindu religion, philosophy and morality), so that any understanding of either Hindu religio-philosophy or morality in simplistic terms results in a grave injustice to the subject matter; and (iii) The limitations of the usual historical method of study in the context of Hindu 'religio-culture', as it fails to appreciate both the immense complexity of and the continuity in the religio-moral thought and values of Hinduism. This work, in a way, is based on the above three contentions which it also seeks to prove through arguments and exhaustive documentation.

Hinduism is an integrated whole in which religion, philosophy, morality and social culture are so intimately related, that neither morality, nor any other aspect of Hinduism, can be studied in isolation without reference to its other aspects. The words Hindu Dharma and Hindu 'religio-culture' are used in the present work to express this holistic concept of Hinduism. Starting with the assumption that Hindu morality is always directly or indirectly influenced by Hindu religio-philosophical thought, I have sought to understand and examine those beliefs and goals of Hindu religion and philosophy which seem to be presupposed by various concepts, norms and values of Hindu morality.

It is my further contention, and the entire work is based on it, that the Hindu Dharma (comprising Hindu religion, philosophy and morality) is a very rich, highly complex and composite whole which cannot be understood in a mono-polar terminology. Often a Western scholar picks up any one aspect of Hindu 'religio-culture', thoughtlessly equates it with the whole of Hinduism and then criticizes it on this faulty premise! Hinduism is so multi-faceted that different writers have been able to propound extremely divergent, highly superficial and one-sided views about it by the simple device of selectively quoting some passages from the Hindu texts and neglecting other equally relevant passages. Thus, there have been several misleading evaluations of Hinduism which understand it as world-and-life-negating, soul-centric and/or degenerate and amoral.

Such caricatures of Hinduism are due to the failure of these writers to comprehend the basic fact that Hinduism is not a unified creed like the Semitic religions, but is rather a complex and composite whole, comprising several religio-philosophical beliefs, values and practices which are often mutually incompatible. Thus, if some of the saints and philosophers of Hinduism advocate world-and-life-negation, there are others who affirm both the reality and worth of a life in the world. If Hinduism contains certain self-centric values and tendencies, it also emphasizes man's socio-moral obligations. On the negative side, if Hinduism affirms one universal Self in all beings, it also believes in the innate inequality of all men. If it expounds highly philosophical ideas, it also encourages crude polytheistic and ritualistic practices. It seems that there is a positive counterpart for every negative idea, value or tendency of Hinduism, and vice versa. Various beliefs, ideas and values of Hinduism are at once mutually contradictory and complementary. We are, therefore, led to the conclusion that Hindu religio-philosophy and morality can be understood in the right perspective only when the multi-dimensional nature and immense diversity of the Hindu 'religio-culture' are frankly recognized.

The present work seeks to take cognizance of and understand this diversity of Hindu Dharma by a working device of segregating it into several parallel religio-philosophical traditions. Such an analytical division of Hinduism helps to bring into focus various divergent religio-philosophical ideas and socio-moral values that constitute the composite Hindu 'religio-culture'. This is not meant to supplant the historical approach; rather it aims at supplementing it. Nor does giving cognizance to the diversity of Hinduism imply an undermining of the fact that Hinduism possesses a basic vision and a certain ethos which underlie all its immense diversity and changing phases. The underlying unity and diversity of Hinduism, as well as its immense adaptability, must be appreciated and understood in the context of their interrelationships, as reflected in the dynamics of Hindu 'religio-culture', for any serious attempt at understanding and evaluating Hindu morality. Such an understanding of Hindu Dharma paves the way for a reconstruction of the Hindu philosophy of morals which can meaningfully synthesize various ideas and values of Hinduism, and also accommodate modern moral perceptions and values.

No understanding of Hindu 'religio-culture' (including its morality) would be complete without reference to what is arguably the most glorious period of Hindu history, namely, that of Hindu renaissance during the nineteenth and first half of the twentieth century. A detailed study of this period is not included in the present work for two reasons: First, since my primary concern has been to relate the values and norms of Hindu morality to various religio-philosophical beliefs of Hinduism, I have relied exclusively on classical religio-philosophical texts, and was forced to leave out modern period of Hindu history. Secondly, there already exists a vast literature on the saints, thinkers and reformers of this period which is very comprehensive in nature, so that whatever I could have written on the subject would have been merely repetitive.

This may provoke an adverse comment, that since there is an equally vast literature on Hindu ethics, there was no need for another work on the same subject either. But except for a few comprehensive works like those of Surama Das Gupta and Cromwell Crawford, the majority of works on Hindu ethics are quite superficial in their understanding and treatment of the subject matter. A large portion of the existing literature on Hindu ethics comes from Western writers, whose critical comments only betray their ignorance and want of sympathetic understanding of the Hindu ethos. Indian authors have also generally failed to do justice to the immense richness and complexity of the

Hindu 'religio-culture' and morality. While most Indian thinkers have adopted an apologetic stance and tried to rationalize the various shortcomings and contradictions of Hindu thought and practice, some others have uncritically rejected Hindu philosophy and spirituo-moral values. And to the best of my knowledge, no one has seriously tried to relate Hindu moral values and norms to its religio-philosophical beliefs and goals, as I have attempted in this work.

In a departure from the usual practice, I have considerably enlarged the field of reference for the present study to include, in addition to the usual texts, the *Mahābhārata* and the Purāṇas. These works contain important discussions on moral issues and reflect the mores and values of the then Hindu society. Hence, they deserve more attention than is usually given to them.

The plan of this work was developed after long discussions with Prof. N.K. Devaraja whose guidance has been with me throughout the long period in which this work has been completed. He has also kindly read the final draft and given me his constructive suggestions. I am extremely grateful to him for his kind guidance. I am also profoundly grateful to Prof. Cromwell Crawford who has gone through two drafts of the work at various stages of its development and has given me extremely valuable suggestions for its improvement. Prof. Crawford has very kindly written the foreword to this work for which also I am very grateful to him. Prof. K.J. Shah has read my manuscript and given me his valuable critical suggestions, and I take this opportunity to thank him. I have also benefited by a long discussion with Prof. R.C. Gandhi who made me see certain shortcomings of my approach, especially concerning my treatment of the tradition of liberation, and I am naturally very grateful to him. My sincere thanks are due to Prof. G.C. Pande for his guidance and encouragement. He has read the final draft of the work and given his 'opinion' on it for which I am grateful to him. I am also thankful to Prof. K.K. Mittal whose kind guidance and constructive suggestions have helped me immensely, especially at the initial stages of this work. My son Dhir has helped in the final editing of the work, especially its language, and I appreciate his help and interest.

New Delhi —*Saral Jhingran*
November 1987

ABBREVIATIONS

Āpast D.S.	Āpastamba Dharmasūtra
B.G.	Bhagavadgītā
Bhāg. P.	Bhāgavata Purāṇa
Br. S.	Brahma Sūtra
Bṛhad. Up.	Bṛhadāraṇyaka Upaniṣad
Chān. Up.	Chāndogya Upaniṣad
Gaut. D.S.	Gautama Dharmasūtra
History	P.V. Kane, History of Dharmaśāstra
M.S.	Manusmṛti
Mbh.	Mahābhārata
Mbh. Anuś. P.	Mahābhārata, Anuśāsana Parva
Mbh. Āraṇ. P.	Mahābhārata, Āraṇyaka Parva
Mbh. Śān. P.	Mahābhārata, Śānti Parva
Ś.B.	Śaṁkara Bhāṣya
Up.	Upaniṣad
Yājñ. S.	Yājñavalkya Smṛti

CONTENTS

CHAPTER 1

HINDUISM THROUGH THE AGES

I. Intimate Relation between Religion, Philosophy and Ethics in Hinduism

As observed in the preface, the present work seeks to understand and evaluate Hindu morality in a new perspective. It takes the integrated nature of Hindu 'religio-culture' as its point of departure, and argues that Hinduism is a complex whole in which religion, philosophy and morality are soi nextricably bound together that a proper understanding of both Hindu religion and philosophy becomes a pre-requisite for any worthwhile attempt at understanding and evaluating Hindu morality. This may provoke a very basic question: Why should the study of Hinduism be a pre-requisite for a study of Hindu morality? This question implies the claim of ethics as an independent branch of learning which refuses to be subordinated to religion. It also raises, an even more basic issue of the relation, if any, between religion and ethics. True, ethical behaviour and ethics as a science do not necessarily presuppose a religio-philosophical creed. However, not only does every activity presuppose some knowledge of pragmatic matters, it also involves ideas or beliefs regarding the nature of the objective world and the subject. In moral behaviour man has to be conscious of himself as a moral agent, and this presupposes some definite concept of the human self, as also of the goal(s) or value(s) which man seeks to realize through his conduct. Human conduct, being a pursuit of moral values, also implies a faith in those values and a hope of their realization and conservation in the existing world order. Kant is right when he contends that our moral consciousness implies certain unprovable ontological beliefs regarding the world, the immortality of the soul and the Divine Providence. This does not mean that ethics is necessarily dependent upon religion for support; but man's metaphysical beliefs do seem to condition his entire approach to life and conduct. In the words of S. Radhakrishnan:

"Any ethical theory must be grounded in metaphysics, in a philosophic concept of the relation between the conduct and the ultimate reality. As we think the ultimate reality to be, so we behave; vision and action go together."[1]

The two, religio-philosophy and conduct, are inextricably linked together in Hinduism. Together they form both a view of life and a way of life. As explained by S.C. Chatterjee:

"In fact, the Hindu code of life never stands divided from Hindu philosophy. Rather, it is a code for a religious mode of life which is organically related to a theory of reality. In truth, Hinduism as a religion is both a view of life and a way of life which are related as the theoretical and practical sides of the same spiritual life."[2]

At the same time, the term religion has to be given a broader meaning in the context of Hinduism. In modern Western thought the term religion has come to mean a determinate theistic world view which generally understands ethical values and norms in terms of God's commands. Hinduism, however, is a curious phenomenon in which ethical problems are rarely discussed independently of religious ones, and yet in which the central ethical term *dharma* is completely independent of any reference to the Creator God. The Lord in Hinduism is the embodiment of all ethical qualities known to man, and yet man's ethical norms are in no way derived from His being or His commands, as in the Semitic religions. The term *dharma*, which is now loosely used as a synonym for religion, is much more profound and comprehensive than the latter. In its original usage *dharma* mainly meant duty or righteousness, both in the moral and the ritualistic contexts. It is this meaning of *dharma* with which we are most concerned in the present work and we shall have occasion to study it in the last section. But *dharma*, specially when it is prefixed by some such proper noun as *Sanātana* (Vedic) or Bauddha, means the whole of religion, philosophy and moral code of a given people or community. By Hindu Dharma we mean that integral way of life advocated in Hinduism which comprehends all the three, namely, religion, metaphysics and moral code.

Anyone wanting to study the morality of Hindus is confronted by the fact that in the Hindu 'religio-culture' there are no such compartmentalized fields of thought and practice, as religion, philosophy and morality. A person who seeks to study anyone aspect of this complex and rich 'religio-culture' will have to study all the related aspects, or else run the risk of distorting his own perception and understanding of the subject matter. It is to be remembered here that the marked distinction between the above three fields of knowledge is a product of modern Western thought. The thinkers of Renaissance were eager to free the mind and life of man from their centuries old bondage to the Church, and hence asserted the total independence of philosophy, morality and secular sciences from religion which was given a very limited deistic interpretation by them. The Western division between religious and secular concerns may be traced further back to the advice of Christ to render unto Ceaser the things that are Ceaser's and to God the things that are God's.[3] But no such division is possible in Hinduism wherein God, as we shall see, is the all-comprehending Absolute. Hinduism affirms a holistic view of life in which there are no marked distinctions between different aspects of life and thought. Thus, ethics has never been a separate subject in Hindu thought. At the same time, every Hindu treatise, whether concerned with religion, rituals, philosophy, polity or narration of stories, discusses moral questions and seeks to provide moral norms. Any study of Hindu ethics ought to take into account innumerable discussions on ethical matters, scattered throughout ancient Indian literature. Also, these diverse ethical viewpoints cannot be properly appreciated without a prior understanding of the different religio-metaphysical stands of various texts. Hence, the necessity of understanding all the facets of Hindu Dharma for a proper understanding of Hindu morality. Assuming that a study of Hindu Dharma is a pre-requisite to a proper understanding of Hindu morality, the next logical question would be: What exactly is meant by Hindu Dharma?

II. Hindu Dharma: A Multi-dimensional 'Religio-culture'

(i) The term Hindu is very wide and nebulous. The inhabitants of this vast sub-continent did not use any labels to describe their 'religio-culture'. The name Hindu was given to them by the Arab invaders very late in their history. As is well known, it does not refer to the religion or philosophy of the people, but only to their habitat, the Sindhu valley. It is our contention that Hinduism is a very complex 'religio-culture' and must not be understood on the basis of analogy with other world religions with definite, uniform creeds and codes of conduct. Any such attempt to understand Hinduism in mono-polar terms tends to misrepresent it. It is very difficult to do justice to the very complex phenomenon of Hindu 'religio-culture' through any one-sided definition. M. Monier Williams is right when he says:

"It may with truth be asserted that no description of Hinduism can be exhaustive which does not touch on almost every religious and philosophical idea that the world has ever known...

"Starting from the Vedas Hinduism has ended in embracing something from all religions and in presenting phases suited to all minds. It is all-tolerant, all-compliant, all-comprehensive, all-absorbing. It has its spiritual and its natural aspect, its esoteric and exoteric, its subjective and its objective, its rational and irrational, its pure and its impure. It may be compared to a huge polygon, an irregular multilateral figure. It has one side for the practical, another for the severely moral, another for the devotional and imaginative, another for the sensuous and sensual, another for the philosophical and speculative...And this capacity for almost endless expansion causes almost endless sectarian divisions..."[4]

Hinduism has always welcomed new ideas and practices, and at the same time it does not usually discard the old. As a result, we find in Hinduism the most profound philosophical speculations, existing side by side with the most primitive magical ideas; sublime ethical conceptions with gross rituals; worship of one God with the worship of serpents and trees etc.

Hinduism is different from other world religions in that it neither owes its origin to a single prophet or religious leader, nor does it have an organised church, or a single determinate creed. In the absence of any central church, Hinduism has ever been in the process of change, absorbing new ideas and creeds and modifying older ones under the impact of the new. The most important fact to be noted in this context is that Hinduism is not a product of a single people, as Christianity and Islam are. Instead, it is the outcome of the interaction between the Aryans and the non-Aryans (Dravidians?). It is generally agreed that when the Aryans came to India they found it already inhabited by people(s) with perhaps richer and more developed civilization(s). From the Vedas to Purāṇas there are innumerable references to wars between *asuras* (demons) and *devas* (gods, presumably the Aryans). Sanskrit texts also speak of various tribes as Vānara, Niṣāda, Nāga, Yavana, Kirāta, Draviḍa, Śaka and Āndhra.[5]

Rāmāyaṇa gives us impressive details of the cities of *vānaras* (monkeys) and *rākṣasas* (demons), as consisting of palatial buildings and beautiful gardens, inhabited by good-looking, well-dressed, soft-spoken natives, engaged in the pursuit of music and other arts.[6] Such descriptions clearly indicate the high level of civilization reached by the non-Aryan natives of India and belie the Aryans' nomenclature of them as monkeys or demons.

At first, the Aryans kept aloof from the non-Aryans. They tried to preserve their racial purity through the device of hardened caste rules which prohibited marriage outside one's caste. Yet such marriages always took place. Śāntanu, the grandsire of the Kauravas and Pāṇḍavas, married Matsyagandhā, a girl belonging to the fishermen's tribe. Arjuna married Ulūpī, belonging to the Nāga tribe, and Bhīma married Hiḍimbā, a *rākṣasī*. King Yayāti married the daughter of the teacher of *asuras*, the enemies of the gods (Aryans), and so on. The classifications of different kinds of marriage and their progeny, found in all the *Dharmaśāstras*[7], are just an attempt to give religio-legal sanction to such unorthodox unions. The non-Aryans were thus gradually abosrbed into the Hindu society, though they often retained some of their individaul customs, social norms and gods. For example, Arjuna and Kṛṣṇa's son and grandson married their cousins, even though such marriages are strictly prohibited in the Hindu Law-codes. There are other similarly interesting stories in the two Epics, suggestive of a matriarchal social organization and a social milieu very different from those of the Aryans.

Gradually a total amalgamation of these different peoples (except a few tribes) was effected through constant interaction, so that we now have neither Aryans nor Dravidians, nor any other people, but only Indians (or Hindus).

The *modus operandi* of this amalgamation is not clear. The conservative opinion, as represented by Prof. P.V. Kane, favours the possibility that the non-Aryans were absorbed into the Hindu society as śūdras. Prof. Kane points out that the word *varṇa* used for distinguishing social classes in the ancient Sanskrit literature, means colour. He argues that though the three classes of brāhmaṇas, kṣatriyas and vaiśyas were distinguished in the Vedic society, there was a much sharper demarcation between the Aryans and the *dāsas* or *dasyus*, suggesting that the two peoples were of different colours.[8] The Dharmaśāstras make a sharp distinction between the three twice-born (*dvija*) 'upper' classes and the śūdras. Gautama refers to the employer of a śūdra as an Arya, suggesting that the śūdras were non-Aryans.[9] The respective nomenclatures, Arya for the three 'upper' classes and dāsa or dasyu (slave) for the śūdras, the use of the term *varṇa* (colour) for classes and the extreme ill-treatment that was meted out to the śūdras, all suggest the possibility that the latter were actually non-Aryans.

At the same time, non-Aryan natives of India boasted of very high standards of civilization, and were probably even more advanced in many fields than the Aryans. It, therefore, does not seem very likely that they would have all accepted the lower-most position of śūdras in the Aryan society. Protima Bowes[10] argues that possibly the non-Aryans also had their class distinctions like the Aryans. For example, *Mahābhārata* speaks of the teacher of *asuras* as a brāhmaṇa. It is possible, therefore, that the non-Aryans were absorbed into classes (*varṇas*) parallel to those to which they originally belonged. As late as 4th or 5th century A.D. the nomadic tribes of Śakas, Kuṣāṇas, Ābhīras and Hūṇas from central Asia were absorbed into the Hindu society. Significantly, they were accommodated somewhere in the middle rung of the social hierarchy. Probably, those who were absorbed into the Hindu (Aryan) society were asked to form new sub-castes, which also explains the later prohibition of marriages and even dining between sub-castes.

There is a very interesting confirmation of this view in *Gautama Dharmasūtra*:

"If the Aryans and the non-Aryans interchange their occupations and conduct, (there is) equality (between them)."[11]

Interestingly, the same text has been quoted by Prof. P.V. Kane in support of his thesis that the Hindu thinkers mostly made a sharp distinction between the Aryans and the non-Aryans. Due to want of any historical evidence we can never be sure of the exact facts about the ancient Hindu society. But we can still be fairly sure that the Aryans did confront other civilized peoples(s), and that the present-day Hindu culture is so complex, varied and heterogeneous that it is best explained on the hypothesis of more than one source.

(ii) The Aryan religion and philosophy were constantly being modified by the inclusion of non-Aryan ideas, beliefs and even gods. The 'religio-culture' that has emerged as a result of the constant interaction between the Aryans and the non-Aryans is a very complex one. Some scholars call it Hinduism in contradistinction to the early Aryan or Vedic religion which is named Brāhmaṇism by them.[12] Hindus themselves do not subscribe to this division and trace their religion directly to the Vedas. We have accepted this distinction for reasons which will become clear as we proceed with our study. If we were to compare modern Hinduism with the Vedic religion, we would find that it contains a lot in the form of beliefs, rituals and values that can be directly traced to the Vedas. But it also contains so much else which has been apparently absorbed from some other source(s), that it cannot be understood exclusively in terms of the Vedic religion. For example, several Hindu gods and goddesses show possible non-Aryan influence. R.G. Bhandarkar has analysed the concepts of two main Hindu deities—Viṣṇu and Śiva, and found that they are composite concepts, some of their constituent ideas being possibly derived from non-Aryan sources.[13] The concept of the mother-goddess is still more significant, as it is more or less absent in the Vedas. Similarly, image worship which is so basic to the present-day Hinduism was unknown in the Vedic and post-Vedic periods, whereas there are indications that it was practised by the people of the Sindhu Valley civilization, and so on.

If we try to analyze the extremely complex 'religio-culture' of present-day Hinduism, we can easily distinguish two divergent traditions, one world-and-life-affirming and the other world-and-life-negating, to borrow the famous twin phrases of Albert Schweitzer. The two traditions have continued almost side by side in Hinduism and are in constant interaction, but have never been fully synthesized. According to Surama Dasgupta:

"Two different currents flowed in different courses (from the Vedas), one in the ritualistic line, then in social and legal laws and rules of conduct in the Sūtras and Dharmaśāstras, and the other in the intellectual and spiritual aspect, culminating in the Upaniṣads and thence in so many philosophical systems. These two ideals are entirely different types."[14]

While Surama Dasgupta thinks that both these currents of thought emanated from one source, the Vedas, others attribute them to two separate sources. Prof. G.C. Pande thinks that the contrast between the two approaches is so fundamental and far-reaching that it warrants the supposition of two divergent ethoses, probably originating among two separate peoples. According to him,

"The Vedic search for the spirit did not deny the world. It rather accepted the world as a gift and an expression of Divine reality. The Upaniṣadic quest seeks to go beyond the life of worldliness and ritualism centred in action, but does not usually advocate a radical renunciation of all life of action. Nor does it condemn the world as a vale of tears, although it recognizes the unsatisfactory character of worldly goods and gains and stresses the need for spiritual enlightenment...A quite different *weltanschauung* is expressed in the spiritual quest and thought of the wandering ascetics and mendicants whom we meet in the 6th century B.C. in north-eastern India."

He further observes,

"Mendicancy was in fact a Śramaṇic institute...His spiritual quest was in sharp contrast to the Vedic one in its attitude towards action and social obligations. Mendicancy implied an irreversible and final rejection of all social claims and obligations and of the efficacy of natural or ritual action in the context of spiritual seeking...

"There may be substantive identity between the Upaniṣadic ideal and the Śramaṇic ideal... (But) it is undeniable that they represented originally distinct approaches and conceptions. It is only through the interaction of these two traditions that the Upaniṣads came to be understood as *nivṛtti-lakṣaṇa* and opposed to the earlier Vedic tradition, characterized as *pravṛtti-lakṣaṇa* by the great Vedic scholar Śaṃkara..."[15]

Prof. G.C. Pande is a profound scholar of both Buddhism and Vedānta, not given to hasty generalizations, and his views are to be respected. But sometimes the thesis of two sources of Hindu culture is presented in such a sweeping manner,[16] that it becomes a mere cliche having no historical basis. The two ethoses found intermixed in the Hindu religio-culture are so distinct that we are often tempted to attribute them to two different peoples, the Aryans and the non-Aryans. At the same time, this is too simplistic an explanation to the very complex phenomenon of Hinduism. It does not explain how Buddhism and Jainism with their marked world-and-life-negation originated among the Aryan kṣatriyas, and how south India is still a stronghold of what we usually call Brāhmaṇism, even though we prefer to understand it as the Dravida region.

The diversity of Hinduism could well have originated within the Aryan society itself. It seeks that the kṣatriya kings not only refused to accept the supremacy of brāhmaṇas in the society, they also rejected the religion of the latter.[17] Probably a very different intellectual atmosphere prevailed in the court circles of kṣatriya kings, where long philosophical debates were held in which brāhmaṇas also participated. The Upaniṣads refer to several kṣatriya kings who were foremost among the teachers of the knowledge of *Brahman.* Thus, not only the heterodox sects of Jainism and Buddhism, but the Sāṁkhya and Vedānta also seem to have developed among the kṣatriyas. Strange though it may seem, the ideal of *ahiṁsā* also seems to have originated among the Aryan kṣatriyas, since there does not seem to be much scope for it in the ritualistic religion of the brāhmaṇas.[18]

The above discussion suggests that we can never be sure regarding the source(s) of the diversity of Hinduism. But we can still be very sure of the fact that the Hindu 'religio-culture' contains ideas, beliefs and attitudes which are quite divergent and even mutually incompatible. This fact is very important for a proper understanding of Hindu Dharma. It also provides the scope for a reformulation of Hindu philosophy of religion and morality, as we shall see in the last chapter.

III. Development of Hindu Moral Ideas Through the Interaction of the Two Religio-moral Traditions

As we have seen in the previous section, Hindu Dharma as it is today is the end result of a long process of interaction between two major and many minor religio-moral traditions. The emergence of this synthetic Hindu 'religio-culture' is best understood in historical perspective.

(i) The Vedic 'religio-culture' represents the first stage of the development of the complex Hindu Dharma, including Hindu morality. The Vedic Aryans were a vigorous people who loved the good things of life and frankly desired and prayed to gods for boons like plenty of cattle, rains, food and sons. Certain Western scholars contend that this positive attitude is no more found in post-Vedic Hindu culture which they characterize as negative and decadent.[19] Such thinkers are entirely mistaken about the philosophy and ethos of Hinduism.

The world-and-life-affirming spirit of the Vedas has persisted in Hinduism through the ages, though it is no more as naive and unconditional as it was in the Vedas. Thinkers like N.K. Devaraja and K. Satchidananda Murty[20] have argued in detail for the positive world-and-life-affirming spirit of Hinduism with the help of copious quotes from Hindu scriptures and Sanskrit literature. It will suffice here to point out that the Vedic-Hindu culture is rich in mundane values and is generally characterized by a positive or affirmative attitude towards the world and life. For example, the seer of *Īśāvāsya Upaniṣad* desires to live a hundred years performing actions in the right spirit; and the teacher of *Taittirīya Upaniṣad* prays for fortune which includes clothes, cattle, food, drink and also many students, renown and fame.[21]

In later Hinduism this positive attitude is all the more pronounced. Prosperity (*artha*) and fulfilment of desires (*kāma*) are given due importance, provided they are pursued according to righteousness (*dharma*), and the three together form the three human goals (*trivarga*) recognized in all the texts.[22] Manu recommends that one should desire the goddess of wealth (Lakṣmī) till death.[23] A typical prayer found in one of the Smṛtis expresses the extremely positive and affirmative Hindu attitude to world and life:

"O, Thou, endowed with lordly powers, give me beauty, fame, good luck; grant me sons and riches, and confer on me all desired objects."[24]

All the characters of *Mahābhārata* sing praises of wealth, saying that no other human value, not even righteousness (*dharma*), can be pursued without wealth.[25] Even today, Lakṣmī, the goddess of prosperity and good fortune, is one of the most popular deities in Hindu homes. Religious festivals and social functions are occasions for lavish spending of wealth which is greatly admired by the masses. The Aryans' love and admiration for world and life are responsible for their unconditional approbation of the life of the householder. It is asserted that a householder alone can realize for himself all the values of life, as well as provide sustenance and support to all other sections of the society.[26] The original Aryan ethos is thus not only a positive one, it is also one of aggressive self-assertion and effort. According to *Mahābhārata*:

"One should never give up effort, even if failure is almost a certainty. If a man acts, there are two possibilities that he may or may not succeed, but if he does not act at all, there is only one possibility that he would never realize his end."

And,

"It is only right for a man never to insult himself, thinking himself to be insignificant, because those who belittle themselves can never acquire fortune or glory".[27]

The ancient Aryans were pragmatic people who even accepted violence as an integral part of life on the plea that it is unavoidable in everyday life.[28] Even *Bhagavadgītā* uses the philosophical beliefs regarding the immortality of the soul and transmigration as arguments in support of Arjuna's duty to wage the war.[29] In fact, killing was the accepted duty of kṣatriyas in the ancient Hindu society, and it was assured that a kṣatriya who is killed in war goes to heaven.[30] In addition, the king was expected to exercise *daṇḍa* or punishment which was even hailed as the only means to preserve the social order and keep people on the path of righteousness.[31]

This Vedic-Hindu approach was also socio-centric. The Vedic seers cherished and prayed for the harmony of thoughts, actions and interests among various members of the society.[32] Religion has all through provided a solid basis for social integration in Hinduism. Socio-cultural functions are presided over by priests and performed with Vedic *mantras* in the Hindu society, or we may say that the Hindu religious rites always have a socio-cultural connotation. For example, the marriage ceremony is performed with elaborate religious rituals; but the chief significance of marriage lies neither in its religious function, nor in its being a personal concern of two individuals, but in its being a social institution. The girl is married not to an individual, but into a family, and the couple start their new life with a very clear concept of their duties towards their family and the society. The original Aryan world-view affirms an organic relation between the individual and the society and emphasizes his indebtedness to his parents, teachers and fellow beings.[33]

Hereditary caste system has long governed not only the Hindu social organization, but also the Hindu way of life. It is responsible for the various evils of Hindu society and morality, and there is no justification whatsoever for its continuance in modern times. But in its original conception the division of society into classes (*varṇas*) was developed with a view to social stability and harmony. In a caste-oriented social organization the interests of the society are the governing consideration in determining the individual's life. According to the Advaita philosopher Sureśvara:

"Duties of four classes lead to common welfare, even as a palanquin is carried by four persons."[34]

This world-and-life-affirming ethos is closely linked with and strengthened by Hindu polytheism and ritualism. The Vedic seers performed their rituals and worshipped their gods with specific desires in mind. The old Vedic gods and rituals have long since been replaced by new Hindu gods and simpler Purāṇic rituals. But the motivation behind the worship of new gods and the performance of later rituals is the same, namely, the desire for the well-being and prosperity of the family. Hindu polytheism is thus constantly strengthened by Hindu appreciation of mundane goods, and vice versa.

The world-and-life-affirmation and the social orientation of the original Aryan tradition has had a very positive influence on Hindu ethics. The moral values and virtues that are affirmed in this tradition are conceived in a pragmatic and social context. Thus, apart from truth (*satya*), magnanimity (*dāna*) is the most admired virtue of Vedic 'religio-culture'. Performing one's religio-moral duties and self-effort are some of the other virtues admired in the Vedic-Dharmaśāstric tradition.

The simple religion of Vedas gradually deteriorated into an extreme form of externalistic ritualism in Brāhmaṇas (around 1000 B.C.). Brāhmaṇas developed Vedic sacrifices into extremely complicated and elaborate affairs and asserted that the correct performance of Vedic ritual(s) automatically resulted in the realization of the desired fruit(s) by the performer. This externalistic approach undermined both religious piety and the moral point of view. The Brāhmaṇical ritualism generally equated moral duty with the performance of Vedic rituals, which further confused the moral point of view. The overriding emphasis on rituals led to the excessive importance of brāhmaṇa priests and thereby strengthened the division of society into hereditary castes.

Though most of the Vedic rituals have now become obsolete, the spirit or approach of the ritualistic religion of the Vedas continues to characterize the present-day Hindu Dharma and enjoys a determinative influence on Hindu morality. Thus, the Vedic 'religio-culture' and all the subsequent stages of the development of Hindu religion and morality are not to be understood as merely stages or phases which Hinduism passed through centuries ago. Rather, every period of Hindu history has contributed to its immense richness and diversity and has survived in it in the form of certain beliefs, values and practices. The usual historical approach generally fails to appreciate this continuity of Hinduism.

(ii) The second stage of the development of Hindu Dharma (which includes both Hindu religio-philosophy and morality) is the one which gave birth to all the great philosophies of India. A great intellectual and spiritual unrest and an urge to question and find answers to the ultimate mystery of life seem to have stirred the Aryans, especially the kṣatriyas, near about the 6th century B.C. Jainism, Buddhism, Sāṁkhya and Vedānta are the products of this spiritual unrest. All of them express the dissatisfaction felt by the intellectual elite of the society against the externalistic approach and violence of Vedic rituals. The various religio-philosophic systems of this period rejected not only the Vedic religion, but also its goals like prosperity here and heaven hereafter. Instead, they sought to transcend them in their quest of liberation. Though they conceived liberation very differently, and also put forward very different ontologies, they shared their spiritual urge and their conviction that the quest of liberation is to be undertaken by turning the mind away from the world and towards the reality within oneself. These philosophies were probably developed independently, but there was continuous interaction between them.

The Vedāntic monism was conceived during the same period (approximately between 1000 to 500 B.C.). Its philosophy and valuational approach were developed in conscious contradiction to the Brāhmaṇical ritualism. Upaniṣads criticize the performers of Vedic sacrifices as blind men led by the blind,[35] and emphasize the worth of inner spirit and experience, as against the external acts. They also affirm the goal of liberation and understand it in terms of mystico-unitive experience. Since liberation can be achieved only through some kind of intuitive realization of the metaphysical truth, neither ritualistic acts, nor ethical conduct can directly be instrumental to the realization of liberation. And yet, ethical discipline and conduct are greatly valued in the Vedāntic tradition as a necessary pre-requisite of any quest of liberation.[36] The most cherished virtues of this tradition are those of self-culture like knowledge of metaphysical truth (*vidyā* or *viveka*), dispassion (*vairāgya*) and control of the senses and mind (*dama* and *śama*), though kindness and forgiveness are also appreciated.

Like all mysticism, the Upaniṣadic mystical philosophy is also transcendentalist in its approach and emphasis; but it is not directly world-and-life-negating. Since the inner Self is also the Creator and the Inner-controller of the world diversity,[37] the latter is not illusory or worthless in the Upaniṣads, as in the later Advaita Vedānta. That is why, the renunciation of the world (*saṁnyāsa*) is not mandatory in them. In fact, the basic philosophy and valuational approach of Upaniṣads is much more balanced and positive than that of Advaita Vedānta and later Hinduism.

At about the same time (660 B.C. onwards), the heterodox sects of Buddhism and Jainism were being developed, (Jainism is possibly older.) The supposedly orthodox system of Sāṁkhya was also probably developed independently during the same period. As convincingly argued by Prof. G.C. Pande, the three religio-philosophical systems of Sāṁkhya, Buddhism and Jainism have much in common and express a very different ethos from that of Vedānta. Here we are mainly concerned with Sāṁkhya which has been recognised as an orthodox system in Hinduism. The ontology, world-view and valuational approach of Sāṁkhya are very different from those of the Vedic-Vedāntic tradition. And yet, Sāṁkhya is the second most important philosophy of Hinduism, the first being Vedānta. In fact, most of the inner tensions and inconsistencies of Hinduism can be traced to this double influence.

Sāṁkhya posits two ultimate realities, *puruṣa* (self) and *prakṛti* (nature). It believes in the plurality of selves, transmigratory existence and the essential duality between self and nature (or body), and conceives liberation as the self's realization of its original pure being. Sāṁkhya also believes in the world as full of suffering and asserts the right of the individual to reject all his socio-moral obligations for the sake of his personal liberation. On the other hand, Vedānta affirms an all-comprehending Absolute, the reality or Self of all individual selves, as well as of the objective world. Though Upaniṣads seem to be familiar with the ideas of karma and transmigratory existence, there are indications that these were rather new ideas for the Upaniṣadic seers.[38] And the idea of the world as full of suffering and hence undesirable is unknown in the Vedic-Vedāntic tradition.

And yet, Advaita Vedāntins conceive their Absolute (*Ātman-Brahman*) in terms of the Sāṁkhya *puruṣa* and liberation (*mokṣa*) in terms of the Sāṁkhya *kaivalya*. The popular religious texts, *Bhagavadgītā*, *Mahābhārata* and Purāṇas, have uncritically accepted the entire Sāṁkhya cosmology, including its doctrine of the plurality of souls and transmigratory existence.

Not only the authors of the popular religious works, but later Advaitins also accepted the Buddhist-Jaina-Sāṁkhya perception of the world as full of suffering, and hence undesirable, a perception so unlike the joyous approach of the Vedic Aryans. This new perception has engendered in the Hindu mind a morbid fear of getting involved in the transmigratory existence and a desire to escape therefrom through the renunciation of the world. The world-and-life-negation inherent in this approach has had a considerable influence on Hindu morality.

The later Vedāntins further imbibed the extreme individualism that goes with the Sāṁkhya ontology. A closer look at the two world-views and valuational approaches would reveal the diversity of the two points of view. Yet, even though Vedānta remains the basic philosophy of Hinduism, Hindu thinkers have incorporated in their thought both Sāṁkhya ontology and its individualism. The latter has had far-reaching negative ramifications for Hindu morality.

(iii) Dharmaśāstras (including both Dharmasūtras and Smṛtis), the two Epics (*Rāmāyaṇa* and *Mahābhārata*) and Purāṇas represent the third stage of the development of Hindu religio-philosophy. They were written and finalised during a very long period, stretching approximately from about 5th century B.C. to 15th century A.D. These religious texts do not propound any well-defined system of philosophy or religion. Yet they express a very important tradition of Hinduism which has gradually become coextensive with entire Hinduism. We can call it popular or synthetic tradition which is the outcome of prolonged interaction between the two religio-philosophical traditions and persistent efforts to synthesize their diverse beliefs, ideas and valuational attitudes. The Dharmaśāstras are in the direct line of the Vedic tradition, though they reflect the influence of the second tradition also and even seek to reconcile the two. The Epics show a much more marked intermixing of the two philosophies and valuational approaches. The Purāṇas are another important source of this synthetic religion and morality of popular Hinduism, and contain all the diverse beliefs, values and attitudes that are found in any of the above traditions of Hinduism.

There are indications of initial antagonism for the creed of world-renunciation among the supporters of the Vedic tradition. Thus, different characters of *Mahābhārata* express divergent philosophico-ethical standpoints and their arguments and counter-arguments make interesting reading. Yudhiṣṭhira, being overwhelmed by the violence and destruction involved in the Mahābhārata war, wanted to give up his kingdom and become a recluse. He argued passionately for absolute freedom, peace and transcendence of worldly concerns enjoyed by a renunciant. His wife, brothers and friends were shocked by such an unmanly desire and rebuked him in no uncertain terms. They declared the life of renunciation as unmanly, unworthy of a king, and even denounced it as un-Vedic. The only life worth living, according to them, is one of manly action, dedicated to the pursuit of three goals of prosperity, desire fulfilment and righteousness. The long dialogue between Yudhiṣṭhira, his brothers and his wife[39] suggests the relative independence of the two traditions. Similarly, *Mokṣādharma Parva* of *Mahābhārata* discusses liberation, but this discussion is constantly interrupted in order to discuss petty rituals, the importance of brāhmaṇas etc. Perhaps till the time of the Epics the creed of renunciation was not fully developed or defined and its implications were not properly understood; it was even less popular.

Various syntheses of the two traditional viewpoints have been attempted in Dharmaśāstras and the Epics. The Dharmaśāstric scheme of four goals of life (*puruṣārthas*), viz. *dharma* (righteousness), *artha* (prosperity), *kāma* (pleasure) and *mokṣa* (liberation), is one such attempt to synthesize the two rather divergent viewpoints. As we shall see in the course of our study, the group of first three goals (*trivarga*) is inconsistent with the final goal of liberation. In fact, the proper eschatological goal of a life dedicated to the realization of the first three goals should have been heaven which has been frankly recognized by various religious texts.[40] Still, instead of heaven, liberation is included as the fourth and final goal of human life. It is argued that the first three are the legitimate goals for the first half of a man's life, while liberation is the proper goal of the latter half. This brings us to the scheme of four stages of life (*āśramas*), i.e. those of the student celibate (*brahmacarya*), the householder (*grahastha*), the forest dweller (*vānaprastha*) and the renunciant (*saṁnyāsa*). There is also a very significant stipulation in *Dharmaśāstras* that a man must not renounce the world without first fulfilling all his socio-moral obligations.[41] This stipulation in a way bridged the gulf between the two valuational approaches, and it was only when this condition was removed that the two ways of life, i.e. those of activity (*pravṛtti*) and withdrawal from activity (*nivṛtti*), were seen as mutually inconsistent and irreconcilable. Again, the first two or even three stages of life express an ethos, entirely different from that of the stage of renunciation which seeks to transcend all the distinctions and values of the first three stages of life.[42] As we shall see in the third chapter *infra*, even though the scheme of four stages of life was formally meant for males of the three upper classes, it was practised by a few spiritually inclined people only.

The two traditions of an active life-in-the-world (*pravṛtti*) and renunciation of the world (*nivṛtti*) have mostly flourished side by side in Hinduism to this day. At the same time, the impact of the second tradition has been intensely felt by the followers of the first tradition. Pessimistic sentiments denouncing life-in-the-world and exalting world-renunciation are found in all Hindu religious texts. Hindus even now admire and venerate the renunciant above all, though they themselves may be leading a very mundane life. The virtues of the second tradition have also been incorporated in the morality of popular religious texts which mainly subscribe to the first, i.e. Vedic world-view. This is amply borne out by the development of the ideal of *ahiṁsā* (*non-injury*) in Hinduism.

As we know, the early Aryan way of life was not particularly given to the ideal of non-violence, while it is the central creed of the heterodox sects of Buddhism and Jainism. At first the Hindu thinkers tried to reconcile the two approaches by saying that all violence is a sin, except that done for the purpose of Vedic rituals.[43] A more meaningful synthesis was later on achieved through the development of non-violent sacrifices in which cereals, butter etc. are poured into the fire.[44] Significantly, while the virtue of *ahiṁsā* is only half-heartedly recognized in Dharmaśastras which are the true heirs to the Vedic tradition, it finds a much stronger exposition in *Mahābhārata*. Non-violence is declared to be the highest duty by the Epic.[45] But it was only with the development of the theistic-devotional (Bhakti) tradition that the ideal of non-violence was fully integrated into the Hindu ethos.

In addition to non-violence, Dharmaśāstras and Epics appreciate and recommend almost all the conceivable personal and inter-personal moral virtues. Sometimes the two sets of virtues, associated with the above two approaches, were reconciled by the artificial device of ascribing them to different stages of life, or different classes of people. Thus, brāhmaṇas and renunciants were expected to be non-violent, forgiving, forbearing and equable towards all and under all circumstances, whereas the kṣatriyas and the householders in general were expected to be extremely active, dutiful and magnanimous. A more meaningful synthesis of the two classes of virtues is achieved in *Bhagavadgītā*'s ideal of the selfless performance of one's duties with kindness and equanimity towards all.

This brings us to *Bhagavadgītā* which is a part of the present *Mahābhārata* and is the greatest syncretizing work, ever produced by man. It accepts from the Vedic tradition the idea of the meaningfulness of the world creation and the necessity of everyone's performing one's allotted duties in order to contribute to the maintenance of the world-order.[46] From the Sāṁkhya tradition it accepts the doctrines of karma, transmigratory existence,[47] the dualism of the self and the body-mind complex and the transcendent, actionless nature of the self.[48] It seeks to reconcile all these heterogeneous ideas in its ideal of desireless performance of all actions. It then adds Vedāntic theism to this unique conglomeration, and concludes that the duties should be performed with detachment, equanimity and a spirit of total self-surrender to the Lord.[49]

The Purāṇic period followed that of the Epics and was co-extensive with a very long period of Hindu 'religio-culture' (from 600 A.D. to about 1500 A.D.). The most significant characteristic of the Purāṇic approach was its new-found concern for the masses who were so far neglected by the Hindu elite. But in their eagerness to provide a religion that could satisfy the needs of the masses, the Purāṇic authors adopted a very irrational (mythological) approach to religion and morality. The religion of Purāṇas is polytheistic and ritualistic; their world-view is marred by their obsession with the other world; and the morality advocated by them is often stale, reactionary and superficial. And yet, in between so much that is inane and worthless, we find glimpses of genuine moral awareness and appreciation of highest moral values. The distinction between the two valuational approaches is obliterated in Purāṇas which advocate the virtues of magnanimity, compassion and non-injury, alongside those of detachment and equanimity.

(iv) The Bhakti movement signifies the fourth stage of the development of Hindu Dharma. Though historically it was concurrent with the Purāṇic period, its spirit and valuational approach are mostly different from those of Purāṇas. The Bhakti tradition originated with the Āḷwar saints of Karnataka in the last two centuries before Christ, spread to Maharashtra and then to the north, and continued to dominate Hindu thought and life till about 16th century A.D. It was developed in contradistinction to Vedic 'religio-culture'. Its greatest contribution to Hindu morality lies in its rejection of the relevance of caste distinctions in determining the worth of a person. Significantly, most of the Bhakti saints came from lower classes. Many of the saints were householders. They lived and preached among the masses and thus helped in sustaining a pretty high level of religio-moral consciousness among the Hindus through a very long period of their history.

This theistic-devotional tradition is essentially Vedāntic in its philosophy and world-view. It has achieved a unique, though not so philosophical, synthesis of Vedāntic monism and theistic-devotional approach in religion. The Lord in this tradition is at once the object of intense devotion (*ekāntika bhakti*) and the innermost Self of all. There was also some influence of Islamic monotheism on some of the later devotional saints like Kabīr and Guru Nānak. But the devotional tradition has been intensely monotheistic since the very beginning; and so the influence of Islam only strengthened its own religious perception.

In its original conception, the devotional philosophy is not world-and-life negating. At the same time, like all mysticism the world over, it has an inner urge for transcendence of the world and its values in order to enjoy the unitive experience. The morality recommended in this tradition is one of spontaneous goodness, love and kindness for all.

(v) The fifth stage of the development of Hindu Dharma begins with the modern age of Indian history. It was preceded by the darkest period of Indian history during the first two centuries of the British rule (from the later half of 17th century to the first half of 19th century). The nineteenth and the first half of the twentieth century saw an unprecedented intellectual and spiritual awakening in the Hindu society. Raja Rammohan Roy (last quarter of eighteenth century) heralded the Hindu renaissance which was carried forward by such spirituo-moral giants as Swami Dayananda Saraswati, Ramakrishna Paramahansa, Swami Vivekananda, Sri Aurobindo, Ramana Maharshi, Ishwara Chandra Vidyasagar and Mahatma Gandhi. Innumerable social reformers, political leaders, intellectuals and scientists contributed towards the liberation of the Hindu mind from the shackles of dogmas and taboos that oppressed it for the past several centuries. There was a marked difference in the philosophy and values of the various thinkers, religious leaders and social reformers of this period. Between them they represented the whole spectrum of the rich Hindu 'religio-culture'. Thus, Ramakrishna Paramahansa was the paradigm of devotional mysticism (*bhakti-mārga*); Ramana Maharshi was a contemplative mystic who exemplified the way of knowledge (*jñāna-mārga*); Sri Aurobindo was, of course, the epitome of the yogic *sādhanā* (discipline) and Swami Vivekananda and Mahatma Gandhi were ideal men of action (*karmayogins*).

At the same time, they all shared certain beliefs and values which characterize the Hindu renaissance. First, all Hindu thinkers of this period were fired by an intense pride for the ancient Hindu religio-cultural heritage. Whether it was Rammohan Roy, Swami Dayananda Saraswati or Swami Vivekananda, they all looked towards the ancient Hindu philosophy and religion for inspiration and guidance. They also idealized the ancient culture and morality and often presented it as a panacea for all the evils of the present-day society.[50]

Secondly, almost all the leaders of Hindu renaissance, with the exception of Swami Dayananda, had Western education and were influenced by modern Western methods of rational inquiry, as also by modern humanitarian and liberal ideas. As we shall see in chapter IV *infra*, ancient Hindu thinkers were capable of the most sublime philosophical vision and religious insight, but they hardly ever tried to develop the practical implications of their vision. In contrast, many modern thinkers, specially Swami Vivekananda, sought to give a new and more meaningful interpretation to the Vedāntic vision of one Self in all and made it the basis of a moral philosophy of the dignity of man as man, the equality of all men and man's duty of love and service of his fellow beings.[51] Other Hindu thinkers like Rammohan Roy, Keshab Chandra Sen and Mahatma Gandhi were similarly influenced by Western liberalism and rationalism, and quite successfully tried to synthesize modern Western values with ancient Hindu philosophy. It goes to the credit of Hinduism that it could accept and absorb radically new ideas and values without in any way feeling endangered by the onslaught of Western thought.

Thirdly, unlike the ancient Hindu thinkers and saints, modern thinkers were eager for social reforms. Perhaps due to the impact of Western thought, they were intensely conscious of the religio-social evils that afflicted the contemporary Hindu society, and attacked them on two fronts, intellectual and practical. Thus, Raja Rammohan Roy successfully campaigned against the inhuman practice of *satī* (self-immolation of widows), and both Swami Dayananda and Mahatma Gandhi waged an incessant war against the hereditary caste system and the practice of untouchability. Many thinkers and social reformers successfully campaigned against caste discriminations, the practice of untouchability and the unjust treatment of womenfolk in the Hindu society. Ishwara Chandra Vidyasagar in Bengal and Jyoti Rao Phule, D.K. Karve and M.G. Ranade in Maharashtra were the pioneers of the struggle for the rights of women, such as equal education, widow marriage etc. Other thinkers of Hindu renaissance like Keshab Chandra Sen, reformers like Swami Dayananda and Jyoti Rao Phule criticized and actively preached against such religious practices as idolatry and polytheism.

Lastly, there was an unprecedented emphasis on personal moral conduct, the employment of fair means to achieve the right ends and the individual's obligations towards the whole of society. All religious thinkers and socio-political leaders of this period were the epitomes of integrity, sincerity and selflessness. Both, the national movement and public life, were governed by highest moral norms, which makes this period the pinnacle of Hindu socio-moral thought and conduct. The contemporary Hindu society falls much short of the level of idealism and morality that was achieved not only by the leaders, but also by the masses during that glorious period of Indian history. Hinduism has been immensely enriched by the lasting contribution of these spirtuo-moral giants of the Hindu renaissance in the fields of thought, morality and social reform; and it will never be the same again after them.

Hinduism thus comes to us as a dynamic religion which has never been presented as a finished product. Several different religio-philosophical traditions and innumerable generations of thinkers, saints and reformers have contributed to its immense richness and complexity, so that it is ever changing under the impact of new ideas and its own inner dynamism.

IV. Causes of the Diversity of Hinduism and Its Immense Adaptability

If someone were to call Hinduism polytheistic, he would be right to a limited extent, and if another described it as monistic, he would also be right, as would be the person who understood it as basically theistic. Some misguided critics call it pantheistic, others soul-centric; and they all find some sort of documentary evidence in support of their mutually contradictory theses. But this is not all; Hinduism also includes in it such lowly beliefs and practices, as the worship of innumerable petty deities, and even trees, snakes and stones.

(i) The question then arises as to how and why such diverse and even self-contradictory practices have continued to flourish side by side in Hinduism. Several related explanations of this unique phenomenon are given. First, it is argued that Hindus worship the 'Divine' in many forms, but know that they are worshipping the same Reality. Sarasvati Chennakesavan has expressed this idea eloquently:

"Each man worships God in the form that most appeals to him and attracts him. When this idea is combined with the idea that God is one, although He appears in many forms, we have the gist of Hindu theology......Every thing great and useful like the rivers, every thing that is strong and monstrous like the creeping contagious diseases are Gods. Evil and good, destruction and preservation are God."[52]

Now, though Ms. Chennakesavan implies as if she is presenting one single argument, in fact the above passage contains two quite unrelated assertions. While the first refers to the basic Hindu faith that the one 'Divine' is worshipped in many forms; the second asserts that the worship of natural forces, inanimate objects and diseases is inspired by the vision of one 'Divine' 'as' all. But the mystical vision of ultimate unity need not inspire the worship of the Supreme in His lowest manifestations. Rather, such objects are worshipped by the aborigines, because their minds are incapable of rising to a higher perception of the 'One'. It is much more likely, therefore, that such practices were borrowed from the tribes that co-inhabited India along with the Aryans.

The first part of the above argument is more relevant. This argument was first formulated by Swami Vivekananda. According to it, Hinduism is widely tolerant and accepts all faiths and gods as so many ways to the one Truth. Not only does Hinduism respect all other faiths, but it is also ready to assimilate any beliefs, values or practices of other faiths which may appeal to it. The ignorant criticism that Hinduism makes no distinction between higher and lower forms of faith is wrong. Hinduism does make such a distinction, though at the same time, it does not condemn the lower as trivial or blasphemous. But, why do we need to preserve the lower faiths in the face of the higher one? And if the lower faiths are not to be condemned and destroyed, should they not be transformed and spiritualized?

This leads us to the second rational explanation or rationalization of the immense diversity of Hinduism in the form of the theory of *adhikāra-bheda*. The doctrine is quite common, but like the doctrines of karma and transmigratory existence, it is generally taken for granted and not clearly formulated. It was again Swami Vivekananda who first used it for a rational defence of Hinduism. According to it, different men have different temperaments, intellectual and emotional needs and equally different capacities, so that one uniform creed cannot possibly suit all persons. Hinduism, therefore, gives the freedom to choose the creed or god (*iṣṭā devatā*) that appeals most to a man's temperament and intellectual capacity, and is best capable of eliciting a proper religious response out of that particular nature.[53] Vivekananda further argued that if a man is allowed to practise the creed that suits his needs most, he would gradually rise to higher levels of religious experience through his own creed. But the writer cannot see how, if one is allowed to indulge in lowest religious practices like the worship of trees and road side stones, one could thereby rise to higher levels of religious experience. The Purāṇas always aimed at providing the masses with a religion that would appeal to their illiterate minds most. While the Hindu intellectual elite, the philosophers and seers, developed esoteric philosophies which were clearly out of the reach of the masses, Purāṇas provided them with a very large variety of dogmatic beliefs and practices, along with the promise that these would lead them to heaven or even liberation. Excepting the Bhakti movement, there was never any genuine attempt to raise the masses above the lowly level of popular religion.

There are other possible causes of the diversity of Hinduism. One obvious cause, of course, is the absence of any central authority or church in Hinduism. This has given vast scope for self-expression and genuine religious experience to the individual. On the other hand, the lack of any central authority has encouraged the writers of Hindu religious texts to indulge in unforgivable flights of imagination regarding gods, rituals and their various fruits; thus misleading the innocent and credulous masses.

Another possible explanation of the immense variety of Hinduism is diametrically opposed to the rational explanation mentioned earlier. That the Hindus worship so many gods may not be because they have a vision of one 'Divine' in all, but because they are basically a polytheistic people. The polytheists, unlike the theists, are naturally a tolerant lot. If they are already worshipping so many gods, they can easily worship a few more!

Hindu thinkers have always been trying to reconcile various religio-philosophical approaches and overcome the contradictions between high philosophical affirmations and lowly social practices. One such philosophic device used to reconcile the varying world-views and approaches is the distinction drawn between the transcendent truth (*pāramārthika satya*) and the empirical truth (*vyāvahārika satya*). This distinction between the two levels of truth helped Śaṁkara in advocating the empirical reality of the world, along with its transcendental unreality. Śaṁkara could also thereby accept the continuity in the empirical dealings of a man of realization who is convinced of the ultimate non-duality and the illusoriness of the world.[54] It is implied that the ultimate truth need not interfere with man's empirical dealings. To a certain extent this is a right approach to mundane life. But in a socio-moral context the practice of adopting double standards has often led to intellectual inconsistency and unconscious hypocrisy in men's inter-personal dealings. Thus, Śaṁkara could at once assert the ultimate universal Self as beyond all class distinctions,[55] and also advocate a very discriminatory and even cruel treatment of śūdras,[56] on the plea that while the first assertion refers to the ultimate truth, the second is relevant in the empirical context (*vyavahāra*) only.

(ii) A few more things should be observed here. First, in spite of its immence diversity and complexity, Hinduism does have a certain vision, underlying all its changing phases through the centuries. It is the vision of the all-comprehending 'Divine' which is the immanent source and essence or Self of all. The second most important tenet of the Vedic-Hindu faith is the universe being a moral order, wherein each man gets only what he deserves and every loss incurred is recompensed in the end. Hinduism has accepted through the centuries only those beliefs and values which can be reconciled with its own fundamental vision and faith, and has rejected others which are contrary to its basic ethos.

Secondly, Hinduism has never been static, except perhaps for a few centuries in the later middle ages. It has been constantly changing under the impact of new ideas. For example, the ideal of non-violence, imbibed from Buddhism and Jainism, transformed the entire Vedic-Hindu 'religio-culture' and morality. Later on Hinduism also welcomed the strict monotheism of Islam and various liberal, humanitarian and positivist ideas of modern Western thought. Hinduism has also been changing due to its own inner dialectics, as also in the process of adapting itself to the changing circumstances.

It is impossible to trace the history of Hinduism on a linear chart. Hinduism can be better understood on the simile of a huge banyan tree with two trunks and several branches. The twin original trunks of Hinduism, the Aryan and the non-Aryan 'religio-cultures', are now lost in the thick jungle, consisting of the various offshoots of the original tree. These offshoots or branches are interrelated, in that they have the same source and yet are widely divergent. Like the huge banyan tree, Hinduism has included at any point of its history beliefs and practices belonging to quite different ages and expressing quite different stages of religio-spiritual development. During any given period, Hinduism has included retrogressive customs and taboos showing signs of decadence and stagnation, as also fresh regenerative ideas which were destined to transform it. At a later stage, these new ideas themselves became heavy with the substance of conservatism and reactionary tendencies and were replaced by new and perhaps more refined ideas. Sometimes the reactionary forces were so strong that the Hindu society continued for long periods in a state of atavism and degeneration. Yet, a closer look would reveal that the seeds of this degeneration were sown much earlier, in perhaps the richest period of Hindu history. At the same time, the most decadent stage of Hindu history contained in it seeds of regeneration.

There were many attempts at systematization and synthesis of various beliefs and attitudes; but mostly divergent beliefs and attitudes were, and even now are, held without any consciousness of contradiction involved. Sometimes new syntheses have been achieved which have replaced old ideas and beliefs; on other occasions old beliefs, practices and attitudes have reasserted themselves. The very self-contradictions involved in Hinduism often work as an impetus to the growth of new syntheses of opposite ideas and approaches. Thus, Hinduism is constantly changing and renovating itself, without ever losing its identity and unique character. The vicissitudes in the Hindu 'religio-culture' have constantly influenced Hindu ethics. Hence, the need to study Hindu religio-philosophy for a better understanding of Hindu ethics.

Generally, a historical study gives a better perspective to the understanding of a particular subject. But it is very difficult to study either Hindu religion or Hindu ethics from a historical point of view. Aryans have left very little information regarding the dates of different literary works. Then, there is the curious phenomenon of cross references. Each single religious text quotes from other texts and is in turn quoted by others, thus making it impossible to estimate the relative dates of their composition. Above all, the history of Hindu 'religio-culture' and thought cannot be divided into artificially separated periods with well-defined characteristics. Hinduism never discards the old, and the new is not born all of a sudden, but is the result of the development of ideas and tendencies which were present in seed form in the earlier ages. For example, Hindu theism, which is understood by Western scholars of such calibre as Ninian Smart to be a later development, has had its origins in *Śvetāśvatara Upaniṣad* and *Bhagavadgitā*; and both of them are works of an era before Christ. On the other hand, Vedic ritualism is popular even today. During any given period, the old and the new have always existed side by side.

(iii) We have, therefore, divided Hindu religio-philosophy and morality into several traditions which have run parallel throughout the history of Hinduism and have together constituted the complex whole of Hindu Dharma. We will, thus, separately study the ritualistic morality of the Vedic tradition, the socio-centric morality of the Dharmaśāstras, the liberation-centric morality of the philosophic schools, the theo-centric morality of the devotional sects and the universal morality which is an amalgamation of all the above moralities and is generally propounded in popular Hindu texts.

We are aware that such an artificial division of the complex Hindu 'religio-culture' into distinct and supposedly independent traditions fails to do justice to its basic unitary character. Various traditions, being distinguished here, have been developed through constant mutual interaction and are often regarded by scholars as complementary to each other. Traditionally, every system of philosophy is concerned with some one aspect of life or thought and elaborates upon it, while accepting the reasoning and conclusions of other systems in other fields of thought and practice.

Thinkers like Prof. K.J. Shah contend that there are no contradictions, not even vertical divisions, in Hindu thought. Various systems of philosophy specialize in their respective fields and together form a homogeneous whole of Hindu religio-philosophy. We are not so sure.

Moreover, tradition also distinguishes several ways (*mārgas*) which roughly correspond to the three broad divisions of Hindu religio-philosophy and morality suggested by us. Though Hinduism expects man strictly to follow his caste profession and generally abide by the customs and norms of the society, it gives him freedom to choose his own way (*mārga*) in his religio-spiritual quest. The way here is understood both as a means of the *summum bonum* of human life and as a right integral approach to life, religion and morality. Tradition distinguishes three major ways of life (*i*) the way of action (*karma-mārga*) which includes both the ritualistic and socio-moral actions or duties, (*ii*) the way of knowledge (*jñāna-mārga*) which is mainly advocated in the systems of philosophy and generally implies a rejection of the worth of action, and (iii) the way of devotion (*bhakti-mārga*) which expresses a theo-centric world-view and a much more comprehensive and positive approach to religion and morality. Sometimes the way of yoga is also listed as an independent way of religious quest. But we have included it in the way of knowledge, as yogic concentration has been traditionally accepted as an integral part of the way of knowledge. The three major traditions distinguished by us are rough equivalents of the above three ways (*mārgas*). Thus, the Vedic-Dharmaśāstric tradition represents the way of action, the tradition of liberation is essentially the same as the way of knowledge, and the tradition of devotion, of course, is the way of devotion (*bhakti*).

Bhagavadgītā has sought to present a meaningful synthesis of the three ways of action, knowledge and devotion. But the three major ways (*mārgas*) have continued to be distinguished in Hindu Dharma. The universally accepted doctrine of *adhikāra-bheda* emphasizes the innate differences between men and asserts that different men should pursue different religio-moral ways which suit their respective temperaments and capacities. Śaṁkara is a strong protagonist of this tradition of allotting different ways to different persons according to their natures and capacities. He presents a strong argument against the interpretation of *Bhagavadgītā* as supporting the synthesis of the way of action and the way of knowledge. According to him, the two ways of action and knowledge are diametrically opposed and are definitely meant for two entirely different temperaments. Therefore, they cannot be simultaneously followed by one and the same man.[57] This only proves our contention that Hindu Dharma is a complex whole which comprehends several parallel traditions, supporting quite different philosophies and valuational approaches, supposedly meant for men of different capacities and inclinations. At the same time, our own division of Hinduism into several parallel traditions is not meant as something final or conclusive, and is to be taken as a working hypothesis which may help us in achieving a better understanding of Hindu religio-philosophy and morality.

V. Some Religio-metaphysical Presuppositions of Hindu Ethics

Charles A. Moore argues for the extreme complexity of Indian mind and civilization and despairs of finding some denominators of mind and practice which may be common to all the religio-philosophical sects and traditions. At the same time, he admits the need to search for such common ideas or concepts and himself proceeds to suggest some. He feels that it is impossible to understand India and its people (and we may add, their morality) without understanding its basic philosophy, because the intimacy of philosophy and life is so fundamental to the whole Indian point of view.[58] Inasmuch as religion and philosophy are so integrally bound together in India, the basic postulates of Indian (Hindu) 'religio-culture' can be termed as religio-metaphysical. A cursory glance at these religio-philosophical beliefs will help in a better understanding of Hindu ethics. Generally, the immortality of the soul, the law of karma, rebirth or transmigration and liberation (*mokṣa*) are regarded as the most basic postulates of Indian (Hindu) thought. The above postulates present a very ego-centric and incomplete view of Hindu thought. Hence to this commonly accepted list we have added polytheism, monism and theism. Hindus, like any other people, are interested in their souls and eschatological destiny, but they are equally interested in the objective world and the Divine reality.

(i) Excepting certain Bhakti (devotional) cults which emphasize exclusive devotion to one God, Hindus have been worshipping innumerable deities from the pre-historic Vedic times to this day. Though the polytheism of the Vedas is frankly recognized by Indian thinkers, they have either ignored or attempted to rationalize later Hindu polytheism. The practice of polytheism is wide-spread and has very important ramifications for Hindu approach to life and morality; and it should therefore be duly recognized. The Vedic gods have long been replaced by new Hindu gods and goddesses, such as Rāma, Kṛṣṇa, Śiva and Śakti or Mother goddess. They are generally affirmed to be different concepts or forms of the 'Divine'. An average Hindu agrees with the above rationalization at the intellectual level; but treats these gods as different deities at the practical (ritualistic) and emotional levles. It is because these deities are conceived in such an elaborate and determinate fashion, with definite abodes, consorts and life histories, that it is difficult to conceive them as different concepts of one and the same God. This is especially true of smaller gods like Gaṇeśa, Hanumān and Santoṣī Mātā who are never even referred to as one supreme God. The Hindu mind is very much at home with the idea of a plurality of gods (*devatā*). The Vedic sacrifices were directed to different gods. A very important *Smārta* sacrifice is addressed to Vaiśvadeva (gods of the universe). The Epics and Purāṇas talk of gods in a very natural and familiar way. Even *Bhagavadgītā*, a theistic work, refers to gods: "Nourished by sacrifices the gods shall indeed bestow on you the enjoyments you desire."[59] The three famous debts of men are towards the seers, the fathers and the gods. Hindus celebrate religious festivals throughout the year and all these festivals are dedicated to different gods. All Hindu temples have idols of various gods, and a Hindu while visiting a temple makes it a point to visit and bow down to all these idols. If the different deities were merely different conceptions of the same Divinity, there would have been no need to do obeisance before so many gods.

The popular Hindu polytheism has very far-reaching implications for Hindu morality. On the one hand, it strengthens the world-and-life-affirmative ethos of the original Aryan tradition; on the other hand, it aligns itself with ritualism and indirectly undermines the ethical point of view.

(ii) Strange as it may seem, Hinduism is at once polytheistic, monistic and theistic. According to it, a monistic world-view refers primarily to the ultimate truth of one all-comprehending Reality, but it does not deny the existence of various gods who derive their being from the 'One', as does the rest of the world. A much quoted verse of *Ṛg Veda* declares: "The Real (*Sat*) is one, the learned call it by many names."[60] The Upaniṣads have presented a moistic world-view which has been imbibed by Hinduism so thoroughly that it has become the constant frame of reference of all Hindu thinking and practice. According to it, every thing, every being 'is' in some way the one *Ātman-Brahman*, not in any pantheistic sense, but in the Vedāntic sense of the 'One' being the source, stay and end of all that there is. The famous Upaniṣadic text, "All this is *Brahman*", contains the further phrase, "all this comes out of, is sustained by and merges into *Brahman*."[61] The ultimate Reality (*Sat* or *Brahman*) is the very essence of the universe, as well as the Self of man.[62]

This vision of one Self in all should have led the Aryans to a morality of love and compassion for all; but it did not. The transcendentalism inherent in the Vedāntic mysticism, instead, led the ancients to the exaltation of the creed of renunciation and its related virtues of detachment etc.

(iii) Characteristically, Hindu theism finds no difficulty in reconciling itself either with popular polytheism or with Vedāntic monism. The existence of smaller gods is accepted alongwith one supreme God who is conceived in terms of the Vedāntic Absolute.

Though the Upaniṣads are largely monistic in their world-view, there are theistic under-currents in several Upaniṣads. The Upaniṣadic Absolute is also the Creator and Governor of the world. But it was in *Bhagavadgītā* that Hindu theism was properly developed. In a typically theistic terminology *Bhagavadgītā* affirms the transcendence of God to the world and the soul, as also the numinous character of God.[63] Like any other theistic text, *Bhagavadgitā* also affirms God's personal Being, and regards the soul as a part of Him (and not as identical with Him).[64] And yet, the Lord of The *Bhagavadgītā* is essentially the same as the Vedāntic Absolute. His transcendence is not the transcendence of a wholly-other Deity, but that of an all-comprehending Absolute. He is the Self residing in all living beings and controlling them from within.[65] The theism of the *Bhagavadgītā* is further developed in several Purāṇas, Bhakti-sūtras, and the writings of Vedāntic teachers and saints belonging to various devotional sects. The advent of devotional theism in the last centuries before Christ transformed Hindu ethics. While the Vedic ritualism is practical and harsh, and Vedāntic monism is intellectual and dry, devotional theism encourages gentle emotions, including love and compassion for all.

(iv) If we were to search for the one most widely shared belief of the Hindus, then it would be their belief in the world order being a moral order which is oriented towards the realization and conservation of moral and spiritual values. It is the belief that the moral law, and not the mechanical forces of nature, governs and controls the world order and all natural processes. It is also the belief in the final victory of justice, better known as truth (*satya*) or right (*dharma*). This belief implies a pious faith that every evil is punished, every virtue rewarded and every suffering compensated in the end. It gives meaning to moral responsibility and a motive for moral conduct, for according to it, as you sow, so shall you reap, that is, each person is allotted the lot which he has earned for himself.

This idea of the world being a moral order was first formulated in the Vedas as *ṛta*. *Ṛta* is the immanent moral order of the universe that governs and controls all phenomena from within.[66] It was also believed that the correct performance of the Vedic rituals leads to an automatic realization of one's desires. The fulfilment of a desire was supposed to materialize through the agency of *apūrva*, the unseen potency generated by the performance of a sacrifice. All these beliefs must have contributed to the development of the theory of karma. The Upaniṣads affirm both karma and transmigratory existence,[67] but fail to relate the two ideas properly. There seems to be some confusion in the minds of the Upaniṣadic seers regarding the mode of recompense for one's actions after death. The *Chāndogya Upaniṣad* posits a double recompense,[68] first in the other world and then again in the next birth. Probably rewards and punishments in the next world and recompense for one's actions in the next life on earth were two independent ideas which were developed in two entirely different traditions, and which have been juxtaposed in the idea of double recompense.

Our actions are further supposed to determine both, our nature or character, as also all the external circumstances of our life, the kind of birth we get, the sufferings and joys we undergo and so on.[69] Nothing happens without a cause and the cause here is to be evaluated in ethical terms. That is to say, the moral quality of our deeds, thoughts and desires not only conditions our future character, but also manipulates the natural world order, so that we are thrown into external circumstances that are most suited to materialize or effect the kind of rewards and punishments which our moral character deserves. The law of karma is thus an explanatory hypothesis, meant to explain and rationally justify the inequalities found in men's characters, capacities and circumstances. This hypothesis has very far-reaching ramifications for Hindu morality. On the one hand, it provides an excellent motive for righteous conduct. Man should act righteously in his own interest, as it is ensured by the world's moral order that every evil action would sooner or later come back to the evil doer and make him miserable. It teaches man to be honest and assume the responsibility or accountability for his deeds, as also to be content and at peace with himself. On the other hand, the law of karma is an extremely individualistic hypothesis which encourages man to be self-centred and indifferent towards others, since the misfortunes of others are easily explained as the results of their own past *karmas*, and hence what they themselves deserve. It is also repeatedly affirmed that each man must suffer the good or bad fruits of his actions and that no one else can suffer for him or help him truly.[70]

The law of karma does not fit very well in the original Aryan ethos. While the universally practised Hindu custom of obsequial rites presupposes that the rites performed by one's progeny ensure one's well-being in the other world,[71] the law of karma categorically affirms that no one else's action can ever help a man. The belief in and the practice of obsequial rites are an integral part of the Vedic tradition, whereas the law of karma seems to express an entirely different and extremely individualistic approach to social life and morality. But characteristically, Hindus accept both beliefs in full faith and even act accordingly.

(v) Another very important postulate of Hindu morality is the immortality of the soul and transmigratory existence. The Upaniṣads have given two types of description of the self (*ātman*), one as the eternal, immutable, unattached and transcendent Pure-consciousness,[72] and the other as the transmigrating soul which wanders from one existence to another due to its desires and actions.[73] Now, transmigratory existence necessarily presupposes separate individual souls which undergo different experiences in innumerable births; and the immutable, transcendent Vedāntic *Ātman* which is the same in all can hardly be conceived as undergoing transmigratory existence. Yet all the Vedāntic texts seem to think that both concepts refer to the same self. The use of the one word *ātman* for both, the transmigrating individual self and the transcendent universal Self, probably led to this confusion in the Vedāntic approach. The entire doctrine of karma and transmigratory existence seems to have borrowed heavily from the Sāṁkhya dualism and generally consists of the following:

1. The plurality of souls,
2. The distinction of the soul from the body,
3. The immortality of the soul and its transmigratory existence,
4. The soul's being a pure detached consciousness and a non-agent, and
5. The soul's transmigration being in accordance with the *karmas* of its body-mind complex with which it has become associated due to the ignorance of its true nature.

A theistic version of the above doctrine of transmigratory existence is presented best in the *Bhagavadgītā* which compares the rebirth of the soul in another body to changing of clothes, thereby emphasizing the essential distinction between the soul and the body-mind complex.[74] This is quite a complex doctrine which suffers from certain philosophical inconsistencies, and is open to certain criticisms. We cannot discuss them here for lack of space. Though philosophically it may not be very defensible, as a metaphysical presupposition of morality it is no less meaningful than Kant's affirmation of the immortality of the soul. It teaches man to look beyond the present moment and conduct himself, so as to ensure a better and worthier future for himself.

(vi) In no other aspect of the Hindu religio-philosophy is the contrast between the two traditions of Hindu 'religio-culture' more prominent than in the concept of the eschatological destiny of the soul. Not only do the Dharmaśāstras and Purāṇas uniformly uphold heaven as the eschatological goal of the righteous soul, it is harmoniously related to the first three goals of life (*trivarga*), affirmed by the first or Vedic-Dharmaśāstric tradition. On the other extreme is the goal of *mokṣa* (liberation), or freedom from and transcendence of the world and all its distinctions and limitations. The Vedāntic *mokṣa* even transcends the limitations of the personality, in that the individual soul which is essentially identical with the supreme Self is merged into the latter in the state of liberation.[75]

Gradually an entirely different concept of liberation emerged. Its chief protagonist was Sāṁkhya, though it came to be shared by almost all the orthodox schools of philosophy, except Vedānta, as also by all the popular religious texts. This second concept implies separate individual souls, transmigratory existence and the transcendent pure nature of the soul. It also affirms that the soul's sojourn in the world is full of suffering and is of the nature of bondage. Soul's liberation, therefore, consists in soul's freedom from transmigratory existence and realization of its original pure nature (*kaivalya*). This concept of liberation is rather self-centric and is quite different from that of Vedānta. The ideas of the soul's ultimate aloneness and the miserable nature of the transmigratory existence were unknown in the Vedic-Vedāntic tradition.

The two concepts of *mokṣa* slowly got merged, so that the Vedāntic writers started explaining liberation in self-centric terms. With the recognition of liberation as the ultimate goal of human life and its conception in self-centric terms, an extremely individualistic approach to morality was engendered which was not intended by the seers of the Upaniṣads.

VI. Morality as Dharma

While the compound word Hindu Dharma means the entire 'religio-culture' of Hinduism, *dharma* as such is almost coextensive with morality. The concept of *dharma* is the most basic and comprehensive and at the same time the most loosely used concept of Hindu thought. It is vital, therefore, to understand this concept before we even attempt to understand Hindu morality. In the Vedas *dharma*, like *ṛta*, is given a near-ontological status. Both are equated to *satya* (truth) and truth is what eternally is. They are also opposed to *anṛta* (falsehood) and false is both ontologically less real and morally reprehensible. *Ṛta* or *dharma* signifies the moral order of the universe that governs and determines the course of events, so as to ensure that truth or *dharma* is always victorious and that untruth or *adharma* (morally wrong or unjust) is finally defeated.[76] In the famous passage of the *Bṛhadāraṇyaka Upaniṣad*, *dharma* is hailed as the highest truth and power, "so that even a weak man hopes to defeat a strong man through *dharma*."[77] It means that the world is a moral order wherein natural events are regulated by moral necessity.

Dharma is mostly understood in Vedas and Dharmaśāstras as the performance of Vedic sacrifices and other rituals, or the merit resulting therefrom. Mīmāṁsā defines *dharma* as what is enjoined in the Vedas,[78] which assertion seems to reduce *dharma* to Vedic rituals. These Vedic rituals are usually divided into three classes, i.e. desire-prompted ones (*kāmya karma*), daily obligatory ones (*nitya karma*) and those which must be performed on specified occasions (*naimittika karma*). Excepting the first, the remaining two categories of Vedic-Dharmaśāstric rituals are to be performed as ends-in-themselves. Though conceived in a purely ritualistic context, *dharma* here is to be understood as duty *par excellence* and appears to be a deontological concept. Specially, Prabhākara school of Mīmāṁsā has unequivocally emphasized that (ritualistic) duties ought to be performed solely because they are perceived to be one's duty, and not for the sake of any desire for their fruits.

But the majority of Hindu thinkers have shown an ambivalent attitude towards the problem of the relation between duty and desire for results. *Dharma* is frequently asserted to be a means of achieving either heaven or a better birth in the next life, or even prosperity here and now.[79] The *Vaiśeṣika Sūtra* frankly defines *dharma* as "that from which (results) the accomplishment of exaltation (*abhyudaya*) and of the supreme goal (*niḥśreyasa*)."[80] This view of *dharma* or morality is apparently influenced by the traditional equation between moral and ritualistic duties (which are mostly undertaken with specific desires).

With the development of the moral consciousness of the Aryans, it was felt that the real worth of *dharma* or righteousness lies, not in the outer act, but in the inner attitude or spirit of the performer. According to Āpastamba the ritualistic and socio-moral duties should be performed for their own sake, and if their performance happens to bring some good fruits, the latter should be taken as additional (and not as the main motive for the discharge of one's duties).[81]

Like the Dharmaśāstras, the *Bhagavadgītā* does not reject the ritualistic concept of *dharma*. But its own understanding of *dharma* is in terms of socio-moral duties or *varṇāśrama dharma*. The *Gītā* further asserts that the various socio-moral duties should be performed without any desire for their fruits and even without any ego of being the agent thereof.[82] The *Bhagavadgītā's* ideal of desireless action comes very close to the Kantian concept of duty for duty's sake. In fact, it is only in the *Gītā* that the concept of *dharma* acquires a truly moral meaning and content. (We shall have occasion to study the *Gītā's* ideal in our chapter VI *infra*.)

The concept of *dharma* has been further enlarged by its association with the concept of debt (*ṛṇa*). A man is supposed to be born with certain debts to parents, seers and gods; and that way of life is *dharma* which helps man discharge his debts to all of them.[83] Gradually the concept of *dharma* has acquired a truly moral meaning as righteous conduct in the society. According to the *Mahābhārata*, "*Dharma* has no limits. It extends to all spheres. It is what sustains the world".[84] It means that *dharma* or righteousness is socially oriented, that is, it largely consists in social morality. Since the aim of *dharma* is to preserve the social order, *dharma* has been generally understood as duties according to one's caste and stage of life (*varṇāśrama-dharma*). It is in this sense that the term *dharma* is mostly used by the Hindu religious texts. The *Bhagavadgītā* has presented a very strong case for the performance of one's duties (*sva-dharma*). But unfortunately it has consistently understood man's duties in terms of his class or caste (*varṇa*)[85]. The ancient texts, thus, often confused man's *dharma* with his externally imposed profession. The referent of the concept of *dharma* was mostly the class (*varṇa*) and not the individual. One's *varṇa* decided not only one's socio-moral duties, but also the spirituo-moral virtues one was expected to practise. While brāhmaṇas were expected to practise calmness, fortitude and forgiveness, kṣatriyas were asked to practise a very different set of manly virtues. Sadly enough, the *dharma* of the 'lower' classes consisted exclusively in the performance of their class duties, and hardly any moral virtues were expected from them.[86]

Dharma also means the moral law within man, so that acting according to *dharma* would mean acting in accordance with one's spiritual nature. It was naively believed by the ancient Hindus that duties in accordance with one's caste and stage of life are also in accordance with one's inclinations or character; and hence performance of one's caste duties (*sva-dharma*) leads to self-fulfilment.[87] Praśastapāda defines *dharma* (virtue) as a quality of the self which is generated by 'means of pure thoughts and determinations.' But then he goes on to explain *dharma* or righteousness in terms of acting according to one's ordained duties.[88] It is in this mixed up comprehensive sense that most of the religious texts, including the *Bhagavadgitā*, use the word *dharma*.

The Hindu concept of *dharma* has thus often been vitiated by its very close association with both ritualistic and caste-ordained duties, so that the purely moral sense of duty is overshadowed by these ideas. Hindu thinkers also appreciate and recommend the practice of moral virtues and moral norms which apply to man as man and are called *sādhāraṇa dharma* or universal duties. But there has been no attempt to systematically relate the two classes of *dharma* or duty, i.e. those based on class distinctions and those applicable to all men.

Above all, *dharma* is a very comprehensive concept which makes it almost coextensive with entire morality. When we say, '*ahiṁsā paramo dharmaḥ*', we mean that it is the highest duty and the highest virtue which should be followed in practice and realized in one's character. Moral virtue finds its true meaning when it is translated in external acts or duty; and duty becomes morally relevant only when it is performed in a virtuous frame of mind. The concept of *dharma* comprehends both concepts of duty and virtue, and becomes a very profound and far-reaching concept of moral thought. A man's *dharma* includes all the duties he ought to perform and all the virtues he ought to practise; that is, *dharma* comprehends all one ought to do and all one ought to be. It also includes all his relative (*varṇāśrama*) and unconditional (*sādhāraṇa*) duties. As ritualistic duty, *dharma* is what is commanded by an external authority (Vedas). At the same time, *dharma* or moral law is innate in man, and by performing one's duties man fulfils his own inner being.[89] Thus, almost everything we can discuss in ethics is included in one way or the other in the concept of *dharma*.

Notes

1. *S. Radhakrishnan, Eastern Religions and Western Thought* (1958), p. 80; cf. "To see the truth deeply is to believe in it fully, to believe intensely is to be or become ....So philosophy is transformed naturally into religion and morality. In India philosophy has seldom dwelt apart from religion. All intellectual speculation had an important bearing on actual life." Surama Dasgupta, *Development of Moral Philosophy in India* (1961), p. 5.

2. *The Fundamentals of Hinduism* (1971), p. 11.

3. *Matthew* 22 : 21.

4. *Hinduism* (1974), pp. 12-13.

5. See *The Cultural Heritage of India* (1975), vol. I, pp. 76 ff. References to various tribes are scattered all through the two Epics and Purāṇas. Also see *M.S.* X. 44.

6. *Rāmāyaṇa, Kiṣkindhā Kāṇḍa*, ch. XXVII; *Sundara Kāṇḍa*, chs. IV to VII.

7. *M.S.* III. 12 ff.; IX. 138 ff. etc.

8. *History* (1974), vol. II, pp. 25 ff.

9. *Gaut. D.S.* X. 61-62.

10. *Hindu Intellectual Tradition* (1979), pp. 95-96.

11. *Gaut. D.S.* X. 67.

12. See M. Monier Williams, op.cit. (1974), pp. 52, 84-85 and H. Zimmer, *Philosophies of India* (1969), pp. 306 ff., 314 ff., 406 ff., 595 ff.

13. *Vaiṣnavism, Śaivism and Minor Religious Systems* (1965), pp. 9 ff., 35 ff., 103, 106, 114-115.

14. Op.cit. (1961), p. 10

15. *Foundation of Indian Culture* (1984), vol. I, *Spiritual Vision and Symbolic Forms in Ancient India*, pp. 60, 71-72. cf. "Throughout the known history of India these two points of view have operatea in a dialectical process of antagonistic co-

operation to bring to pass the majestic evolution of... (that) which we know today as the miracle of Indian civilization." H. Zimmer, op.cit., p. 539.

16. See *The Cultural Heritage of India*, vol. I, pp. 80 ff.

17. See G.C. Pande, op.cit., vol. II, *Dimensions of Indian Social History* (1984), pp. 210 ff.

18. N.V. Banerjee, *The Spirit of Indian Philosophy* (1974), p. 291.

19. M. Monier Williams, op.cit. (1974), pp. 84-85, 168-169, 184 ff.; Maurice Phillips, *The Teaching of the Vedas* (1978), pp. 226 ff.

20. See N.K. Devaraja, *The Mind and Spirit of India* (1967), pp. 39, 81 ff.; 96 ff.; 107 ff. and K. Satchidananda Murty, *The Indian Spirit* (1965), pp. 8 ff.; 82 ff.; 87.

21. *Īśā. Up.* 1-2; *Taittirīya Up.* I. 4. 3.

22. *M.S.* II. 224; *Mbh. Śān. P.* VII. 17; XII. 17; CLXI. 2 ff. etc.—Note: We have used the Hindi transl. of the *Mahābhārata*, edited by Damodar Satavalekar (1968) which is based on the original Sanskrit edition of the Bhandarkar Research Institute, Poona.

23. *M.S.* IV. 137.

24. *Yājñ. S.* I. 291.

25. *Mbh. Udyoga Parva* LXX. 18 ff.; *Śān. P.* VIII. 6 ff.; XV. 48; XVIII. 22-23 etc.

26. *M.S.* III. 75 ff.; *Mbh. Śān. P.* XI. 15 ff.

27. *Mbh. Āran. P.* XXXII. 47, 54; cf. ibid XXXII. 11 ff., 39 ff., 54.

28. Ibid, *Āran. P.* CIC. 3 ff., 19 ff.; *Śān. P.* XV. 20 ff.

29. *B.G.* II. 11-13; cf. *Mbh. Śān. P.* XIII. 6; XV. 56.

30. *B.G.* II. 32-33, 37.

31. *M.S.* VII. 14 ff.; VIII. 124 ff., 306; *Mbh. Śān. P.* XIV. 14 ff.; XV. 2 ff.

32. "Assemble together, speak with one voice, let your mind be of one accord, united be the thoughts of all, that all may live happily." *Ṛg Veda* X. 192. 2-4 quoted in *The Cultural Heritage of India*, vol. I, p. 198.

33. "Every Aryan is born with a three-fold obligation: first to the gods which he discharges by sacrifices, second to *ṛṣis* which he should discharge by studying Vedas and third to his ancestors which he should discharge by getting sons." *Taittirīya Saṁhitā* VI. 3.10.5, quoted in M. Hiriyanna, *Indian Conception of Values* (1975), p. 151.

34. Quoted in ibid, p. 199.

35. *Muṇḍaka Up.* I. 2. 7 ff.

36. See *Kaṭha Up.* 1. 2. 23-24; I. 3. 4-9; *Taittirīya Up.* I.11.1; *Muṇḍaka Up.* III.1.5; *Ś.B. Br.S.* I.1.1; *M.S.* II. 97, 118.

37. *Chān. Up.* VI. 1.4-6, VI. 7.7; *Taittirīya Up.* III. 1.1 *Bṛhad. Up.* III. 7.3 ff. etc.

38. *Bṛhad. Up.* III. 2.13.

39. *Mbh. Śān. P.*, chs. VII to XXV; XXXIV, LVII, LXVI to LXVIII.

40. *B.G.* II. 37; *Mbh. Āran. P.* XXXII. 22; *Śāṇ. P.* XXVI. 34, *Svargārohaṇa Parva*, ch. III; *Āpast. D.S.* II. 7.16. 1; II. 9.24.5 etc.

41. *M.S.* VI. 35; *Mbh. Śāṇ. P.* XXV. 6; CCLXI. 15 etc.

42. *Chān. Up.* II. 23.1; *Ś.B., Br.S.* I.1.4; *Ś.B., B.G.*, introd. to ch. III etc.

43. *M.S.* V. 22 ff., 31, 39, 44.

44. *Mbh. Śān. P.* CCLV. 24 ff.; CCLVII. 4 ff. CCLXI. 19; CCLXIV. 17 etc.
45. Ibid, *Śān. P.* CCXXXVII 17 ff.; CCLXIV. 19 ff.; *Anuś. P.* CXVI. 72; CXVII. 37-39.
46. *B.G.* III. 8 ff., 19 ff, 35; XVIII 5-9, 45.
47. Ibid, II. 13, 22.
48. Ibid, II. 18 ff.; III. 27 ff.
49. Ibid, II. 38; IV. 22-23; IX-27.
50. *Selections from Swami Vivekananda* (1957), pp. 178 ff., 243 ff.
51. Ibid, pp, 39 ff., 280 ff.
52. *A Critical Study of Hinduism* (1970), p. 97. Interestingly, M. Monier Williams had earlier used almost identical words to express the Hindu willingness to worship each and every thing as divine; but he understands this practice in terms of aboriginal fetishism and Brāhmaṇical pantheism; and both these terms are used by him in a derogatory sense. See op.cit. (1977), pp. 168-169.
53. Op.cit. (1957), pp. 185 ff.; cf. Sri Aurobindo, *The Foundations of Indian Culture* (1968), pp. 134 ff., 172 ff.
54. *Ś.B., Br.S.* II. 1.14; *Ś.B., Chān. Up.* VI. 2.1-3; *S.B., Bṛhad. Up.* I. 4.10; III. 5.1.
55. *Ś.B., Br.S.*, introd.; I.1.4.
56. Ibid, I. 3. 34.
57. *Ś.B., B.G.* introd. to ch. III; III. 4, 16; IV. 18-19; introd. to ch. V. etc.
58. Charles A. Moore, ed., *The Indian Mind* (1967), pp. 1, 4.
59. *B.G.* III. 11-12.
60. *Ṛg. Veda* I. 164. 46.
61. *Chān. Up.* III. 14.1; cf. *Bṛhad. Up.* II. 1.20; II. 4.6; *Taittirīya Up.* II. 5.1; III. 1.1.
62. *Chān. Up.* VI. 8.4-7; *Bṛhad. Up.* III. 7.3 ff.
63. *B.G.* VII. 12-13, 24-25; X. 41-42; XI. 15 ff.
64. Ibid, XV. 7.
65. Ibid, IX. 17-18; X.20; XVIII. 61.
66. *Ṛg Veda* I. 24.8; IV. 23.9, quoted in S. Radhakrishnan, *Indian Philosophy* (1956), vol. I. p. 79.
67. *Bṛhad. Up.* III. 2.13; IV. 4.5; IV. 3.35 ff.
68. *Chān. Up.* V. 10.1-8; cf. *Bṛhad. Up.* IV. 4.6
69. *M.S.* XII. 52ff., especially 81; *Mbh. Śān. P.* CLXXIV. 8 ff.; CCLXXXVII. 28, 43 etc.
70. *M.S.* IV. 239; XII. 18 ff.; *Mbh. Śān. P.* CCLXXIX. 21; CCLXXXVII. 37 etc. Also see G.C. Pande, op.cit. (1982), vol. I, pp. 64 ff.
71. *M.S.* III. 274-275; IX. 138.
72. *Bṛhad. Up.* III. 4. 1—III. 5.1; IV. 2.4; IV. 3.15.
73. Ibid, IV. 3. 35 ff.; IV. 4.6.
74. *B.G.* II. 13, 18 ff.
75. *Muṇḍaka Up.* III. 2.8-9; *Bṛhad. Up.* II. 4.12.
76. *M.S.* VIII. 15-17; *Mbh. Śān. P.* XCIII. 6; XCVI, 16-19.
77. *Bṛhad. Up.* I. 4.14.
78. *Mīmāṁsā Sūtra* I. 1.2.

79. *Āpast. D.S.* II. 2. 4.9; II. 5.11. 10-11.
80. *Vaiśeṣika Sūtra* I. 1.2.
81. *Āpast. D.S.* I. 7. 20. 1-3.
82. *B.G.* II. 47; III. 7, 19, 25-30; IV. 22 etc.
83. M. Hiriyanna, op.cit. (1976), pp. 150-152.
84. *Mbh. Śān. P.* CX. 11; cf. ibid XCI. 5-14.
85. *B.G.* III. 35; XVIII. 47-48; cf. *M.S.* X. 96-97.
86. *B.G.* IV. 13; XVIII. 41-46; *M.S.* I. 87-91.
87. *B.G.* III. 5, 33, 35.
88. Praśastapāda, *Padārthadharma Saṁgraha*, as quoted in Cromwell Crawford, *Evolution of Hindu Ethical Ideals* (1974), p. 141.
89. *B.G.* XVIII. 45.

Chapter II

RITUAL-CENTRIC MORALITY OF THE VEDIC-DHARMAŚĀSTRIC TRADITION

I. Amoral Nature of the Brāhmaṇic Rituals

Karma-kāṇḍa or the way of rituals is the oldest of the several parallel traditions constituting Hinduism. It had its origins in the Vedas around 2000 B.C. and was developed in an extreme form in Brāhmaṇas which were probably compiled around 1000 B.C. The Vedic ritualism continued to be a dominant trend in the Dharmaśāstras which were written approximately during the period between 3rd century B.C. to around 3rd century A.D. Rituals did not form the chief concern of the Epics which were probably written and finalized during the same period as the Dharmaśāstras and Purāṇas which came much later. But even they advocated Vedic and other rituals in the characteristic spirit of the Vedic tradition.

(i) During the Vedic period *yajña* (sacrifice) was the pivot round which the entire Aryan 'religio-culture' was evolved. In the beginning, these sacrifices were relatively simple affairs and expressed the religious piety of the early Aryans. The sacrifice was originally conceived as a literal offering of nourishment to the gods who were then expected to shower prosperity and other desired gifts on the sacrificer. For the simple Aryans prosperity, moral purity and religious piety were not disparate values; rather, they were seen as necessary ingredients of a desirable life. Vedic rituals were understood and practised as a means, as well as an integral part, of a worthy life. Thus, many of the Vedic sacrifices, especially the daily rituals, were performed as symbolic acts expressing harmony or rapport with the forces of nature, without any desire for their fruits. Ritualistic and moral purity was regarded as a necessary pre-requisite of the performance of such sacrifices. There were detailed instructions concerning the norms of purity to be observed by the performer before and during the sacrifice. While harmony with nature could supposedly be achieved through Vedic rituals, it was felt that harmony within the human society is best achieved through the practice of such moral virtues as friendliness, magnanimity etc. Truthfulness is another virtue greatly admired by the Vedic Aryans.

Certain Western writers idealize Vedic religion as an expression of genuine religious piety, and even present it as a monotheistic religion, which it is not. They underplay its polytheism and ritualism and over-emphasize those passages of the Vedas which express a relatively high level of moral consciousness and religious piety.[1] But this form of selective presentation never does justice to the subject. If we try to understand the early Vedic religion comprehensively, we would find it to be an expression of simple religious piety which was necessarily developed in a ritualistic-polytheistic context.

(ii) Vedic sacrifices became progressively more elaborate with a concomitant decrease in their religio-moral content in the Brāhmaṇas. V.M. Apte observes:

"So implicit was the belief of the ancient Aryans in the efficacy of their rituals which practically dominated every phase of their life, and so firm their faith in almost unlimited powers of the rituals in ensuring prosperity and averting misfortunes, that quite a number of interesting ritual practices and performances were formulated for this purpose."[2]

Every stage of life from birth (or rather existence in the womb) to death was marked by a corresponding sacrament. In addition, there were rituals for the attainment of specific wishes and averting misfortunes. There were rites for prosperity in trade or victory in dispute, rites for procuring gold and other objects or finding lost property, as also those for guarding one's wife's fidelity ! There were specific instructions in the Brāhmaṇas regarding the details of each and every aspect of various sacrifices, such as the construction of the altar, preparation and lighting of various fires, the manner of grinding *soma* leaves and the utensils to be used etc. The main sacrifice apart, even the erection of the altar became a very elaborate affair requiring specific number of muds and metals which were to be spread in various specified layers, and so on.[3] There were also detailed instructions regarding the ending of the sacrifice and the disposal of the material used in it.[4] Both the grandeur and the degeneration of the Vedic rituals are best exemplified in the major Vedic (*Śrauta*) sacrifices, such as *Agniṣṭoma, Aśvamedha, Darśapūrṇamāsa* etc. All of these sacrifices were real elaborate affairs requiring a lot of preparation and expenditure, as well as time. Most of these sacrifices took several days to complete, and some stretched to a whole year, or even continued for an indefinite number of years !

Gradually the violence in these sacrifices increased. Scores and probably hundreds of animals were sacrificed in the major sacrifices. Cow, the most sacred animal of the present-day Hinduism, was one of the important victims in several Vedic sacrifices. Even man was included among the list of victims of some sacrifices, such as *Sarvamedha* (sacrifice of all). An important Vedic ritual—*Agnicayana* (erection of the fire altar) included man as one of the five victims whose heads were to be walled up in the construction of the altar. Thus, the human sacrifice was not beyond the thinking of the Aryans, though in all probability it was usually not carried out.[5]

The role of the priests became more and more important and the number of priests required in a sacrifice multiplied, till sixteen or more priests were required for the bigger sacrifices. Every priest had a very specialized function to perform in the sacrifice, and priesthood became hereditary. Significantly, the host (*yajamāna*) had no role to play in the sacrifice, even though he was the one who was expected to reap the fruits of the sacrifice by virtue of having paid for the expenses of the sacrifice and large fees to the brāhmaṇa priests. The host was thus expected to reap the fruits of actions performed by others (priests).

A Vedic sacrifice, if correctly performed, was supposed to automatically effect the realization of the desires of the subject or the host. The Brāhmaṇas affirmed the self-efficacy of the Vedic rituals, and there is a suggestion in them that gods, religious piety and morality are secondary in the successful performance of Vedic sacrifices. Prof. P.V. Kane has quoted the *Mīmāṁsā Sūtra*[6] to the effect that in the Vedic sacrifices it is the oblation into fire (*havi*) which is principal, while gods (*devatā*) are secondary. Fruits of Vedic sacrifices (*phala*) are conferred by the sacrifices and not by the deity; and the words, that 'Indra and Agni confer progeny to the sacrificer', are purely laudatory. That is to say, gods are mere accompaniments of rituals and the rituals alone directly effect the desired results (*phala*).

V.M. Apte has pointed out certain magical elements in the Vedic rituals.[7] For example, in the *Śyena* sacrifice, aiming at the destruction of the enemy, the priests wore red garments and the sacrificial butter was made of the milk of a sick cow ! Slightest error in the ritualistic details was supposed to be disastrous. The Brāhmaṇas abound in examples of men losing their limbs or life due to some ritualistic error. As Cromwell Crawford says,

"The error and its punishment were not related to any moral aspects of sacrifice, but to its magical and mechanical sides."[8]

Moral qualifications were generally not needed for the efficacy of these sacrifices, as affirmed in the following passage of the *Aitareya Brāhmaṇa*:

"Even if the performing priest is not a brāhmaṇa (in the strict sense), or even if he is pronounced to be an ill-reputed man, the sacrifice nevertheless goes up to gods and becomes not polluted by its contagion with a wicked man."[9]

The moral character of the performer of the sacrifice was hardly ever considered as a relevant qualification, the only requirement being ritualistic purity. Similarly, the rightness or wrongness of the purpose of the sacrifice was usually considered irrelevant for its successful performance. Sacrifices were performed for all sorts of immoral purposes, including the destruction of the enemy which was the professed aim of the *Śyena* sacrifice. Cromwell Crawford is right when he remarks that Vedic rituals were quite frequently used for immoral purposes, and no stigma was attached to such practices. The following passage of the *Aitareya Brāhmaṇa* seems to prove his observation:

"Should a *hotṛ* (priest) wish to deprive any sacrificer of his standing place, then he must not repeat the 'silent prayer' at his sacrifice; the sacrificer then perishes along with his sacrifice which thus has become rootless".[10]

The Gṛhya Sūtras which followed the *Brāhmaṇas* prescribed their own rituals, called *Gṛhya* (domestic) sacrifices. Some of these sacrifices (five daily sacrifices and morning and evening prayers) were to be performed daily, while others were meant for special occasions. Both groups of sacrifices were obligatory on the householders of the three 'upper' classes. The daily domestic sacrifices of Gṛhya Sūtras were relatively simple rituals. They expressed a certain amount of religious piety and a desire to establish harmonious relations with the universe which characterized the early Vedic religion. At the same time, it should not be forgotten that the Gṛhya Sūtras accepted and endorsed all major Vedic (*Śrauta*) sacrifices and whatever else they implied.[11]

(iii) The Dharmaśāstras are the main source books of present-day Hindu Dharma. Though Hinduism originated in the Vedas, it is the later texts, specially the Dharmaśāstras, which have provided it with its most important religious beliefs and practices.

Dharmaśāstras accepted Vedic rituals, but often simplified them. They also developed rituals of their own. The most important group of rituals advocated unanimously by the Dharmaśāstras, is that of *Pañca-mahāyajñas* (five great sacrifices) which are to be performed daily by all the householders of three 'upper' classes. They consist of *Brahmayajña* (regular study of the Vedas), *Pitṛyajña* or *tarpaṇa* (offering water to the forefathers), *Devayajña* or *homa* (oblations into fire with recitation of *mantras*), *Bhūtayajña* or *Balivaiśvadeva* (offering food to fire, water and other natural forces or nature deities, as well as to all living creatures) and *Manuṣyayajña* (giving food to the guests).[12] Now, the study of Vedas may have religious worth, but it is mainly conceived and practised as a daily ritual. The next two sacrifices of offering water to the forefathers and oblations into the fire are nothing but rituals to be performed more or less mechanically. The fourth or *Balivaiśvadeva* sacrifice is more important and is also recognized as an independent ritual. The sacrifice consists of offering food in the fire for various gods; after which some of it is to be thrown into different directions for various smaller deities and living beings. And the remaining portion is to be left on the ground outside the house 'for persons suffering from sin-originated diseases, outcastes, dogs, crows and worms.'[13] Apart from the unthinkable indignity associated with such food left on the ground, the intention here is obviously not to feed human beings, but to fulfil a ritualistic obligation. Even in modern times, though very few men perform all the five sacrifices, many householders of 'upper' castes do take out a microscopic quantity of food out of their plate and put it on the ground for different living beings !

The last sacrifice of feeding the guest also had ritualistic overtones, but gradually developed into an independent practice with socio-moral significance. It would be discussed in our next chapter.

Another related and very important ritual of the Dharmaśāstras is *śrāddha* (obsequial rites). *Śrāddha* consists of feeding brāhmaṇas with the specific aim of giving satisfaction to the forefathers. The ancestors are said to eagerly wait for dutiful sons and grandsons who would perform their obsequial rites and thereby secure a long stay in heaven for them.[14] Dharmaśāstras give detailed instructions regarding the brāhmaṇas to be called for the feeding, the manner of welcoming and serving the brāhmaṇas and the food to be offered to them. The food eaten by the brāhmaṇas is supposed to reach the ancestors in some literal sense. Various Law-givers, as Manu and Āpastamba, have given the relative efficacy of various kinds of food to be offered in a *śrāddha*. Thus, if sesame seeds, rice, barley and fruits are offered (to the forefathers through the mouths of the brāhmaṇas), the forefathers are supposedly satisfied for a month; if fish is offered, they are satisfied for two months; if meat of red he-goat is offered, their satisfaction continues for ever ![15]

It is believed that if the funeral rites are not properly performed, the departed soul becomes a ghost (*preta*). Therefore, there is tremendous religio-social pressure on sons and relatives to perform the rites in an elaborate fashion, which leaves a majority of them under heavy debts. The belief in funeral rites means that the rites performed by one's heirs can secure one's eschatological destiny. As we know, the Vedic ritualistic tradition emphasized the ritualistic act more than the inner spirit, and asserted that it is possible for the host to reap the fruits of the sacrifice performed by the priests. That is how the funeral rites, even though they are a later innovation, are harmoniously related to the Vedic religion.

Often irrational sanctions and comparisons were offered to ensure that people performed various rituals. For example, Manu equated the non-performance of *Agnihotra* sacrifice to the murder of a son and prescribed a rigorous penance for the lapse.[16] Everywhere in this tradition the emphasis was on the performance of outward act and not on the inner spirit. Too much attention was bestowed on ritualistic cleanliness (*śauca*) and uncleanliness (*aśauca*). There were innumerable taboos regarding ritualistic defilement, resulting from the death of someone or the birth of a child. A man was supposed to become impure by touching or even talking to an outcaste, a dog and a woman under certain natural conditions, such as child birth or menstruation. He also became impure if a death occurred in the family.[17] While bathing or merely rinsing the mouth with water purified a man in certain cases of defilement, in other cases detailed ritualistic baths were prescribed at the end of specified periods of defilement (*aśauca*). Many of these ritualistic observances are still practised by the caste Hindus.

Another subject that seems to have engrossed our Law-givers (*Smṛtikāras*) is food. They have given elaborate and irrational instructions regarding the eatability or otherwise of various kinds of food. Not only was the food spoilt by dirty objects or animals thought to be unfit for human consumption, but the food which was touched or even looked at by an untouchable or a sinful person was declared to be uneatable.[18] Though meat as such was not prohibited, the meat of certain animals and birds was so, as also certain innocent things like garlic.[19] And reading these lists one cannot detect a single reason for the choice of various taboos.

Smṛtis abound in innumerable other taboos which could hardly be given any rational explanation. A graduate householder was enjoined by Manu that he should not see the sun or its reflection in water, or his own reflection in water; he should not cross over the rope binding a calf, nor should he write on the ground, or grind a lump of mud with his hands; he should also not point out a rainbow to others, and should cross a mud-heap, a brāhmaṇa and certain trees in a prescribed manner.[20] Now, most of these taboos are irrational and amoral, and must have, therefore, encouraged an equally irrational and amoral approach to life and morality. The Dharmaśāstras were supposed to regulate the entire life of man, and if they chose to prescribe the above amoral taboos, instead of giving meaningful moral commands and prohibitions, it may suggest that these ritualistic concerns were more important for them than moral ones. Moreover, if so much time and thought were devoted to such irrational matters, naturally much less time and thought would have been spared for moral concerns.

(iv) Though the main stance of the Epics and the Purāṇas was not ritualistic, the rituals found an important place in their total concept of the right way of life. The two Epics and scores of major and minor Purāṇas cover almost one and a half millenniums of Hindu history. So much changed during this period. Vedic sacrifices became increasingly less popular, first, because they involved so much violence which had gradually become abhorrent to the Hindu mind; and secondly, because they necessitated huge expenditure and were restricted to the three 'upper' castes, thus being beyond the reach of the masses. The *Mahābhārata* and Purāṇas frankly admitted that the poor and the lowly were offered no religious solace by the Vedic tradition. They were also conscious of the attraction of the heterodox sects of Buddhism and Jainism for such people. The Purāṇic writers, therefore, set upon the task of wooing the 'lower' castes, the poor, the illiterate and women away from the lure of Buddhism by providing them with an alternative religion. This new religion mainly consists of various ritualistic fasts or vows (*vratas*) and pilgrimages,[21] and forms the bulk of present-day popular Hinduism.

The Purāṇic rituals are much simpler than the Vedic ones and universal in their appeal; but the general approach of the authors of the Epics and Purāṇas is no different from that of the Vedic-Dharmaśāstric tradition. The ritual of *śrāddha* is given great importance in the *Mahābhārata* and Purāṇas. It is joined together in the Purāṇas with the ritual of pilgrimage. Pilgrimage is the chief of Purāṇic rituals and is popular even now among all classes of Hindus. Each Purāṇa has its own favourite *tīrtha* or pilgrimage centre and devotes several chapters eulogizing the amazing potency or power of that particular *tīrtha* to absolve men of all sins. Prayāga, Vārāṇasī, Haridwāra, Gayā and Puṣkara are among the more important pilgrimage centres; but there are innumerable others. In the *Āraṇyaka Parva* of *Mahābhārata* scores of sacred places are enumerated in a short span of ten chapters (chs. 80 to 89); and almost identical claims are made on behalf of each of them.

Vratas (religious vows and fasts) are another set of rituals, greatly cherished by the Purāṇas. *Vratas* are mostly religious fasts undertaken on specific religious occasions and are usually consummated with the observance of certain rituals. There are innumerable such *vratas*. P.V. Kane has enumerated as many as 1238 *vratas* in the fourth volume of his *History of Dharmaśāstra.* Many of these *vratas* have now become obsolete; but there is still a very large number of such fast-cum-festivals observed by people belonging to different regions, castes and sects. Though they are supposed to be voluntary, like all Hindu rituals a certain obligation is associated with them. Purāṇas invented exaggerated sanctions to induce people to observe these *vratas.* To give but one example, the omission of the observance of *Janmāṣṭamī*, the festival associated with the birth of lord Kṛṣṇa, is compared in *Brahma-vaivarta Purāṇa* to the murder of hundred brāhmaṇas ![22] Perhaps the most important of these Purāṇic rituals is that of the *ekādaśī vrata*[23] or the fast on both the eleventh days of the lunar calendar, followed by the worship of Viṣṇu on the twelfth day. The *Padma Purāṇa* hails the practice of the *ekādaśī* fast as of tremendous merit in the present age of degeneration (*Kali yuga*). According to the *Garuḍa Purāṇa*, the merits of the observance of the fast and its associated rituals on the eleventh day of the lunar calendar are greater than the giving away of the entire earth.[24] *Nārada Purāṇa* narrates the story of king Rukmāṅgada who, when offered the option of either renouncing the *ekādaśī* fast or putting his son to death, opted to kill his son, rather than to forego the fast ![25] Such stories are highly fantastic and suggest a total reversal of all moral values. Religious sanction in favour of these fasts is so strong that a vast majority of Hindus still observe them. They even force other members of the family, specially ladies, to observe these fasts, sometimes even at the cost of their lives. (Such extreme practices are becoming increasingly less common.)

On the credit side, these religious fasts demand great self-restraint on the part of the subject and express a strong faith and an equally strong will. Similarly, pilgrimages used to and even now involve great hardships, so that it is something a person does or undergoes that is supposed to secure the fruits of the ritual, and not merely some ritual performed by the priests, as in the Vedic tradition. On the whole, these Purāṇic rituals are very different from, much less elaborate and much more universal than, the Vedic rituals. But the spirit in which they are performed is more or less the same as that of Vedic ritualism. External act or observance, and not inner spirit or any moral qualification, is more important and is supposedly conducive to the attainment of the desired result. For example, a person desirous to observe the fast dedicated to Santoṣī Mātā is expected to eat only once and avoid all sour things on Fridays. This simple observance is expected to secure the fulfilment of all one's desires ! And if one fails in the above ritualistic observance, one is sure to incur the wrath of the goddess and suffer all sorts of calamities !

(v) The Tāntric tradition not only exalted the rituals, it declared them to be capable of sanctifying apparently immoral acts. Tantras are a class apart and do not represent the main stream of Hindu religio-philosophy. We would have left them, but for the fact that Tantras are even now popular among certain sections of the Hindu society. Tantras expressed a strong world-and-life-affirmation and advocated the well-known practice of *pañca-makāras* or five prohibited objects which should instead be made a means of final liberation, viz. wine, meat, fish, *mudrā* (ritualistic configuration of fingers or the woman as a partner in the Tāntric practice) and sex. It was argued that these objects or various enjoyments are sinful in themselves, but if they are enjoyed according to the rules and with the recitation of *mantras*, they become conducive to final liberation.

Tantras openly upheld magical powers (*siddhis*) which could be used for the following six ends—avoidance of some evil or physical illness (*śānti*), bringing people and gods under one's control (*vaśīkaraṇa*), blocking other men's activities (*stambhana*), creating enmity among friends (*vidveṣaṇa*), causing the ouster of some person from one's territory (*uccāṭana*) and killing or inflicting fatal injuries on others (*māraṇa*). Various Purāṇas, especially the *Matsya Purāṇa*, have recognized these Tāntric powers.[26]

Men everywhere have their baser desires; and it is the task of religion and morality to control or sublimate them and not to encourage and sanction them. When this is done in the name of religion, both religion and morality suffer as a consequence. Though theoretically the Tāntric way of life is supposed to lead one to the realization of one's transcendent nature, in practice, Tāntric practices are mostly undertaken with the purpose of acquiring ritualistic powers (*siddhis*). The masses are not permitted to participate in the Tāntric rituals; but they are often eager to benefit from the Tāntric powers that are supposedly acquired by the adepts. Now, inasmuch as the acquisition of these powers does not usually require any moral qualifications, and they can be used for highly immoral purposes without inviting any censure from the society, the Tāntric way implies a total negation of all ethical norms and values.

Luckily the inherent moral consciousness of Indians (Hindus) was too strong to accept such a perversion of values, and there was a persistent outcry against the Tāntric practices which found frequent expression in ancient literature.[27] This forced the Tāntrikas to remain largely an esoteric group and protected the masses from its evil influence.

We admit that our understanding of the Tāntric tradition is necessarily incomplete and superficial. We have not at all considered the philosophical aspects of the tradition or the rationalizations of the Tāntric philosophy and practices offered by such modern scholars as Gopinath Kaviraja. Given the limitation of our understanding, we still think that the Tāntric tradition has exerted an unhealthy influence on Hindu morality.

II. Equation of Morality with Ritualistic Religion

It may be argued here that we might well have successfully criticized Hindu ritualism, but it does not necessarily follow that the same criticism would apply to Hindu ethics. But the truth of the matter is that Hinduism hardly ever makes a distinction between rituals and morality proper. These religious or semi-religious rituals would not have mattered much, had they not claimed to exhaust the entire field of *dharma* or morality. The hold of ritualistic tradition on Hindu morality is possibly due to the one word *dharma* being used for both ritualistic acts (misnamed religion in the English language) and what we now consider morality proper.

(i) The philosophy of Mīmāṁsā has played a very important role in the development of the ritualistic tradition. The main subject matter of Mīmāṁsā inquiry is *dharma*, as is clear from the very first Mīmāṁsā Sūtra—"*Athāto dharma-jijñāsā* (now begins an enquiry into *dharma*)." According to Śabara, *dharma* being a supernatural object, it cannot be known either through perception, or on the authority of other persons, as human intellect is fallible. Vedas are, therefore, the only source of knowledge of *dharma*. Mīmāṁsā asserts the infallibility of Vedas and the absoluteness of Vedic commands regarding *dharma*. Those Smṛti texts which are not opposed to *Śruti* (Vedas) are also to be followed in the performance of *dharma*.[28]

This is a doctrine which understands morality exhaustively in terms of Vedic commands (*vidhi*) and prohibitions (*niṣedha*). The second *Mīmāṁsā Sūtra* gives the famous definition of *dharma*—'*Codanālakṣaṇortho dharmaḥ*', that is to say, *dharma* is that good (*artha*) which is characterized by Vedic injunctions or commands (*codanā*).

A few things are to be noted here. First, all *dharma* necessarily means *karma* or action and hence is related to the will which is supposed to be impelled by the Vedic commands. Secondly, this *dharma* cannot be known by man's reason, so that it is solely derivable from the Vedic commands. That means, no act is good or bad in itself, but is so because and only because it is commanded or prohibited in Vedas. This denies all autonomy to morality and completely subordinates it to a very narrow ritualistic concept of religion. Śabara was of the opinion that only those acts which are of the nature of *artha* (good) and are enjoined by the Vedas are to be regarded as *dharma*, and not those actions which are of the nature of *anartha* (evil), a stock example of the latter being the *Śyena* sacrifice. According to him, inasmuch as violence cannot be commanded, Vedic injunctions pertaining to such acts cannot be called *dharma*. They are just hypothetical imperatives to the effect that whosoever wants to destroy his enemies should perform the *Śyena* sacrifice.[29] While Prabhākara agreed with Śabara, writers like Umbeka Bhaṭṭa and Kumārila emphatically argued that whatever is enjoined by the Vedas is *dharma*; and that positively includes *Śyena* sacrifice which is to be regarded as *dharma*, since it has been enjoined by the Vedas ! This discussion absolutely and irrevocably reduces morality to Vedic commands. Thirdly, not to leave any doubts, Mīmāṁsā thinkers have affirmed that by *dharma* is meant Vedic sacrifices and not such altruistic acts (*paropakāra*) as digging wells and planting trees.[30] The Mīmāṁsakas thus seem to have no confusion regarding *dharma* which they regard as consisting of ritualistic acts only.

It is, therefore, sometimes suggested that since Mīmāṁsā concerns itself exclusively with Vedic rituals, the *dharma* of Mīmāṁsā need not be understood in the same sense as the *dharma* or duty in the moral context. It is argued here that the 'ought' in the ritualistic context is not the same as the 'ought' in the moral context. But this is not the case. The meaning of the term *dharma* in Mīmāṁsā is what ought to be done or duty. It is in this sense only that *dharma* is considered as an object of Vedic commands. The form of the command or the meaning of the 'ought' in the ritualistic context is exactly the same as that in the moral context. According to Mīmāṁsā, the central idea in the Vedic command or imperative (*vidhi*) is action; and the *vidhi* is recognized by its formal character which includes some verb in the imperative mood. Śabara has quoted some old verse to the effect that *vidhi* or command is known by such phrases as, 'one should do it', 'it should be done', 'it ought to be done', 'it should be so' and 'it ought to be so'.[31] This means that the Vedic command is expressed by, and *dharma* is known through, the verb in the imperative mood (*vidhi liṅ*). In the imperative sentence the verb used, as *yajeta* (you ought to perform the sacrifice), consists of two parts—while the first part consists of the root form (*dhātu*) of the verb expressing the nature of the act, the second part or the suffix (*pratyaya*) is in the imperative mood (*vidhi liṅ*). *Liṅtva* or the imperatival form of the verb is thus the essence of the command, and inasmuch as *dharma* is what is commanded by the Vedas, it becomes the essence of *dharma* also.

According to Prabhākara, the Vedic command (*niyoga*) does not impel the will, but constitutes an authoritative suggestion to the will (*preraṇā*) which results in the appropriation by the self of the commanded act as one which ought to be done by oneself. The power of motivation of the command lies in this cognition of obligation by the self. Prabhākara also insists that the expectation of some good to be attained does not at all enter into one's performance of duties, especially the unconditional ones (*nitya karma*)[32]. Now, if Prabhākara first explains *dharma* in terms reminiscent of Kant's categorical imperative, that is, in strictly ethical terms, and then understands *dharma* exclusively as ritualistic acts commanded by the Vedas, it means that ritualistic acts and moral duty are not differentiated by Prabhākara.

The idea of 'ought' is central to the ritualistic concept of *dharma*, and it is the same as the 'ought' of morality. When Mīmāṁsā, Vedas and Dharmaśāstras tell a man that a given ritual is what he ought to perform, and when another thinker commands that he ought to speak the truth, an average Hindu does not think that they are speaking of different things. The same is true of prohibitions. Most of the Vedic prohibitions are of a ritualistic nature, the conventional example being, 'you ought not to eat *kalañja*'. The logical form of the negative command (*niṣedha*) is in no way different from the negative moral commands, as 'you ought not to commit adultery.' Thus, the entire discussion of *dharma* by Mīmāṁsā unequivocally identifies ritualistic duty with moral duty, both being understood as what ought to be done or *dharma*.

(ii) Dharmaśāstras equally make no distinction between *dharma* as ritualistic duty and *dharma* as moral duty. All their discussions of duty, sin and repentence refer to ritualistic and moral duties jointly. As we have seen in our previous section, most of the *Smārta* taboos are amoral and irrational, but they are given in a typically moralistic language, such as, "Let him never look at the sun... Let him never cross over the rope binding a calf..."[33] Since the Smṛtis are supposed to govern the entire life of the Hindus, presentation of amoral acts as one's duty must create confusion in their minds regarding the meaning and content of moral duty.

All Dharmaśāstras indiscriminately combine the two kinds of duties while giving the duties of the four classes (*varṇas*).[34] For example, the duties of the three upper classes include the study of Vedas and performance of Vedic sacrifices which are clearly ritualistic duties. In addition, they have their specific caste duties (*varṇāśrama dharma*), and all of them are denoted by the word *dharma*. In fact, the meaning of the term *dharma* has very important ritualistic overtones. Vedas and after them Smṛtis are universally regarded as the chief sources of *dharma*[35]. Since the chief concern of the Vedas is ritualistic acts, it can be taken for granted that the *dharma* which is based on the Vedas would be largely ritualistic in character.

(iii) Even other religious texts like the *Bhagavadgītā* have used the term *dharma* for both ritualistic and socio-moral duties. It is to be remembered that there is no separate term for moral duty in Sanskrit. The two terms, *dharma* and *karma*, have been indiscriminately used both for ritualistic and moral duties. In the following passages of the *Bhagavadgītā* the term *karma* is used for socio-moral duty:

"Thy concern is with action or duty (*karma*) alone, never with results. Let not the fruits of action be thy motive."[36] And,

"Devoted each to his own duty (*karma*) man attains perfection."[37]

In the famous verses exhorting men to follow their respective caste duties the *Gītā* has used both terms, *karma* and *dharma*, to indicate one's socio-moral duties.[38] At the same time, the *Gītā* also uses both the terms to denote ritualistic duties or sacrifices. It asserts that the ordained duties (*niyata karma*) should always be performed, and explains them in terms of sacrifice (*yajña*). Of course, sacrifice has got a very broad meaning in the *Bhagavadgītā*, but its ritualistic content is undeniable.[39] Śaṁkara also understands the term *niyata karma* used in the *Gītā* as *nitya karma* (daily obligatory rituals).[40] According to the *Bhagavadgītā*, *dharma* or *karma* consists of all the duties which have been enjoined in the scriptures, and they include both ritualistic and caste duties. It is the *Gītā's* contention that the ritualistic duties help in the harmonious functioning of the world order, while the caste duties are essential for the smooth functioning and stability of the social order. And there is no distinction between the ritualistic and caste or socio-moral duties for the *Bhagavadgītā*.

The *Bhagavadgītā* is not a work belonging to the ritualistic tradition. Yet it understands duty (*dharma* or *karma*) in terms of Vedic sacrifices (*yajña*), and confuses between the ritualistic and moral meanings of the term *dharma* (duty). We can discern here the overwhelming influence of the ritualistic tradition on entrei Hindu ethical thought. It is our contention, therefore, that the ritualistic tradition unequivocally identifies morality with rituals, generally reduces moral duty to ritualistic acts and conceives sin and repentance in entirely externalistic terms. This equation between the ritualistic and the moral meanings of *dharma* (duty) has constantly undermined a rational approach to moral matters, and indirectly discouraged truly moral concerns.

III. An Amoral Concept of Sin

The confusion between the ritualistic and moral points of view is similarly expressed in the popular Hindu concept of sin.

(i) The externalistic ritualism of the Brāhmaṇas naturally resulted in an equally externalistic and amoral conception of sin. The Brāhmaṇas with their ritualistic bias conceived sin as some external matter which can be washed off with water or holy grass. Sin was supposed to be the effect of some ritualistic transgression. Truth was a highly valued moral virtue in the Brāhmaṇas; but even the sin accruing from the transgression of truth was declared to be washable with external means.[41]

(ii) The Dharmaśāstric stance in this matter is no less unfortunate. The *Gautama-Dharmasūtra* defines sin as:

"Man becomes sinful in this world by evil acts, such as performing sacrifice for undeserving persons, eating uneatable things like garlic, speaking untruth or indecent things, not doing ordained rituals or doing prohibited acts."[42]

All the Smṛtis agree on the list of five great sins, viz. murder of a brāhmaṇa, drinking, adultery with one's teacher's wife (or some close elderly relative), stealing a brāhmaṇa's gold and association with the above four sinners. There follows a list of sins which are equal to the above sins in gravity, and this second list includes eating uneatable things! The list of minor sins (*up-pātaka*), given in all the Smṛtis, consists of petty acts of commission and omission, such as selling prohibited objects, felling trees, eating prohibited food and working in mines or on machines etc.[43] The damage to a healthy ethical approach was even greater, as such ritualistic offences were grouped together with the murder of all human beings, except brāhmaṇas (yes, murder was a minor crime in the Smṛtis). On another occasion, Manu has given the list of brāhmaṇas who are not worthy of being invited for a *śrāddha* rites and who should not be given gifts, presumably because they are sinners. The offences which disqualified a brāhmaṇa consisted of acts of moral transgression like theft, adultery etc. as also morally innocent acts like teaching a śūdra, selling prohibited objects, or even marrying before one's elder brother ! Even innocent professions like being a courier of the king were regarded as disqualifying. Certain physical defects, such as being one-eyed or bald or having ugly teeth or nails, were treated as detestable and sure signs of one's being a sinner.[44]

Thus, sin was mostly conceived in the Dharmaśāstras as a result of the commission of certain amoral acts or omission of certain other ritualistic acts. One of the most important subjects of discussion of the Dharmaśāstras and later Nibandhas is penance. Penance was first conceived as voluntarily undergoing severe mortification of the flesh in repentance for one's sins. All Dharmaśāstras prescribe most severe penances for the major sins.[45] Such severe mortification of the body would naturally purge the heart of its sinful tendencies. But the Law-givers soon realized that very few people would be capable of undertaking such severe penances, and so they went on to prescribe petty ritualistic acts as substitutes for the harsh penances. Manu gives a list of several alternative penances, such as studying the Vedas, performing five daily sacrifices, undertaking certain specified fasts, giving gifts, performing yoga exercises and repeating the sacred syallable *Om*, all guaranteed as capable of absolving men of all sins. He then goes on to offer several Vedic texts and promises that a ritualistic repetition of either one of them for a prescribed number of times absolves a man of all but the most heinous sins.[46] At one place Manu prescribes a ritual for a man who has violated his vow of celibacy during studenthood. It consists of a sacrifice with the tallow of a one-eyed donkey at the road crossing ![47] How this magical rite can purify a man's heart is anyone's guess.

Of course, Manu and other Law-givers equally emphasized moral duty, right moral attitude and true heart-felt repentance. But the fact that they prescribed petty amoral ritualistic acts as penances for almost all sins must have eroded the consciousness of moral responsibility among the masses and distorted their moral perspective.

(iii) If Manu and other Law-givers had any reservations about the efficacy of rituals in absolving men of all sins, they were shed by the authors of the Epics and Purāṇas. As we have seen, they advocated rituals of their own and claimed that these rituals, especially pilgrimages, are capable of destroying all one's sins. It was claimed for each and every pilgrimage centre (*tīrtha*) that a visit to it, or a bath in its river destroys all one's sins. It was further declared by several Purāṇas and *Mahābhārata* that all who die in the Avimukta region of Vārāṇasī, including the gravest sinners and even sub-human beings, are automatically released from transmigratory existence.[48] The *Mahābhārata* eulogizes river Gaṅgā and declares that not only are its sacred waters capable of destroying all one's sins, bathing in it results in freedom from transmigratory existence of several generations of one's ancestors and even that of the future progeny ! It adds that mere remembrance of the river Gaṅgā destroys all one's sins.[49] Even after leaving allowance for poetic exaggeration, such pronouncements do belittle the idea of the gravity of sin and suggest an undermining of the idea of moral accountability.

As we have seen, the Brāhmaṇas conceived sin as some external pollution which can be got rid off with the use of water or holy grass. The Dharmaśāstras corrected this externalistic concept to a certain extent, though their perception of sin was marred by their ritualistic bias. The Purāṇas apparently reverted to the view of the Brāhmaṇas and conceived sin as something to be washed off by a dip in the holy waters of various sacred rivers. If sin generally results from the commission of some external act, and if it can be got rid off by some ritualistic act, then, sin must pertain to the body and cannot involve one's inmost being. Such a view goes against the moral point of view according to which it is the inner attitude that determines the moral quality of an act, and indulgence in sin leaves a deep scar on one's inner being which cannot be healed so easily by petty ritualistic observances.

IV. The Fruits of Rituals and the Desire For Them As the Motive

(i) Traditionally, all Hindu religious texts, from the Vedas to Purāṇas, claim that the religious practices or rituals advocated by them, if practised properly, would bring prosperity and happiness to the devout. The Brāhmaṇas regarded their rituals as sufficiently potent to bring about the desired results without the mediation of gods. They also gave fantastic stories regarding certain persons who supposedly benefited from the performance of their rituals. The Dharmaśāstras and Purāṇas substituted their own simpler rituals for the more expensive and elaborate Vedic rituals. But the general approach, the ritualistic bias and the tendency to make fantastic claims for the rituals, found in the Brāhmaṇas, continued to characterize the later works. The authors of Dharmaśāstras and Purāṇas made similarly exaggerated and irrational claims regarding the efficacy of their rituals in producing the desired results. For example, Āpastamba has listed days when if a *śrāddha* is performed, it is sure to bring about certain results. Thus, if a *śrāddha* is performed on the third day of the second half of the month, one would have sons; but if it is performed on the first day, one would have only daughters ![50] Such fanciful claims encourage dogmatism which naturally hampers the development of a positive rational morality.

Purāṇas and the Epics sought to give the masses a religion suited to their needs and intellectual capacities. Lest the masses feel deprived of their right to learn the Vedas and perform Vedic sacrifices, extravagant claims were made on behalf of the new rituals. The *Viṣṇu Purāṇa* describes Vyāsa as praising *Kali yuga* (the present age of moral degeneration), as it is only in *Kali yuga* that a very small amount of effort results in great merit (*dharma*), whereas in earlier ages, when moral and spiritual values prevailed, much greater effort, in the form of sacrifices and hard austerities was needed in order to secure the same amount of merit.[51] The sentiment is repeated in other Purāṇas also. But no rational explanation is given as to why in the present age, when man has become degenerate, he has to put in less, instead of more, effort in order to secure merit or moral excellence. Their only intention being popular appeal, the authors of Purāṇas competed with each other in offering the easiest possible panacea for all the ills of life. For example, both *Mahābhārata* and *Padma Purāṇa* contend that since the Vedic and Smārta sacrifices cannot be performed in the present *Kali* age, people should undertake fasting on both the eleventh days (*ekādaśi*) of the lunar calendar which involves very little botheration and expenditure, but is sure to give the greatest fruit.[52] On another occasion, the *Padma Purāṇa* declares that the merit of the man who gives a single candle (*dīpa*) on the eleventh lunar day of the month of *kārttika* is beyond measure ![53]

The *Brahma-vaivarta Purāṇa* assures that the man who forms a single *Śivaliṅga* of clay would reside in heaven for hundred long ages (*kalpas*).[54] The *Padma Purāṇa* narrates the story of two brothers who had wasted their lives in carnal pleasures. After death, one was awarded hell, while the other was sent to heaven. It was so because the latter had once bathed in the Yamunā river in the month of *Māgha* ![55]

Similarly fantastic claims were made for each and every Purāṇic ritual, as pilgrimage, bathing in certain rivers, especially on certain days, performance of obsequial rites (*śrāddha*), observance of religious vows or fasts, giving gifts to brāhmaṇas, reading Purāṇas and repeating (*japa*) some religious text or formula (*mantra*). Each Purāṇa had its own favourite pilgrimage centre and claimed that a visit to that *tīrtha*, or even mere remembrance thereof, would not only absolve a man of all sins, but also secure heaven or even release from transmigratory existence for him.

Reading or listening to Purāṇas and other religious texts was another typical Purāṇic ritual for which similar tall claims were made. The Epics, Purāṇas and other religious texts, all end with lengthy benedictory statements promising the highest merit and all imaginable rewards to the man or woman who listens to their stories. To give a typical example, the *Rāmāyaṇa* claims:

"Should anybody read or adore this old history, he or she will be absolved of all sins and will enjoy longevity. Kṣatriyas should hear this tale from brāhmaṇas and they will get wealth and sons... If one hears the whole of *Rāmāyaṇa* he (lord Rāma) will be pleased. This history is so very efficacious."[56]

Listening to the stories of Purāṇas, especially the *Bhāgavata Purāṇa*, is even now regarded as of tremendous merit, the emphasis being on mere listening and not on conduct or right inner attitude. Purāṇas contain excellent moral precepts, but their major bulk consists of mythological stories. These stories are narrated in an extremely exaggerated style which has fascinated the masses for centuries. The illiterate credulous listeners of the Purāṇic stories do not have enough discrimination to discount such exaggerations as mere poetic licence. A heavy and regular dose of Purāṇic mythology must necessarily engender dogmatism or an irrational approach to life and morality, and thus confuse the moral perspective.

(ii) This tradition frankly admits that the universal motive for the performance of *dharma*, both in the ritualistic and moral contexts, is the desire for the good fruits that are expected to accrue from the performance. Śabara and Kumārila of Mīmāṁsā school of philosophy emphasized the role of desire for some specific gain in inducing a man to obey a Vedic command or perform some ritual. The Vedic command was generally understood as a hypothetical imperative, the hackneyed example being, 'if you desire heaven perform this sacrifice (*svargakāmo yajeta*)!' According to Śabara, Vedic commands are of the form, 'you ought to perform *Agniṣṭoma*'. If it is asked how, the answer is, 'with *soma*'; if it is asked why, the answer is 'for heaven'.[57] For Kumārila, the attainment of some good (*hita-prāpti*) is the motive behind all positive willing or activity (*pravṛtti*), while the avoidance of evil (*ahita-parihāra*) is the universal motive for desisting from willing (*nivṛtti*).[58] Most Mīmāṁsā thinkers, with the exception of Prabhākara, contend that even though the authority of the scriptural imperative is independent of the desire on the part of the individual, a man does not take up any duty commanded by the scriptures, unless he is prompted by desire for some end to be attained by the act commanded. Kumārila has categorically affirmed that all men act with some specific gain in mind and that, "not even fools act without some purpose in view..."[59]

Interestingly, all orthodox schools of thought accept the Mīmāṁsā view of action or duty. According to the *Vaiśeṣika Sūtras*, "*Dharma* is that from which (results) the accomplishment of exaltation or well-being (*abhyudaya*) and the realization of the highest good (*niḥśreyasa*)".[60] *Dharma* or duty here is conceived not as an end-in-itself, but as a means of the realization of well-being here and release or heaven hereafter.

The Dharmaśāstras clearly follow the ritualistic tradition and acknowledge the role of desires in inducing man to follow the path of *dharma*. According to Āpastamba, a man who fulfils his assigned duties properly enjoys birth in a distinguished family, beauty of form, wisdom and wealth here and heavenly bliss hereafter.[61] It suggests that the desire for the good fruits of the performance of one's duties is a legitimate motive for their performance. Manu has frankly accepted personal gain as the most significant motive for the performance of one's duties:

"It is not good to desire the fruits of actions, but it is not necessary to give up desires. Both the acceptance of Vedas and the performance of Vedic acts are motivated by desire. . . .

"No act is undertaken by a man without desire in this world. Whatever a man does is the result of desire..."[62]

This necessary relation between desire and duty has been further strengthened by the exaggerated claims of Purāṇic authors regarding the fruits of their particular rituals. These claims have engendered an attitude of expectation among the masses regarding the beneficial results of various rituals. As a result, most of the Hindu *vratas* are undertaken by people, especially ladies, with specific desires for the long life and prosperity of their loved ones. Since moral duties are scarcely distinguished from religious acts in Hinduism, the habit of performing one's religious duties with the definite expectation of rewards can easily transfer itself to socio-moral duties. If it happens, it would naturally be detrimental to the interests of genuine morality which necessarily judges the moral worth of an action on the basis of the motive for its performance.

V. Amoral Implications of Hindu Polytheism

Brāhmaṇical ritualism has been closely allied to popular polytheism since the Vedic times. While various gods occupied quite a prominent place in the Vedas, their role became rather secondary in the Brāhmaṇas. The same is also true of the Dharmaśāstras in which gods seem to be mere abstractions, referred to and worshipped as a class only. There was a resurrection of Vedic polytheism with the Epics and Purāṇas. Or it may be that polytheism continued to dominate popular religion all the while; only it found a fresh expression in Purāṇas which were avowedly concerned with the religion of the masses. By the time of Purāṇas almost all Vedic gods were replaced by new Hindu gods. Similarly, old Vedic sacrifices were substituted by simpler Purāṇic rituals, as *vratas* and pilgrimages. But though both gods and rituals have changed, the approach of the devout Hindus towards their gods has continued to be the same through the centuries. The Vedic seers sang hymns and performed sacrifices with the firm expectation that the gods, thus appeased, would confer the desired boons on them. The present-day Hindus similarly visit various holy places and temples, perform certain rituals, observe certain fasts or religious vows (*vratas*) with the expectation of receiving favours from the gods in return. The entire relation between the devotee and the gods in the polytheistic tradition seems to be based on the spirit of business transaction. Even the *Bhagavadgītā*, a highly ethical and theistic work, has accepted the legitimacy of such an approach:

"With this (sacrifice) do you nourish the gods, and the gods shall nourish you...

"Nourished by the sacrifice, the gods shall indeed bestow on you the enjoyments you desire..."[63]

Hindu polytheism has exerted some rather unhealthy influence on Hindu morality. Since various gods are mostly worshipped by their devotees with some personal motive, the practice of polytheism in the Hindu society has reinforced the old Vedic connection between *dharma* or duty and desire-fulfilment, and has thereby undermined the very basis of genuine morality.

This approach has also cheapened religious piety and by implication has made ethical qualifications irrelevant for both religion and social life. As the goal of desire-fulfilment can be achieved by appeasing anyone of the various gods through the observance of some ritual or the other, moral considerations become rather secondary in this approach, at least at the level of popular religion. Purāṇas have given stories of gods, especially Śiva, giving all sorts of boons, including vastly destructive weapons, to blatantly immoral persons. Many of the heroes of Mahābhārata war, belonging to the two opposing camps, possessed highly destructive weapons, given to them by lord Śiva, thus ensuring the mutual destruction of both the armies. A widely repeated mythological story tells how the gods (*devas*) deprived the demons (*asuras*) of their share of the nectar which the two had churned together out of the ocean. The *Mahābhārata* frankly points out that the gods (*devas*) could secure heaven only by deceiving their half-brothers (*asuras*).[64] Purāṇas narrate innumerable stories in which gods are portrayed as no better than humans. The Purāṇic gods constantly suffered from jealousy, fear and lust, were often faced with difficult situations and were quite willing to use immoral means to achieve their ends. The *Bhāgavata Purāṇa* and other religious texts give stories of Kṛṣṇa's amorous plays with the milk-maids of Vṛndāvana. These stories can be allegorically explained as the soul's love for her Divine Beloved. But the masses who have been listening to these stories for centuries do not understand the mystical language and take them literally. In the *Mahābhārata* Kṛṣṇa emerges as a man of practical wisdom who is not very particular about moral norms.

In fact, excepting Rāma, most other Hindu gods are generally portrayed as amoral persons. When a devotee worships them and constantly hears the narrations of their deeds with the firm conviction that it would bring great merit to him, the moral values (or lack of them), as exemplified by the divine heroes of Purāṇic stories, are bound to affect him. Add to it the general conviction in the Hindu mind that a man can appease these gods by the observance of certain rituals and get the desired boon(s), and we get a rather amoral approach to religion. The ubiquitous presence of religion in Hindu society may well lead to a certain transference of this amoral attitude to socio-moral matters, thus undermining a truly moral approach to life.

VI. Conclusion

We are here aware that our version of Hindu ritualism is possibly a one-sided one. Every religion has its own rituals and most of these rituals are amoral. The Eucharist of the Christians is in no way more moral or spiritual than the *śrāddha* of the Hindus. Taken individually, there is nothing morally objectionable in most Hindu rituals. Rituals, in fact, are an integral part of every religion and culture. Every society has its own rituals and social customs, and their observance by the members of that society binds them together in fellowship and harmony. Our criticism of the ritualistic approach in Hinduism is mostly based on certain observations concerning its ramifications for the morality of Hindu society.

First, we feel that when there is an unchecked proliferation of rituals, it necessarily diverts the mind from the more vital issues of religion and morality. Rituals are hardly ever conceived and executed at a rational level, and they generally discourage a rational approach to life and morality. Also, the emphasis on the external act in the ritualistic tradition endangers the moral approach for which the inner attitude is far more important than the external act. When rituals take the centre of stage in a man's life, the practice of virtues and righteous conduct become rather secondary for him. Those men who are extremely religious, i.e. perform all possible rituals and spend hours in morning *pūjā* (idol worship), are generally quite casual about their socio-moral duties. Secondly, the ritualistic approach has persistently undermined morality by neglecting to include moral character and conduct among the qualifications for the performance of rituals. In fact, moral qualities are often implicitly assumed to be irrelevant for the performance of various rituals. There has been a complete sundering of morality from religion in the ritualistic tradition. One can be religious and hope to earn religious merit through the performance of rituals without being a morally upright person. Given the central place and prestige of religion in the Hindu society, the negative ramifications of this approach for practical morality are too obvious to be argued in detail.

Thirdly, the traditional understanding of duty largely in terms of ritualistic acts, and the use of identical terminology to express both ritualistic and moral commands and prohibitions have confused the moral perspective of the Hindus, resulting in a general undermining of true moral concerns. Most Hindus take recourse to this equation between ritualistic and moral duty in order to avoid their actual socio-moral obligations in daily life. The performance of funeral rites is given greater importance than actually caring for, or serving, one's parents. The duties towards one's fellow beings are supposedly discharged by throwing a microscopic quantity of food on the ground, and so on.

Fourthly, the assertion of a necessary ralation between desire for fruits and the performance of (ritualistic) duty denies the worth of the true moral motive, i.e. the performance of the duty for duty's sake. It may be argued here that actions can still be moral if they are performed with some utilitarian end in view. But such an end or good must have intrinsic worth in order to confer moral worth on duty which is instrumental to it; and the desire for some personal gain as the motive for the performance of rituals does not have any intrinsic worth.

Lastly, the excessive importance given to ritualistic purity in this tradition has continuously strengthened caste discriminations and even the practice of untouchability. This tradition has also contributed to the general undermining of the position of women in the society, both because they are considered to be less pure than men, and because they cannot perform the funeral rites which are extremely important in this tradition. The ritualistic tradition has thus been the greatest cause of the practice of social discriminations in the Hindu society.

At the same time, the above is only one side of the medal. *Dharma* not only means ritualistic duty, it also means morality or righteousness. And it is in this sense that the term *dharma* is mostly used in the *Dharmaśāstras*, Epics and Purāṇas. The aim of our discussion has only been to point out certain negative contributions of the ritualistic tradition to the development of Hindu morality. We believe that they can easily be counterbalanced by a renewed emphasis on the genuinely moral aspects of the Brāhmaṇical tradition and a deliberate distinction between the ritualistic and moral meanings of *dharma* or duty (ought).

Notes

1. Maurice Phillips, *The Teaching of the Vedas* (1976), pp. 29 ff., 40 ff., 139 ff., 190ff. Roderick Hindery, *Comparative Ethics in Hindu and Buddhist Traditions* (1978), pp. 43 ff.
2. *Social and Religious Life in the Gṛhya Sūtras* (1954), p. 65; also see ibid, pp. 66 ff., 72 ff.
3. For a detailed account of Vedic rituals see *The Cultural Heritage of India* (1975), vol. I, pp. 237 ff., 248 ff., and *History* (1974), vol. II, chs. XXIX to XXXV.
4. See *The Cultural Heritage of India*, vol. I, p. 251.
5. See ibid, p. 253; *History*, vol. II p. 1247; Maurice Phillips, op. cit., pp. 190 ff.
6. *Mīmāṁsā Sūtra* VIII, 1. 32-34, quoted in *History* (1975), vol. V, p. 1270.
7. *The Cultural Heritage of India*, vol. I, pp. 234, 236, 245, 251.
8. *Evolution of Hindu Ethical Ideals* (1974), p. 26.
9. *Aitareya Brāhmaṇa* I. 26, quoted in ibid, p. 27
10. Ibid I. 25, quoted in ibid, p. 27.

11. Foı an account of *Gṛhya* rituals see *The Cultural Heritage of India*, vol. I, pp. 254 ff.
12. *M.S.* III. 68 ff.
13. Ibid II. 92.
14. Ibid III. 274-275; IX. 137-138.
15. Ibid III. 266 ff.; *Āpast. D.S.* II. 7.16.23 to II. 7.17.3.
16. *M.S.* XI. 41.
17. Ibid V. 57 ff., 85-86; *Āpast D.S.* I. 5.15.8 ff.; I. 5. 16. 18 ff.
18. *M.S.* IV. 205 ff.; *Āpast D.S.* I.5.16.22 ff., I.5.17.1 ff.
19. *M.S.* V. 5 ff., 19-20.
20. Ibid IV. 37 ff.; *Gaut. D.S.* IX. 8 ff., 38 ff.
21. *See History*, vol. V, pp. 913 ff.
22. Vide H.H. Wilson, *Analysis of Purāṇas* (1976), p. 48.
23. Vide *History*, vol. V, pp. 43-45, 93, 96-99, 104, 934.
24. Vide ibid, vol. V, p. 99.
25. Vide H.H. Wilson, op.cit., preface, p. 32.
26. *See History*, vol. V, pp. 1113-14.
27. Ibid, vol. V, pp. 1073-76.
28. *Mīmāṁsā Sūtra, Śabara Bhāṣya* I.1.5; also see *History*, vol. V, pp. 1202-4, 1224.
29. Ibid I.1.2.
30. Ibid I. 3.2.
31. Ibid IV, 3.3, quoted in *History*, vol. V, p. 1226.
32. See S.K. Maitra, *The Ethics of the Hindus* (1963), pp. 29 ff., 136 ff.
33. *M.S.* IV. 37 ff.
34. Ibid I. 87-91; cf. *B.G.* XVIII. 41-45.
35. Ibid II. 6-11.
36. *B.G.* II. 47.
37. Ibid XVIII. 45.
38. Ibid XVIII. 45-48
39. Ibid III. 8 ff.; XVIII. 7, 23.
40. *Ś.B.*, *B.G.* III. 8
41. *Śatapatha Brāhmaṇa* III. 1.2.10; III. 1.3. 18.
42. *Gaut. D.S.* XIX. 2; cf. *M.S.* V. 4.
43. *M.S.* XI. 56 ff.
44. Ibid III. 151 ff.; *Gaut. D.S.* XV. 16 ff.
45. *M.S.* XI. 71 ff.
46. Ibid XI. 210 ff., 245 ff., 258 ff.
47. Ibid XI. 118-120; cf. *Āpast. D.S.* I. 9.26.8.
48. See *History* (1974), vol. IV, pp. 629-630.
49. *Mbh. Anuś P.* XXVII. 25 ff., especially 45, 61, 92.
50. *Āpast. D.S.* II. 7. 16. 7 ff.
51. *Viṣṇu Purāṇa*, bk. VI, ch. 2 (1972, pp. 491-492).
52. Vide *History*, vol. V, p. 934.
53. Vide ibid, vol. V, p. 45; H.H. Wilson, op.cit., p. 64.
54. Vide H.H. Wilson, op.cit., p. 114.

55. Ibid, p. 55.
56. *Rāmāyaṇa, Yuddha Kāṇḍa*, ch. LXXXVI (1978, pp. 562, 563).
57. *Mīmāṁsā Sūtra, Śabara Bhāṣya* I. 1.32; II. 1.1.
58. See S.K. Maitra, op.cit. (1963), pp. 176 ff.; and *History*, vol. V, p. 1246.
59. *Ślokavārttika*, quoted in M. Hiriyanna, *The Outlines of Indian Philosophy* (1956) pp. 328-329.
60. *Vaiśeṣika Sūtra* I.1.2.
61. *Āpast, D.S.* II. 1.2. 2-3.
62. *M.S.* II. 1-4.
63. *B.G.* III. 11-12.
64. *Mbh. Śān. P.* VIII. 28.

Chapter III

SOCIO-CENTRIC MORALITY OF DHARMASASTRAS AND EPICS

1. The Relativistic Approach of Hindu Social Morality

Dharmaśāstras are the main source-books of both Hindu ritualism and Hindu social morality. The inter-personal morality of Hinduism has been developed in the same Vedic-Dharmaśāstric tradition which is so much concerned with rituals. Ritualism, in a way, pervades the entire outlook of Hindu religious texts. But their main concerns are often the stability of the social organization and the advocacy of a social morality that would be conducive to it. The ethos behind the two moralities, ritualistic and social, is equally one of world-and-life-affirmation. The perception of the world as real and meaningful is presupposed both by the performance of rituals and the fulfilment of one's social obligations. A unique feature of this whole Vedic-Dharmaśāstric tradition is that it affirms the legitimacy of the pursuit of one's self-interest, but at the same time contends that there is no conflict between the good of the individual and that of the society. This reflects a pious faith in the moral governance of the world and the harmony of interests in such a moral order.

Granting that the two moralities of Hindus, social and ritualistic, have originated in the same religio-cultural tradition, they should still be distinguished for two reasons. First, while the norms of socio-moral duties, as given in the Dharmaśāstras, have been almost unanimously accepted by Hindu thinkers, excepting some followers of the tradition of liberation, the tenets of Vedic ritualism have been frequently questioned by the philosophers of liberation and the saints of devotional sects. Secondly, even though the Dharmaśāstras are a very important source of Hindu social morality, the latter has been constantly enriched by the contribution of other Sanskrit works, especially the Epics. On the other hand, the Dharmaśāstras are the supreme, or almost the only, source of present-day Hindu ritualism.

Morality has never been discussed in Hindu works as a separate discipline. But the genuineness of the socio-moral concerns of Hindu thinkers and Law-givers (*Smṛtikāras*) is un-deniable. The term *dharma* is derived from the root *dhṛ*, meaning to sustain or support; that is, *dharma* is what sustains or supports the society.[1] This definition of *dharma* has given a slight bias to the entire Hindu thought in favour of social stability. The main emphasis of Hindu Law-givers has been on those duties of the individual which directly contribute to the stability and harmonious preservation of the social order. The Hindu thinkers recognize both, man's universal duties (*sādhāraṇa dharma*) which appertain to him as man and his specific or class duties which are obligatory upon him by virtue of his class and stage of life (*varṇāśrama dharma*). But their chief concern being social stability, they are mainly interested in setting forth the *varṇāśrama dharma* which expresses an essentially social, but relativistic, approach to morality.

Hindu social morality is relativistic on several counts. First, man's duties are frankly accepted to be relative to time (*yuga*) and place (*deśa*), so that the *dharma* of one age and region is acknowledged to be non-applicable to another age and place. Secondly, the duties of a person are also strictly relative to his *varṇa* (class) and the stage of life (*āśrama*). The two together are called *varṇāśrama dharma.* Thirdly, the individual's duties are also relative to one's sex. Thus, women of all *varṇas* are treated as a class apart, their duties and virtues being very different from those of their menfolk.

Both Manu and Āpastamba contend that along with Vedas and Smṛtis, the conduct (*ācāra*) of those Aryans of the three 'upper' classes, who are humble, have full control over their senses and are free from moral vices, is the source of *dharma*; that is, it forms the standard or criterion of man's conduct.[2] Since the Smṛtis aim at presenting guidelines for conducting a man's entire life which includes religion, morality, culture and socio-legal matters, the importance given by the Smṛtis to the conduct of good men signifies the essentially social character of Dharmaśāstric morality. Āpastamba distinguishes between the *Śrauta* or Vedic *dharma* and the *samayācārika dharma*, i.e. the *dharma* that has been determined by the *samaya* or pronouncements (agreements) of learned men.[3] Here *ācāra* or conduct means an ideal mode of conduct; but gradually any mode of conduct which was practised by the people of a given community came to be known as *ācāra*.[4] The importance given to the customs as a source or criterion of man's *dharma* (righteous conduct) expresses the essentially social and relativistic stance of Hindu ethical thinkers.

These customs are necessarily relative to time, place and other such factors. The Aryans were fully aware of the differences in the customs and conduct of people of different regions of this vast subcontinent. True to their syncretic spirit, they accepted these differences and affirmed that customs are relative both to time (*yuga*) and place (*deśa*), as also to caste, guild and even family.[5] These customs (*ācāra*) are to be accepted as valid for the particular region in which they are in vogue, with only one condition that they should not contradict the Vedas. But these very customs, as marriage between near relations, would be invalid if practised by the people of other regions. Similarly, actions and practices, such as *niyoga* which were accepted in the earlier ages, are prohibited in the modern age of *Kali yuga*.

All Dharmaśāstras seek to protect the various customs and practices of people belonging to different castes, communities and professions. They instruct the king that not only should he respect these different customs, but also judge legal cases according to them, as far as possible. According to Gautama, the king should accept (in addition to the Vedas and Smṛtis) 'the laws of countries, castes and families which are not opposed to the sacred texts' as authoritative in his 'administration of justice'.[6] The Dharmaśāstras and the *Arthaśāstra* of Kauṭilya also instruct the king that he should never seek to impose the customs and practice of his people on the vanquished people, but let them continue to practise their own customs.[7]

Now, custom or *ācāra* in this sense is very different from *dharma*. The first is what is actually practised by the people, whereas the second refers to what ought to be practised. Also, custom refers mostly to amoral practices, such as those followed at the time of various socio-religious functions, as marriage; while *dharma* should refer strictly to moral matters. Hindu thinkers made the mistakes, committed by all naturalistic thinkers of the world, in that they confused the actual practice with the ideal or norm of conduct.

II. *Duties According to One's Caste and Stage of Life*

The real emphasis in the social morality of the Dharmaśāstras and Epics is on the relativity of all duties to the subject's class (*varṇa*) and stage of life (*āśrama*). *Varṇāśrama dharma* is a compound of the twin concepts of *varṇa dharma* and *āśrama dharma*. The two concepts are quite independent of each other; while the first is essentially a social concept, the second is more meaningful in the context of personal morality.

(i) We would like to take up the scheme of *āśrama dharma* first. It was more of an ideal scheme of life, which was probably followed in its totality by a very few spiritually inclined persons only. A few men renounce the world even now, but the complete scheme of four stages of life has become obsolete. Of the four stages of life, only that of the householder was conceived in a social context, so that its ideal remains relevant even today. The remaining three stages of studenthood, dwelling in the forest and renunciation of the world were mainly concerned with individual self-culture.

Theoretically, all males of the three 'upper' classes were expected to follow the scheme of four stages of life. But in practice the four consecutive orders were not usually adopted by people, other than the brāhmaṇas. It is significant that Manu, after describing the duties of four classes (*varṇas*), discusses the four stages under the duties of brāhmaṇas.[8] It is but to be expected. Not many would have liked to spend a large portion of their lives in theoretical learning alone. While the royal sons preferred to have their education at home under expert coaches, vaiśyas found apprenticeship with their fathers more useful than lengthy Vedic learning. Brāhmaṇas alone adopted regular *brahmacarya*, as a detailed knowledge of the Vedas and allied subjects was required for their particular profession of teaching and priesthood. Most people entered the second stage of *gṛhastha* (married life) after having spent only a few years in formal education.

The last two stages of *vānaprastha* (forest-dwelling) and *saṁnyāsa* (renunciation) were similarly not very common. The *Mahābhārata* clearly states that the stage of renunciation (*saṁnyāsa*) was meant for the brahmaṇas only.[9] Moreover, if any man wanted to renounce the world, he went to the forest and did not generally become a renunciant. And those who went to the forest did so after living very long and full lives as householders, and not in the beginning of the second half of their lives, as stipulated in the scheme of four stages. Daśaratha, Dhṛtarāṣṭra etc. were very old indeed when they thought of retiring to the forest. Taking up of *saṁnyāsa* was quite rare in ancient times, and it was only under the impact of the heterodox sects of Buddhism and Jainism that the practice became so prestigious. The Dharmaśāstras and Epics even show some confusion regarding the order and relative worth of these last two stages. Both Gautama and Āpastamba regarded the order of the forest-dweller as the highest and the last of all,[10] while the order of the renunciant was recognized as the final one by all the rest.[11] When Yudhiṣṭhira wanted to renounce the world, he sought to present an ideal picture of a renunciant before his friends. But his description shows considerable confusion between the two stages of the forest-dweller and the renunciant.[12] It may well suggest that the disciplines of the last two stages were not properly understood till the time of the Epics and Dharmaśāstras.

Of the four orders, the three, i.e. those of the student-celibates, forest-dwellers and renunciants, were largely conceived in the context of self-culture. The first or *brahmacarya āśrama*, as its name indicates, was a period of learning and strict self-discipline. The student-celibates were supposed to have no direct contact with and no definite responsibilities towards the society and dedicated themselves mainly to the quest of personal liberation. At the same time, even though no active participation in social matters was expected from men belonging to these three stages of life, they were expected to observe the rules of morality (*dharma*) and ideal social culture (*śiṣṭācāra*). There were detailed guidelines for the student-celibates, the forest-dwellers and the renunciants, regarding the proper mode of conduct before one's elders, equals and juniors. For example, the list of injunctions and prohibitions for a student-celibate includes total obedience to the teacher, conducting oneself before the teacher and other elders in the most humble manner, as also never indulging in any sensual pleasures or luxuries, practising the virtues of forgiveness, self-control and perseverance, as also abstaining from the vices of anger, jealousy etc.[13] And though many of the virtues of this stage of life were not required to be practised by a graduate-householder (*snātaka*), we can presume that the habits of discipline, self-restraint, and humility, developed during the period of celibacy, would have persisted throughout a man's life.

The Dharmaśāstras prescribe a separate set of virtues for the forest-dwellers and another for the renunciants. The morality expected from these two classes was quite similar, the emphasis being on utmost self-restraint. Both the forest-dweller and the renunciant, were expected to practise total control of the senses and the mind, forbearance and equanimity, as also the virtues of friendliness and kindness towards all.[14] Though the forest-dweller was expected to live away from the society, in a way his mode of life was a continuation of the householder's life. Often accompanied by his wife, he performed all Dharmaśāstric rituals, maintained the household fire, received guests and gave gifts. As depicted in the Epics, the forest-dwellers mostly lived in hermitages, had pupils, maintained communication with the society and played host to kings and others. On the other hand, the morality of the renunciants was almost asocial in its conception. Unlike the forest-dweller, the renunciant lived in the society and ate cooked food; yet he was constantly admonished to remain alone and completely detached towards all.

Unlike the above three orders, that of the householder has been conceived in a decidedly social context. Most Hindu religious texts hail the life of the householder as the most worthy mode of life.[15] Gautama goes as far as to say that the order of the householder is the only one prescribed by the Vedas and the Dharmaśāstras.[16] What is more, the householder is expected not only to practise all the virtues and perform all the duties which are specifically meant for him, he is also expected to practise virtues like humility and utmost self-restraint which were originally conceived in the context of other orders of life.[17] Thus, the morality of the householder is a truly comprehensive one which includes both sets of moral values, concerning inter-personal morality and self-culture.

(ii) *Varṇa dharma* (the duties according to one's caste) refers mainly to the duties of the householders. While the scheme of *āśramas* was more or less optional, that of *varṇas* was and even now is compulsory. All religious texts agree with the fourfold division of the society into brāhmaṇas, kṣatriyas, vaiśyas and śūdras. Traditionally, the four *varṇas* have been grouped into two classes—the twice-born who, having undergone the initiation ceremony (*upanayana*), form the three 'upper' classes and the once-born or śūdras. They are also arranged in a hierarchical order—brāhmaṇas, kṣatriyas and then vaiśyas, with śūdras forming the lowermost rung of the social hierarchy. Briefly, the duties of the four *varṇas* were as follows: Teaching and study of Vedas, giving and taking gifts (*dāna*) and performing sacrifices for oneself and others were the duties of brāhmaṇas. Kṣatriyas and vaiśyas could not teach Vedas or conduct sacrifices for others, but the daily reading of the Vedas and the performance of daily sacrifices were the duties of all the three classes. In addition, kṣatriyas were expected to take up arms for the protection of the people, and vaiśyas were to engage in business, agriculture and cattle rearing. The only duty of the fourth class of śūdras was to serve the three 'upper' classes.[18] During emergencies men were allowed to take up the profession of the next 'lower' class, but in no case a man of a 'lower' class was allowed to take up the profession of a 'higher' class.[19]

This was the ideal scheme of social organization. It was perhaps not always followed in practice, and there was a certain interchange of professions, especially between the topmost classes of brāhmaṇas and kṣatriyas. Thus, while brāhmaṇas like Droṇa and Kṛpa were teachers of martial arts, kings like Janaka and Pravāhaṇa were teachers of supreme knowledge of *Brahman*. The same interchange seems to have taken place between the two 'lower' classes of vaiśyas and śūdras, at least in the early stages of Aryan expansion. Though in actual practice an interchange of professions constantly took place, in theory it was never encouraged. Specially brāhmaṇas remained aloof and supreme. We have the story of king Mataṅga who performed the severest penances to attain brāhmaṇahood, but failed. He was told that brāhmaṇahood could not be achieved by any means.[20] Since the time of Brāhmaṇas these different classes (*varṇas*) have been divided into various castes and sub-castes. What is more, gradually they have become hereditary, so that one belongs to a caste one is born into, irrespective of one's profession and other qualifications.

Prof. P.V. Kane[21] has given following broad characteristics of the caste system: i. hereditary character, ii. prohibition of inter-caste marriages, iii. prohibition of inter-caste dining, iv. profession according to caste, and v. the hierarchical order of the castes. As the civilization developed, there was naturally greater specialization and greater division of labour, so that new professions came into being and were converted into castes. The number of castes and sub-castes has multiplied to an extent that it is no longer possible to arrange them in a hierarchical order. These hereditary castes are organized on a more strict basis than earlier *varṇas*, resulting in the stratification of the society into innumerable sub-castes. The four *varṇas* now represent only broad categories into which the innumerable sub-castes can be grouped in a very general way. This subject has been studied and discussed at length by various thinkers of such eminence as P.V. Kane, G.S. Ghurye, J.H. Hutton, K.M. Panikker and Andrey Beteille, that we can hardly hope to add anything new. At the same time, the stratification of society into innumerable castes and sub-castes is the one most important factor that has determined the Hindu social organization, its practices and moral values for ages and is, therefore, very important and relevant for our study.

It seems to us that three factors contributed most to the development of a rigid caste system—religious sanction, concern for the stability of the society and the racial prejudices of the Aryans, combined with their obsession with ritualistic cleanliness. First, religious sanction has been unfortunately quite strong in favour of the caste system. The advocates of the caste system happily quote the *Puruṣa Sūkta*[22] according to which different classes (*varṇas*) were produced from different parts of the body of the primeval Being (*Puruṣa*). The strongest sanction for the caste system comes, however, from the *Bhagavadgītā*. Lord Kṛṣṇa declares that the fourfold order was created by God himself according to the division of *guṇas* (constituent elements of *prakṛti*) and *karmas* (actions of individual selves).[23] The *Gītā* puts forward the thesis that man's station in life and the duties he is supposed to discharge are in strict accordance with (a) the divine order which is morally just and (b)man's own nature and his past actions. It repeatedly affirms that every man acts according to his own nature and the caste ordained duty is the one to which a man is naturally suited.[24] It is so, because both the outward circumstances of a man's life and his inner constitution or nature are the result of his own past actions. By implication, if a man is born a śūdra and is forced to do menial jobs, it is what he deserves because of his past actions, and above all, it is what his nature is best suited to do. The *Bhagavadgītā*, therefore, advises:

"Better is one's own caste duty (*sva-dharma*), though imperfectly carried out, than the *dharma* of another, even if carried out perfectly. Better is death in the fulfilment of one's duty, for to follow another's *dharma* is perilous."[25]

Manu, a strong protagonist of caste distinctions, naturally repeats this advice.[26] Religious scriptures have thus strongly supported the caste system which they generally consider under the category of *varṇa*.

Secondly, the division of society into various classes and castes was encouraged for its supposedly positive contribution to social harmony. It was believed that if people did not submit to the limitations of their respective classes and professions, there would result an overall confusion or chaos in the form of mixing up of classes[27] (which seemed to the ancient Aryans a big catastrophe). On the other hand, if all persons followed their respective class professions, it would help in the preservation of a stable social order. Sureśvara (vide ch. I, section III *supra*) compares the four *varṇas* to the four carriers of a palanquin. Just as the carrying of a palanquin requires the harmonious motion of the four carriers, so the society requires the harmonious functioning of its four constituent classes.

Thirdly, the sharp demarcation between the three twice-born (*dvija*) 'upper' classes and the once-born śūdras possibly originated in the fact that the two, the 'upper' class Hindus and śūdras, originally belonged to two different racial groups. As we have seen (ch. I, section II *supra*), scholars like P.V. Kane attach much importance to the meaning of the term *varṇa* used in the Sanskrit texts to denote various classes. According to this view, śūdras were non-Aryans who were accepted into the Aryan society, but were never fully integrated into it. Prof. Kane points out that the Hindu Law-givers often call śūdras non-Aryans and describe them in contradistinction to the Aryans.[28] The sharp distinction that is everywhere made between the three twice-born classes and śūdras and the extreme ill-treatment of the latter by the former might well have originated in the racial prejudices of the fair-skinned Aryans who looked down upon the relatively dark-complexioned non-Aryans.

This possible racial prejudice was combined with ritualistic prejudice against certain professions which seemed to be unclean to the Aryans. Hindu obsession with cleanliness thus resulted in a complete segregation of śūdras who followed supposedly unclean professions. The list of unclean professions was very wide and not only included cleaners, public executors, meat cutters and fishermen, but also carpenters, iron-mongers, architects, painters and doctors.[29] This class of śūdras was further being swelled by the addition of all those 'upper' caste persons who were ousted from their castes due to some ritualistic or moral offence.

Manu and other Law-givers have given an entirely different explanation for the development of mixed castes which were invariably adjusted among the lower rungs of the social hierarchy. According to it, these mixed castes were the products of inter-caste (*pratiloma*) marriages in which the female spouse is of a higher caste than the male.[30] But this could hardly explain the very large number of 'lower' caste people in the Hindu society.

Food was the most important field in which the concept of cleanliness was rigorously applied. Not only was the food touched by a śūdra considered unfit for consumption, but that touched by any person other than one's near relations or brāhmaṇas was also not to be eaten. If one cannot eat the food touched by others, that certainly creates barriers between oneself and others, and must erode fellow-feeling among different members of the society. Those who avoid others, lest they pollute their food, can hardly be expected to help them in times of their need.

III. Exaltation of Brāhmaṇas, Degradation of Śūdras and The Miscarriage of Justice

(i) Various Dharmaśāstras, Purāṇas and the Epics vied with each other in declaring the supremacy of brāhmaṇas. Brāhmaṇas were constantly being compared to gods and were unanimously declared the highest beings on earth. According to the *Śatapatha Brāhmaṇa*:

"Gods are of two kinds, gods of heaven and learned brāhmaṇas. In *yajña* heavenly gods get the oblations and the fees are given to brāhmaṇas."[31]

According to Manu, brāhmaṇa, having been born out of the mouth of Brahmā, is the highest being or lord of the creation and is the personification of *dharma*. He is also great because he mediates between men and gods and is equal to, or even greater than, gods.[32] The *Mahābhārata* is equally categorical in its praise of brāhmaṇas as the highest beings on earth, worthy of the greatest reverence and deserving utmost protection and all kinds of gifts from the king.[33]

A brāhmaṇa was beyond any physical or verbal offence. Severest punishments were prescribed for the offender of a brāhmaṇa, especially if he happened to be a śūdra.[34] Manu and others even invented terror-inspiring punishments in hell for the offender of a brāhmaṇa.[35] The brāhmaṇas could not be given any corporal punishment, were exempt from the state taxes and were thus in general above the law.[36] The excessive exaltation of brāhmaṇas not only resulted in a social order wherein men were basically unequal, it also encouraged the brāhmaṇas to claim transcendence over all law, civil and moral.

According to all religious texts, a brāhmaṇa deserved reverence simply by virtue of his very birth. Thus, a brāhmaṇa boy of ten years was to be respected by a kṣatriya man of hundred years,[37] and a brāhmaṇa would still command the respect of all other classes, even if he indulged in immoral acts.[38] All religious texts were furthermore unanimous in declaring the merits of making gifts to brāhmaṇas. While the Dharmaśāstras and Epics generally stipulated that only those brāhmaṇas, who were learned and were of high moral character, deserved gifts and invitations for dining,[39] Purāṇas removed this condition. Gradually, it came to be believed that a brāhmaṇa unconditionally deserved greatest honour and all kinds of gifts, so that his moral qualifications (or want of them) became a totally irrelevant factor.

(ii) The degradation of śūdras is directly proportional to the excessive exaltation of brāhmaṇas. Śūdras were, and even now are, denied the right of undertaking the purificatory rite in the form of investiture of sacred thread (*upanayana*) which is supposed to give a man his second birth. Thus a śūdra was compulsorily distinguished as once-born from the twice-born (*dvija*) 'upper' classes. A śūdra was not allowed to perform Vedic sacrifices or read or listen to the Vedas; worse still, severest punishments were prescribed and even carried out, if a śūdra even dared to recite, or chanced to hear the Vedas.[40] Even Rāma killed a śūdra who dared to perform some penance which was the prerogative of 'upper' classes only.[41] Śaṁkara, the philosopher who proclaimed one universal Self that is beyond all caste and other distinctions, denied the right of studying Vedas to śūdras. He lamely argued that since śūdras cannot undertake the initiatory rite (*upanayana*), they cannot study Vedas. What is worse, Śaṁkara has quoted with approval the *Gautama Dharmasūtra* prescribing that the tongue of that śūdra who dared to recite Vedas should be pierced with a hot iron nail and the ears of that śūdra who ever dared to listen to Vedas should be filled with molten lead.[42] It shows how bias can lead to the dehumanization of human conscience and result in the sacrifice of all humanitarian values.

The Law-givers (*Smṛtikāras*) repeatedly asserted that the only duty of śūdras was the service of the three 'upper' classes.[43] The *Viṣṇu Purāṇa*, trying to be liberal, affirmed that śūdras were lucky or blessed, because while the three 'upper' classes had to put in a lot of effort to earn religious merit, śūdras could secure it simply by serving the three 'upper' classes[44]! Such assertions are nothing more than an attempt to deprive śūdras of their birth right to be responsible moral agents.

The right to property was denied to them;[45] they had no social rights as citizens, no right, in fact, as human beings. Manu declares:

"A śūdra, whether bought or unbought, may be compelled to do servile work; for he was created by the Self-existent to be the slave of a brāhmaṇa.

"A śūdra, though emancipated by his master, is not released from servitude...Since that is innate in him, who can set him free from it?"[46]

The Law-givers thus seem to have taken pains to ensure that no shred of human dignity should be left with śūdras. Śūdras were considered so unholy that they could not be given even the left over food eaten by a brāhmaṇa or a student-celibate.[47] Certain sub-castes of śūdras, as cāṇḍālas, were very early declared untouchables. Not only was the food touched by a cāṇḍāla uneatable, even that seen by him was so! Āpastamba even prescribed that one should speak to a brāhmaṇa after speaking to a low caste śūdra (cāṇḍāla), so as to get rid of the impurity![48] The 'untouchables' were forced to live outside the villages, or near burning grounds. Their property consisted only of dogs and donkeys. They were expected to wear clothes used for covering dead bodies, eat in broken utensils, and so on.[49] They were and even now in practice are prohibited to visit temples or use community wells, even though the modern Indian law prohibits any discrimination against them. Śūdras, especially certain lowermost sub-castes of śūdras, were often treated as sub-humans. They were constantly compared to dogs, crows and even worms;[50] and the killing of a śūdra required a penance similar to the one required for the killing of crows, peacocks, frogs, etc.[51]

(iii) The most significant difference between śūdras and the three 'upper' classes was the one before the law. The concept of equality before the law seems to be unknown to the ancient Aryans. While the killing of a brāhmaṇa was a 'great (major) sin' (*mahā-pātaka*) or a 'super (extreme) sin' (*ati-pātaka*) from which no redemption was possible,[52] the killing of persons of the remaining three classes (*varṇas*) was but a minor sin. The penances for the murder of a member belonging to any of the three remaining classes were prescribed in such a way that the rigour of the penance decreased with the decrease in the class of the victim in the class hierarchy.[53]

The Dharmaśāstras stipulated that if a śūdra committed adultery with a higher caste woman, his organ ought to be cut off, or he ought to be executed. But if an 'upper' caste man had adulterous relations with a woman of the same caste, he was only to be fined. The fine was reduced further if the woman belonged to any of the 'lower' classes.[54] If a śūdra spoke offensively to a brāhmaṇa, either his tongue was to be cut off, or pierced with a red hot iron nail, or his mouth and ears were to be filled with burning oil.[55] If a śūdra attacked a twice-born, that part of his body which was used for the offence was to be cut off.[56] And so on. On the other hand, the 'higher' caste Hindus, especially brāhmaṇas, were not deemed to be fit for punishment if they injured or even killed a śūdra. Only in the case of thefts a 'higher' caste person was sometimes awarded a higher fine. But even here Gautama prescribed that if a śūdra stole something, he should be made to pay eightfold the amount of the property stolen, whereas the three 'upper' classes need pay only double the amount in fine.[57] A moral code which constantly discriminates against the underprivileged and the down-trodden can hardly claim to represent an ideal social morality.

(iv) In all probability, the above picture of the Hindu society's attitude towards śūdras is not wholly true. No doubt, śūdras were ill treated and discriminated against; but they were generally not treated cruelly by the caste Hindus. The harsh punishments prescribed in the religious texts were probably not carried out in everyday life. The prescriptions of Dharmaśāstras are not obligatory in a strict sense. The day-to-day business of the society and decisions in the law courts were generally governed more by local practices, advice of the wise men of the community and the laws and stipulations of such down-to-earth works as the *Arthaśāstra* and later Nibandhas. They are definitely less harsh towards the śūdras than the Dharmaśāstras.

The religious texts also advise a considerate and humane treatment of śūdras. Śūdras who served in the homes of the 'upper' class Hindus were without doubt treated with consideration and kindness. Āpastamba even allows a śūdra servant to cook food.[58] All the religious texts emphasize the householder's duty to provide for his śūdra servants. According to Āpastamba :

"The division of the food must be made in such a manner that those who receive daily portions (servants) do not suffer by it.

"At his pleasure he may stint himself, his wife or his children, but by no means a slave who does his work."[59]

Manu gives the same advice that the servants should be fed first before the householder and his wife partake of their food.[60] At another place he is even more specific about the duty of the master towards his śūdra servants:

"They (the 'upper' class men) must allot to him (a śūdra) out of their own family property a suitable maintenance, after considering his ability, his industry and the number of those he is bound to support."[61]

The above advice may still not be sufficient to counterbalance the generally harsh attitude of the Law-givers towards śūdras. But it does suggest that at the practical level they were mostly treated humanely. The *Rāmāyaṇa* gives several stories of Rāma's dealings with the tribes who inhabited the jungles, such as Niṣādas, Vānaras etc. They were definitely śūdras from the orthodox point of view; but Rāma always treated them with respect and affection. He even accepted the hospitality of many of them, including Śabarī, the tribal woman. His most faithful servant Hanumān, belonging to the Vānara tribe, has been made into a god by the Hindus.

There were also dissenting voices which asserted that a man's worth must be judged not by his hereditary caste, but by his moral character. Yudhiṣṭhira is the chief exponent of this view in the *Mahābhārata*.[62] Such views, even though they are much less frequently expressed than the anti-śūdra feelings, should be taken into account while attempting a general assessment of the ancient Hindu society.

Perhaps due to the influence of Buddhism, there was a general softening of the Hindu society's attitude towards śūdras. Hindu theism also contributed towards a better deal for them, as it affirmed that all those who love God are equal before Him. At the same time, Vaiṣṇavas quite inconsistently emphasized various food taboos which resulted in a further hardening of barriers between 'upper' caste Hindus and śūdras. Thus we find that caste distinctions have been a constant source of tension and disparity between Hindu philosophy and Hindu practice. They have always hampered the emergence of a truly universal social morality. We have caste distinctions even now, though hopefully they will gradually disappear under the impact of industrialization, urbanization and modern Indian law.

IV. The Ideal of Justice and the Preservation of Status quo

(i) Dispensing justice means in Hindu thought arranging matters so as to ensure the victory of *dharma* or *satya* (right or truth) over *adharma* or *asatya* (wrong or untruth). *Dharma* is always considered as a power which preserves, so that if a king or any other person helps in the victory of *dharma* over *adharma*, he would surely gain well-being; and if he does not take the side of truth, he would be destroyed by his own *adharma*.[63] Characteristically, there is no specific word in Sanskrit literature for the modern concept of justice. *Dharma*, *vyavahāra* (law suits) and *daṇḍa* (punishment) are used to express the idea of justice according to the particular context. In spite of this looseness of expression, the Hindu Law-givers were genuinely concerned with justice and related issues

Rendering justice was regarded as the second most important duty of the king, the first being the protection of the masses from external enemies. *Daṇḍa* or punishment was seen as the chief instrument of rendering justice, or setting things right in the society. The Aryans professed a realistic, or rather cynical view, of man and society. According to this view, the human society is governed in its natural state by the law of the survival of the fittest, called *matsya nyāya* (the law of the ocean). It was accepted that when left unchecked, men always indulge in the pursuit of self-interest at the cost of others, which may well lead to a state of anarchy. It was, therefore, advised that men should be kept under control and forced to tread the path of righteousness (*dharma*) through a judicious use of punishment.[64] All Dharmaśāstras and Epics hail *daṇḍa* as the chief means of preserving *dharma*, and the king as the protector thereof. *Dharma* which the king was expected to protect was understood as a just social order. But unfortunately this just order was conceived in terms of class hierarchy or *varṇāśrama dharma*. The king was expected to preserve the caste order. He was further expected to use his power of punishment not only against criminals, but also against anyone who dared to overstep the limitations of his class (caste) profession and thereby threatened the stability of the society.[65]

The Law-givers have made several suggestions with regard to the dispensing of justice which do them credit. For example, it is stipulated that the punishment should be in proportion to the crime; that is, the injury inflicted upon, or the loss incurred by, the victim of offence (*sāhasa*) should determine the nature and amount of punishment.[66] It should also be taken into consideration whether the offender of the law is a hardened criminal, or the given instance is his first crime.[67] Āpastamba makes a valuable observation that the man who acts, the one who prompts and the one who helps are equally responsible for the crime.[68]

(ii) Theoretically, all were equal before the law and that included the king's relatives and the king himself. Manu even opines that a king should be fined a thousand times more than the common man for the same offence.[69] But actually, all were definitely not equal before the law. Brāhmaṇas were mostly above the law and śūdras were given a very prejudicial treatment by the law. Manu stipulates that the punishments should be awarded strictly in accordance with the relative castes of the offender and the victim.[70] The preservation of the *status quo* seems to be the basic motive behind all Dharmaśāstric stipulations. The *status quo* which was sought to be preserved referred not only to class (caste) hierarchy, but also to the class distinction between the rich and the poor. A major concern of the Dharmaśāstras seems to be the protection of the property of the rich. The theft of a brāhmaṇa's gold was universally regarded as one of the five major sins (*mahā-pātaka*), the other four being murder of a brāhmaṇa, adultery with a respectable lady, drinking and association with the above four kinds of criminals. Every Smṛti also gives another list of crimes that are morally equivalent to the five great sins. This list includes theft of certain things like horses, silver, diamond and men as morally equivalent to the stealing of a brāhmaṇa's gold.[71] Thus, while theft is mentioned twice in the list of grave sins, murder does not find a place even in this second list. Murder of anyone, except brāhmaṇa males, was unanimously considered a minor sin. While very harsh or even cruel penances were prescribed for the four major sins, only mild penances were required for the murder of all women and males of the three classes, other than brāhmaṇas.

Not life, but property seems to be the main concern of the Hindu Law-givers. Manu's three chapters on king's duties and the administration of justice are primarily concerned with matters relating to property. Of the eighteen topics of legal dispute, all but five deal with property, such as rules of inheritance, guidelines for the payment of debts, return of stolen property.[72] While no specific punishment is prescribed by him for the murder of human beings, except brāhmaṇas, very harsh punishments are prescribed for various kinds of thefts. For example, the thief of a brāhmaṇa's gold was expected to go to the king with a heavy instrument and get himself killed by the king.[73] *Vadha* (killing or severe physical punishment) has been prescribed for almost all kinds of thefts. Worse still, it was advised that first a thief's hands should be cut off, then he should be executed. And a goldsmith who adulterated gold was to be killed by hacking his body to pieces.[74]

Of course, violence is also condemned by the authors of the Dharmaśāstras from time to time.[75] But it does not seem to be the main concern of the Law-givers. Perhaps violence was accepted as an integral part of day-to-day life and did not bother them, unless it threatened the stability of the social order. At least, it suggests that the ideal of non-violence (*ahiṁsā*) was not fully integrated into the Hindu social ethos till the time of Dharmaśāstras and Epics.

As compared to the Dharmaśāstras, Kauṭilya's treatment of the subject of punishment for various crimes in his *Arthaśāstra* (between 300 B.C. to 100 A.D.) is refreshingly reasonable and liberal. While all Dharmaśāstras prescribe severe physical punishment or even death (*vadha*) for thefts, Kauṭilya prescribes only various amounts of fines, proportional to the stolen property.[76] On the other hand, the use of violence in the society is taken very seriously by Kauṭilya. Capital punishment is prescribed for all murders, and it is advised that more painful forms of death penalty should be given to those men who are guilty of more reprehensible kinds of violence.[77] According to Kauṭilya, only brāhmaṇas were to be exempt from capital punishment; but even they were to be branded on the face, or imprisoned for life, if they indulged in serious crimes of violence.[78]

We may say in conclusion that the Hindu social morality and ideal of justice are generally vitiated by the inherent flaw of social discrimination against the 'lower' classes. People belonging to different classes (*varṇas*) were essentially unequal both in the society and before the law. Inter-personal morality was determined by class (caste) distinctions and hierarchy, resulting in grave injustice to the 'lower' classes and an overall undermining of a healthy social or inter-personal morality.

V. Sex Morality and the Treatment of Women

It is again a very much discussed topic, and yet we have to consider it here, as a people's morality can best be judged by their treatment of weaker classes and the weaker sex.

(i) There was a steady deterioration in the condition of women in Hindu society. It is a matter of common knowledge that the Aryan women enjoyed considerable freedom and a very respectable position in the Vedic society. If we compare the evidence regarding the society's attitude towards women found in the Vedas to the known historical facts about the Hindu society's attitude towards the weaker sex in later middle ages, we would find a world of difference between the two. Several factors have been responsible for this negative trend in the Hindu thinking and practice towards women. First, the wide-spread practice of polygamy among higher class Aryans was responsible to a considerable extent for the devaluation of the position of women in the society. There are even indications of a deplorable practice of giving several maids in gift to an honoured guest, or as dowry to the bridegroom.[79] We can hardly expect that women would have been respected and valued as independent persons in a society in which they were viewed as an object of enjoyment, or as something which can be given away as a gift to anyone.

Secondly, the later denial of the right to practise the Vedic *dharma* to women resulted in the depreciation of their worth. Probably, in the beginning women could perform at least some of the Vedic sacrifices and recite Vedic *mantras*. But gradually these rights were denied to them, including the right to undertake the initiation ceremony (*upanayana*). The *Śatapatha Brāhmaṇa* compares women with śūdras, dogs and crows and declares them as personifications of untruth and impurity.[80] Very early the idea of ritualistic impurity, from which women were supposed to suffer at certain periods of their life, was used to emphasize the impurity and inferior being of women. Thus, all women were reduced to the status of 'once-born' or śūdras. Manu contends that since women cannot recite Vedic *mantras*, they are essentially impure or sinful.[81] Since all women, irrespective of their class (*varṇa*), were equal to śūdras, killing a woman came to be accepted as a crime equal to killing a śūdra.[82]

Thirdly, the growing importance of rituals, especially the funeral rites, further contributed to the devaluation of women in the Hindu society. The importance of sons grew with the importance of obsequial rites which were supposedly essential to ensure a man's eschatological destiny, and which, as we have seen in our second chapter, could be performed only by sons. The *Aitareya Brāhmaṇa* gives the story of Hariścandra's desire for a son and justifies it as follows:

"The father who looks upon the face of his son, born living to him, discharges his debt in him...... The son is to him a rescuing boat...... In him you have the blameless world of heaven. The daughter is a sorrow, while the son is light in the highest regions of heaven to his father."[83]

Shakuntala Rao Shastry observes that the growing importance of funeral rites and sons resulted in a proportional devaluation of women in the Vedic and post-Vedic society:

"The imperative necessity of a son who could offer oblations dominated the whole sphere of thought...... Women, who hitherto had a share in the intellectual and religious field, came to be considered as having no purpose in life except that of being the mothers of sons."[84]

Fourthly, the gradual change in the Aryans' attitude towards sex also contributed to the steady deterioration in the condition of women in the society. Dhairyabala P. Vora has very ably argued for the intimate relation between the growing emphasis on the virginity of women and the deterioration in their social condition.[85] It seems that the early Aryans were not very particular about sex mores and a considerable amount of promiscuity in sex relations was tolerated in the society. The *Mahābhārata* gives innumerable instances of extra-marital unions. Many of the heroes of the Epic were the offsprings of such unions (or *niyoga*) and were gladly accepted by the society.

Apparently, there was some disparity between moral norms and actual practice. The wise men of the society did not approve of the sexual licence prevalent in the society and condemned it. At the same time, they tried to legitimize such unorthodox unions, lest they destabilize the caste-based social structure. Thus, the Dharmaśāstras discuss eight kinds of marriage, the last four being only unions of love or even sexual assault.[86] They also discuss several kinds of progeny, and many of them are nothing but offsprings of extra-marital unions. These classifications express the Law-givers' desire to legitimize such issues.[87] There is a very curious discussion, found in various sacred books, as to whether the issue of an extra-marital union belongs to the biological father, or to the husband of the mother.[88] The fact that this problem is taken seriously suggests that extra-marital unions were quite common. Not only was *niyoga* allowed in the case of childless widows,[89] it was practised by women with impotent husbands. While all the Law-givers accepted such unions, most of them, at the same time, disapproved of them. Thus, we find two opposite opinions regarding *niyoga* in the *Manusmṛti*. Having admitted the custom of *niyoga*, Manu goes on to condemn it as immoral and against the duty (*dharma*) of the wife to remain loyal to her husband in life and death.[90]

There was gradually a new formulation of sex mores. Adultery in general was disapproved, and adultery with ladies who deserved one's respect, e.g. mother, teacher's wife and other immediate relations, came to be regarded as one of the five gravest sins. This sin was asserted to be so great that it could be expiated only by a very cruel penance ending in one's death.[91] As the Aryans grew more zealous about the chastity of their womenfolk, they put more and more restraints on their freedom and other rights. The marriage age of the girls was constantly lowered, till the ridiculous norm was reached that the girl should be married while she is still naked (*nagnikā*).[92] The participation of women in social functions was prohibited; they were expected to live indoors, and were mostly treated as second class citizens.

Fifthly, the gradual emergence of a new perception of the world and life by the Hindus, especially in the tradition of liberation, also contributed to the general depreciation of women. As we know, the original Aryan ethos was favourably disposed towards both sex and women. Sons were welcome and the act of procreation was heralded as a sacrifice. Women were viewed as partners-in-life, needed both for enjoyment of life and performance of religio-moral duties. But as the Aryan mind matured, it became sensitive to the transience and sufferings of mundane life and began to appreciate the ideal of detachment to, and mental transcendence of, mundane pleasures. Pleasure-seeking was condemned, and it somehow entailed an equal deprecation or condemnation of women. Women were perceived by thinkers belonging to the tradition of liberation as the source of all temptations and an obstruction in a man's quest for liberation. They were pictured as frivolous and lustful creatures and men were advised to avoid them as a plague. Aryans became afraid of getting involved in the world; but instead of controlling their own minds and desires, they preferred to control their womenfolk and condemned them as the cause of men's bondage.[93]

The depreciation of women, along with their unjust portrayal as lustful and pleasure-seeking persons, might have originated in the tradition of liberation. But it was soon adopted by the thinkers of the Vedic tradition. That is how we find that even Dharmaśāstras and Purāṇas often speak of women derogatively. According to Manu, women are naturally lustful and ever ready to seduce men. He adds that they have an unsatiable passion for men, so much so that they are not even bothered as to who their partner is. They are frivolous, heartless and full of untruth and malice.[94] Manu, therefore, firmly believes that the wife must be carefully guarded by her husband. In an oft-quoted piece of advice, various Law-givers and authors of Epics and Purāṇas agree that a woman must never be left independent. She should be under the protective guardianship of either father, husband, or son.[95] This steady deterioration in the condition of women seems to have been influenced by two quite different trends within the Hindu 'religio-culture', viz. the extreme ritualism of the Brāhmaṇical religion and the world-and-life negation of the tradition of liberation. The two religio-moral approaches are diametrically opposed, and yet they apparently combined forces against the weaker sex.

Moreover, later Hinduism contains ideas and practices (concerning women) which seem alien to both the above traditions. For example, the Hindu ideal of extreme loyalty to one's husband (*pativrata dharma*) cannot be traced to the Vedas. Nor can it find any justification in the world-and-life-negating ethos of the tradition of liberation. And yet, it is the sixth and probably the most important factor, responsible for the total suppression of women in the Hindu society. Manu and other Law-givers never tire of listing the duties of wives towards their husbands. All

Dharmaśāstras, Purāṇas and Epics are unanimous in declaring that the service of her husband is the only duty (*dharma*) of a woman, and that she would achieve heaven just by scrupulously performing her 'supreme duty'.[96] According to the *Rāmāyaṇa*, a woman should sacrifice her insignificant life (*sic*) for the good of her husband.[97] The wife was expected to remain totally obedient and loyal to her husband and worship him as a god, even if he was full of blemishes.[98] She was to remain loyal to him even after his death. There was no question of the remarriage of the widow or the deserted wife. After her husband's death, or in his absence, a woman was forced to live a life of total deprivation and strictest self-discipline.[99]

The custom of *satī* (self-immolation of the widow) was not very popular in ancient times, though there were occasional cases of self-immolation even then. The *Dharmaśāstras* have discussed the ideal mode of conduct of the widow, as also the rules of inheritance of the family property by her in the absence of any male issue. They even allowed the widow to have a son through *niyoga* or intercourse with a man appointed by the elders for that purpose. All this means that they expected the widow to live in the society after her husband's death. The practice of *satī* gained popularity during middle ages only. There is no doubt that it was the religio-social pressure that forced most of the widows to accept this ghastly end. For the last one hundred and fifty years the custom of *satī* has been legally banned. But even now we occasionally have cases of *satī*, and always the instance is highlighted by a great fanfare. Once she is burnt, she is declared a *satī* and people gather round the place to get their desires fulfilled! It is sad how religious dogmas can turn normal good-natured human beings into blood-thirsty brutes.

(ii) But the above is only one side of the medal. Those thinkers, who are very critical of the treatment meted out to women in the Hindu society, generally quote selected passages from the texts which seem to support their own one-sided version of the issue, while completely ignoring other equally relevant passages. Thus, we find an altogether different approach towards women, alongside the one discussed above, in all religious texts, from the Vedas to the Dharmaśāstras and Purāṇas.

As is well-known, women enjoyed quite a respectable position in the Vedic society. Girls married late and they even participated in philosophical debates and other social functions. Of course, the main field of work for woman was recognized to be the hearth and home, but there she enjoyed maximum freedom and power. There are beautiful marriage hymns in Vedas expressing hope for a life of togetherness and sharing for the married couple. One hymn blesses the bride, saying that she may rule over her husband's household, including the parents-in-law and servants.[100] And there are hardly any injunctions to the wife for the practice of extreme loyalty towards her husband (*pativrata dharma*) which are so common in later Hindu texts.

Not only did Hinduism originate in the Vedas, the central Hindu ethos is even now Vedic to a large extent. That is how we find quite positive sentiments regarding women in all Hindu texts. Women of all four classes are declared unslayable and worthy of protection in almost all religious texts. Manu equates the murder of a woman to that of a brāhmaṇa or a child and declares it as the greatest crime, from which no redemption is possible.[101] It is also gratifying to note that the Aryans held the male partner responsible for any adulterous relation and tried to minimize the guilt of the female. At one place the *Mahābhārata* gives a passionate plea in defence of women who are involved in such extramarital relations. According to it, women hardly go in for such relations, unless they are tempted and misguided by men.[102] In cases of adultery the Dharmaśāstras prescribe very harsh punishments and penances for men. All men, excepting brāhmaṇas could be given capital punishment for adultery, especially if the woman was an unwilling partner.[103] The king was expected to protect the victim of a sexual assault and return her to her family after she had performed the prescribed penance.[104]

Unlike man, an adulterous woman was asked to undergo very easy penances, after which she was declared to be fit to be accepted by her family and society.[105] It was also stipulated that the fallen woman must be given refuge in the house and provided with food and shelter.[106] Both Manu and Yājñavalkya chivalrously declare that a woman does not need any purificatory rites, as she is always pure.[107] All Dharmaśāstras recognize certain rights of women, including their right over their personal property.[108]

Significantly, Kauṭilya is much more liberal and considerate towards the fair sex than the authors of Dharmaśāstras, probably because his views are based on practical considerations and not on religious bias. He allows considerable portion of the family property as the personal property of women (*strī-dhana*). But his real revolutionary views are regarding the compensation to be paid to the wife in case the husband marries again, and the remarriage of the widows and the deserted wives. Kauṭilya prescribes that a woman is free to remarry after waiting for a short period (varying from a few months to two years) for a husband who has gone to foreign lands.[109] Other Law-givers like Nārada have also allowed the remarriage of widows, especially those whose marriage has not been consummated.

True, it was a men's world and women had to live under the constant protection of their men-folk, but there were repeated admonitions for husbands, fathers and sons to look after their female relations well and to keep them well satisfied.[110] According to the *Mahābhārata*, the husband is called *bhartā* (protector and provider), but that man is no more a *bhartā* who does not provide for his wife.[111] The emphasis on the duties of the wife was sought to be counterbalanced by the emphasis on the duties of the husband. Manu points out that women are like the goddess Lakṣmī, as they bring prosperity to the household. According to him, women are essential for the welfare of the family, for they give birth to children, bring them up, serve the elders of the family and look after the entire household and all socio-religious customs. Above all, a wife is a must for the proper fulfilment of a man's religious duties.[112] Though the ancient Hindus often practised polygamy, the practice was never encouraged by the Hindu religious texts. The Dharmaśāstras even sought to safeguard the interests of the wife by stipulating conditions under which alone a man may remarry. And deserting a wife is declared a serious crime.[113]

Mothers are the most respected and loved persons in Hindu homes. In an oft-quoted passage, Manu declares the mother to be the one deserving greatest respect, much more than either the father or the teacher.[114] According to Āpastamba, a mother should be served properly, even if she has become a fallen woman.[115] Hindu thinkers and writers have been eloquent in their praise of the mother who symbolises unselfish love, tender care and willingness for utmost self-sacrifice.[116]

The Vedic religion should be given the credit for the high position of women in family life. Only the householder with a wife could maintain the family fire and perform sacrifices. The recognition of their worth in the family life gave the Indian women moral strength and self-respect. Whenever our legendary heroines were mistreated by their spouses, they rose valiantly in self-defence and scoffed at their tormentors. The personalities of Sītā, Damayantī, Śakuntalā and Sāvitrī outshine those of their spouses. In the hour of crisis all of them showed a ready intelligence, a very strong moral character and a determination to get back what was most dear to them. True, these ladies were also the epitomes of the conventional ideal of loyalty to one's husband (*pativrata dharma*), and their mental horizons would seem limited to a modern reader. But they all married of their free choice, knew their duties and rights and in general asserted themselves remarkably well, and can in no way be considered as the poor weaker sex.

At first glance the two viewpoints, regarding the nature and worth of women, discussed above, seem diametrically opposed. If they had come from different writers, or had been professed during different periods of Hindu history, it would have been easy to understand or evaluate them. But it is not so. Both the viewpoints and their concomitant attitudes towards women are found side by side in all Hindu works, from the *Manusmṛti* to *Mahābhārata* and Purāṇas. A few passages in some works might be later interpolations. But generally, both kinds of description of women, their nature and worth represent the views of the author of a given text. It is so, because most Hindu thinkers have an ambivalent attitude towards women and look upon them from two or three very different perspectives. From the point of view of worldly pleasures (*kāma*) which was symbolized by women for the Aryans, they were deprecated and condemned as obstacles in the path of spiritual quest. From the point of view of *dharma* (comprehending both religion and morality), they were seen as wives and mothers and were well respected. (Even now the Hindu masses cherish the image of women as mothers.) But from the point of view of ritualistic purity they were again deprecated. This last is unfortunate, as the ritualistic tradition is an integral part of the Vedic tradition which is otherwise very positive and affirmative in its approach to world and life.

VI. The Pivotal Position of Family in the Hindu Social Morality

Manu presents a very charming picture of the Hindu family. According to him, a man is incomplete without his wife and son.[117] And wife and husband should always be together in the performance of all their religio-moral duties (*dharma*), the aim being that they should never be separated from each other.[118] According to Āpastamba, there can be no division or separation between husband and wife, either in the enjoyment of prosperity, or in the performance of duties. They share everything, including the merits of their acts.[119] The key to marital happiness, according to Manu, is mutual consideration and affection:

"The welfare of that family is always secure wherein the woman is always satisfied with the man and the man with the woman."[120]

Hindu family has been a very harmonious and homogeneous whole from time immemorial; and though the external circumstances changed with time, they did not touch the Hindu family which has remained the backbone of Hindu society. A salient point of Hindu morality has been the pivotal place of family in a person's life. Man's primary duty is always towards his family. Manu has stipulated that though charity (*dāna*) is of highest merit, it should be practised only after ensuring the needs of the entire family, including those of the servants.[121]

The family is the most basic unit of the Aryan culture; even castes developed afterwards. An average Indian (Hindu) family usually consists of parents, their sons and their families. The old are not only very well cared after in India, they have a very important say in the lives of the younger generation. Man is supposed to be born with three debts, the first being towards his parents. The concept of one's debt to, and the concomitant value of care and service of, one's parents are unique to the Indian culture. It is said that the parents not only give birth to and bring up the children, they are also the children's true well-wishers, friends in need and guides in moral matters (*dharma*). The debt one incurs to one's parents is so great that one can never be free from it.[122] Parents, therefore, deserve life-long service and obedience. The teacher is the third person who has been unanimously regarded as deserving enormous respect and obedience. Manu rhetorically affirms that respect and service of the above three is the greatest duty of a man, and all other duties are secondary to it.[123]

The householder and his wife should not only serve their parents, they should be equally kind and considerate towards their dependents. All Smṛtis stipulate that the daughters and daughters-in-law, especially the pregnant ones, should be given food before everybody else, and that the couple should take food after feeding everybody, from the guests to the servants.[124] The Epics describe, both in theory and by way of example, the ideal interrelationships between different members of the family in the context of real life situations. The attitude and conduct of different characters of the *Mahābhārata* and the *Rāmāyaṇa* express a very high level of self-restraint and inter-personal morality. For example, though unjustly treated by his step mother, Rāma never once showed disrespect towards her. Even though Rāma's mother, Kauśalyā had to suffer the separation of her only son due to Kaikeyī, she never condemned her. The relationship between Sītā and Rāma was one of love, companionship and mutual concern. And the mutual brotherly love of the four step-brothers of the *Rāmāyaṇa* is a thing of pleasure to read.

The Hindu families are built on the solid foundation of mutual consideration and duty. The reason for the exceptional harmony in a Hindu family lies in the fact that the couple enter into wedlock, not as independent individuals whose sole commitment lies towards each other, but as members of a family who are responsible for the welfare of the entire family. There are very few orphanages and hardly any old age homes in India. Old relatives and small children are very well looked after in Indian joint families. After the demise of the father or mother, the eldest brother or sister still takes up the place of the late parent and brings up the younger brothers and sisters as one's own children. In cities these large families are breaking up for several socio-economic reasons, but they still exist in the villages and small towns. Even if the families are not very large nowadays, one's parents are always considered an integral part of the family unit and never left uncared for.

The most important moral virtues, like self-restraint, kindness, unselfishness and the habit of sharing one's possessions with others, are learnt and practised in Hindu joint families. The Hindu joint family has thus been the foundation of the entire superstructure of the society.

VII. Social Responsibilities of the Individual

(i) The key concept of Hindu socio-moral thought is *dharma*, meaning righteousness or duty. There is no discussion of men's rights (with the exception of those of brāhmaṇas) in the entire Dharmaśāstric literature. If ever the Law-givers wanted to discuss the rights of some class of persons (rights of the individuals were never discussed), they would discuss them as the duties of another class of persons towards the given class. Thus, the rights of the masses are attended to not as rights, but as duties of the king. The rights of the husband were guaranteed by emphasizing the duties of the wife, and those of the wife were assured by insisting on the duties of the husband. Even the rights of the widows, issueless women and orphans were taken care of, but only in the form of duties, either of the members of the family or of the king.[125]

Here we may contrast Hindu social philosophy with Western social thought. The basic emphasis in the Western thought is on the rights of the individual; and his duties are mostly conceived negatively as non-interference in the enjoyment of similar rights by other members of the society. But in Indian (Hindu) thought the basic emphasis is always on duties, and these duties are mostly conceived positively, requiring positive effort on the part of the individual towards the well-being of other members of the society.

Another important difference between the two approaches, the Western and the Indian, is in their respective conceptions of the relation between the individual and the society. Broadly speaking, the Western social philosophy regards the individual as the basic unit of the society. This individual is an autonomous self and is free to pursue his personal goals and live his own life. At the same time, he has very definite obligations towards the society. And the relations of the individual with the society as a whole are non-mediate or direct. On the other hand, the Hindu social thought does not usually consider man in his capacity as an autonomous self. It is not the individual, but the class or group which is generally the main referent of all socio-moral norms and values. The individual's rights in and his duties towards the society are determined on the basis of the class to which he may belong. The various classes are defined in terms of either hereditary caste, sex or stage of life.

While the three classes of student-celibates, forest-dwellers and renunciants did not have many social responsibilities, the class of householders was conceived in a thoroughly social context. This class of householders included the members of all the four classes (*varṇas*), so that the duties of householders, such as providing for one's family, earning one's livelihood righteously and giving magnanimously, are more or less coextensive with the entire Hindu social morality. A householder was expected to provide not only for his family, but for all who needed food and succour. This included the student-celibates who compulsorily begged for food, guests who were temporarily in need of food and shelter, brāhmaṇas or teachers who usually did not have any other source of income, and renunciants. It has been unanimously agreed that the life of a householder is the support (*āśraya*) of all human beings belonging to the other three stages of life. Manu compares the life of a householder to the life-sustaining air (*prāṇa vāyu*), and the *Mahābhārata* compares it to the mother who cares for and looks after the welfare of her children. All living beings are similarly supported or looked after by the householder. And hence the conclusion, that the order of the householder is the best of the four orders.[126]

As we know, a man is said to be born with various debts (*ṛṇa*). His first debt is to the Vedic teachers which is symbolic of man's indebtedness to the entire religio-cultural heritage. His second debt is to his ancestors which affirms the value of life and procreation. And his third debt is to the gods to whom he owes his life.[127] He is also indebted to entire mankind and all other living beings. This affirms man's solidarity with all his fellow humans and the entire creation. The concept of man's indebtedness to the society and the entire creation is perhaps the most positive and morally meaningful concept, ever developed in the history of ethical thought. It is asserted that each man owes his life to his parents, teachers and society; and that he must live in a way so as to be able to repay his debts to them. The debt to parents can be repaid, as we have seen, by serving them and continuing the family line through procreation. The debt to teachers can be repaid by the regular study of Vedas. And the debt to human beings or society has to be repaid by feeding guests and helping anyone in need of help and succour. According to this tradition, even the quest of one's liberation cannot be undertaken without first fulfilling all one's socio-moral obligations,[128] especially those towards one's immediate relations.

The life of the householder is thus oriented towards the well-being of the society (*lokahita* or *lokasaṁgraha*). Though the householder is supposedly free to pursue the values of pleasure or desire-fulfilment (*kāma*) and prosperity (*artha*), in fact it is the value of righteousness (*dharma*) that is expected to govern his entire life. Utmost self-restraint and dedication to duty are expected from him. The concept of the ideal householder is unique in Hindu thought. It seeks to include and synthesize the two sets of values, viz. those relating to the enjoyment of the world and those concerned with self-discipline. There is an overwhelming emphasis on duties and self-abnegation in the Hindu ideal of the householder.

The householder is constantly held responsible towards the society. The twin duties of charity (*dāna*) and entertaining the guests (*atithi-satkāra*) express the individual's obligation towards the society. While magnanimity has been one of the most cherished values of the Aryan ethos, hospitality became obligatory because of being included in the five daily sacrifices. As we have seen, a householder was expected to feed each and every person who came to him. A text, common to both the *Bhagavadgītā* and the *Manusmṛti*, says that one who cooks food for the purpose of sacrifice (which includes offering food to the gods and all living beings) eats well, but one who cooks for himself eats in sin.[129] Roderick Hindery has pointed out that charity (*dāna*) was understood in Vedas as sharing one's food and wealth with others; he seems to imply that this sense of sharing is lost in later Hinduism.[130] But it is not so. The obligatory duty of feeding the guests, as affirmed in later Hinduism, is nothing but sharing one's food with others. Sharing one's wealth with others (*saṁvibhāga*) is a virtue often included in the description of an ideal man.[131] The *Mahābhārata* advises that one should spend one-third portion of one's income for religio-moral duties (*dharma*) which include both ritualistic acts (*iṣṭa*) like sacrifices and philanthropic acts (*pūrta*) like digging wells, planting trees etc.[132] We have seen in the previous chapter that the ritualistic tradition does not give any importance to philanthropic acts; but these are highly valued by popular religious texts.

At first, the chief beneficiaries of both charity and hospitality were brāhmaṇas. As brāhmaṇas were forbidden to teach for fees, the society acknowledged its responsibility to look after their material needs. The custom of giving liberally to brāhmaṇas expresses a high regard for knowledge and a desire to keep education within the reach of all deserving students. Later on the weak, the old and the homeless were also included, along with the renunciants, in the category of the persons deserving charity. Brāhmaṇas were still regarded as the most deserving recipients of charity; but the popular tradition affirmed that in addition to brāhmaṇas all those who are in need of food and shelter deserve help and charity.

Giving food and shelter to guests is one of the most important traditional duties of a householder. In ancient times receiving a guest was an elaborate social ritual. The guest was not only given food and shelter, he was elaborately received and honoured.[133] Though generally the guest was either a brāhmaṇa or a respected relative, the Dharmaśāstras stipulate that anyone who comes after a householder has performed the *Vaiśvadeva* sacrifice should be given food. If he is a śūdra or even an untouchable (*cāṇḍāla*), he should be given food after taking some work from him.[134] It is agreed that food should be given to all, except men of immoral character; some opine that even these should be given uncooked food. Thus, to feed all in need of nourishment is the most sacred duty of every householder. And nothing is ever expected in return.

(ii) A man is held responsible towards the society in more than one way. He is not only expected to fulfil all his obligations towards his fellow beings, he is also held accountable to the society for his conduct. Hindu legislators prescribe the ouster of the individual sinner from the society. They even stipulate that the offenders of moral code must not be associated with in any manner. Significantly, the rule of the individual's accountability to the society applies to all men, belonging to any stage of life. Though student-celibates, forest-dwellers and renunciants were not expected to engage in any socially useful work, they were strictly accountable to the society for their conduct. Rather, breach of moral code by any one of them was regarded as much more serious than an equivalent lapse by a householder.

In order to expiate for his sins, a sinner was expected to willingly undertake certain prescribed penances (*prāyaścitta*). The penance for each act of breach of moral code was decided by a group of village elders, to whom the offender was expected to report his crime. The prescribed penance was to be in accordance with the gravity of the offence. Sometimes the capacity of the sinner was also taken into consideration. Penance is one of the most discussed topics in the Dharmaśāstras and later Nibandhas (commentaries). A distinction is also made between voluntary and involuntary, major and minor sins. According to Yājñavalkya, a penance cannot expiate a sin, but can make one worthy of social intercourse,[135] implying that one becomes unworthy of social intercourse the moment one commits a sin. The *Mitākṣarā* explains this statement by pointing out that all sins have two kinds of effects—securing punishment in hell for the evil-doer and ouster of the sinner by the society.[136] A social outcaste was expected not only to live by begging, but also to loudly pronounce his sin to the society while begging.[137] Confessing one's sin before the society requires real moral courage and must have had tremendous purgatory value.

The Hindu texts have persistently tried to instil in the individual the idea of his being organically related to the society. Nothing pertaining to the life of the individual is exclusively his personal concern. Nowhere is this social bias more prominent than in the context of moral sin. Sin is neither a mere personal affair which can be confessed to a priest in private and done away with, nor a mere legal offence, punishable by the state. It is not even a moral offence, or a breach of *dharma* alone which will be punished in the other world. Rather, it is mainly a social offence. The individual forefeits his right of social membership by his moral offence, which means that the individual's membership of the society is based on the condition of his adhering to the path of *dharma*. The whole system very effectively affirms the accountability of the individual towards the society. A positive aspect of this tradition is that the individual is willingly accepted back into the society after performing due penance. Manu contends that the society should not keep any contact with the unrepentant sinner, but adds that a man who has duly repented for his sin by performing the prescribed penance must never be humiliated by reminding him of his past crime.[138]

The above concept of man's accountability to the society is not formally developed in Indian thought, but is implied in various injunctions against association with the sinners. Even the concept of society is not properly defined. Mostly it means either the caste or the village community. Even today village assemblies (*pañcāyatas*) are organized on the basis of caste. In fact, the concept of a nation or society as a whole is hardly found in the ancient literature. There may be several reasons for this. First, the ethical deliberations of ancient Hindu thinkers were largely governed by pragmatic considerations like the stability and harmonious functioning of the social order. Most of the Hindu socio-moral thought thus comes to us in the form of simple commands and statements, approving or disapproving certain forms of conduct, and we hardly ever find any deliberate effort at systematic thinking. Secondly, it seems that the leaders and thinkers of Hindu society were very conscious of the fact that it was constituted by several heterogeneous 'religio-cultural' (racial) groups. Eager to accommodate all of them within Hindu society, they neglected to develop a comprehensive concept of society. As a result, the potentially cogent idea of the individual's accountability to the society could not be given any worthwhile socio-moral content.

Since the individual was accountable to the society for his moral conduct, he was often asked to undergo some penance as a token of repentance for every breach of religio-moral laws. This gave a tool in the hands of society, especially the priestly class, to victimize and harass the simple poor folk. New petty sins were invented and the poor people's hard earned money was extracted from them in the name of expiation of sins. Thus, giving food to the whole community, earlier a symbolic act of re-entry into the community, was required on every occasion of some petty ritualistic offence. All pretence to moral relevance was given up. Crossing the sea, or killing or injuring a cow became very important sins. Village assemblies (*pañcāyatas*) have always played a very important role in the Indian life. As times changed, these assemblies became the strongholds of all that was conservative and reactionary in the Hindu society. Its members, being very old, always resisted, and still do, any change desired by the younger generation. This is perhaps an inevitable, though very unfortunate, by-product of the system.

VIII. *Some Concluding Observations*

The Hindu social morality, like everything Hindu, or rather like everything human, is a very complex phenomenon. On the one hand, the entire Hindu ethos centres round the concept of *dharma* or righteousness, and the Hindu social structure is based on the firm foundation of a harmonious family life. The individual is not lost in an impersonal social organization, so that his interests are much better safeguarded in the Indian (Hindu) social order. The individual belongs to a family and sub-caste and is never forsaken during the times of adversity. Specially, the welfare of the weaker sections of society, e.g. the old, the women and the orphaned children, is much better ensured in the Hindu social organization than anywhere else in the world.

Hindu socio-moral thought contains several very valuable ideas which have been the cause of the stability of the Hindu social organization and the basis or source of a relatively quite high level of inter-personal morality in the Hindu society through its long history. We refer here to—i) The idea of man's being born with several debts to various members of the society, as also to all his fellow beings, and the need to repay these debts by discharging all his responsibilities towards others; ii) The universal emphasis on the duties, instead of the rights, of the individual; iii) The equal emphasis on self-restraint and self-denial to be practised by the householder in order to be better able to perform all his socio-moral duties; iv) The value of sharing the goods of life with one's fellow-beings, as enshrined in the virtues of charity and hospitality which are practised even now; and v) The accountability of every member of the society to the latter for his moral conduct. The above ideas have never been systematically presented in Hindu works. But together they form a highly valuable integrated approach to social or inter-personal morality. The basic idea of Hindu socio-moral thought seems to be that man is a social animal, a product of his family and society, so that his life and conduct can never be his personal concern alone. Man's socio-moral behaviour, therefore, must be determined by his place and role in the society, as well as by the needs of those around him. If properly developed, this idea can provide a valuable basis for a healthy, positive social morality.

On the other hand, all Hindu ideals of *dharma* (righteousness), justice and social harmony are permanently vitiated by its basic assumption of the inequality of men. The division of society into hereditary, exclusive and hierarchically arranged classes (castes), as also the determination of all social relations and even justice by class considerations are expressions of the above assumption. Apart from the injustice of treating half of the population as śūdras or even untouchables, the structuring of the society into separate castes with specific duties has created insurmountable barriers between man and man.

The existence of the joint families and the division of the society into castes and sub-castes are interrelated. Both express the ethos in which the individual is not seen as an independent unit of society, but as a member of some bigger unit, a family or a caste. Till recently the individual's relations with the society were generally mediated through his caste community or *pañcāyata*. The latter exercised considerable control over the conduct of the individuals belonging to that particular caste or sub-caste and ensured that the individual did not overreach his limits and harm the interests of the society. Now, when the caste order and village communities are disintegrating due to the impact of industrialization and urbanization, the individual finds himself in direct relation with the society. It may well be that the Hindu socio-cultural tradition has not prepared the individual well to shoulder his responsibilities towards the society directly. An Indian (Hindu) usually feels himself solely responsible towards his family and close with his clan (sub-caste), so that he often unintentionally indulges in acts which are detrimental to the larger interests of the society.

Changing times have transformed the Hindu society, but in the process the entire Hindu social structure is put to great strain. Most Hindus have retained their religion, but are no more as keen on ancient socio-moral values which seem to them to come in the way of their newly acquired craze for modern ways and material comforts. There is an urgent need, therefore, to present the Hindu philosophy of morals to the people in such a way that it can provide a basis for a meaningful social morality suited to the needs of modern times. As we shall see in our VIIth chapter *infra*, this would require a reconstruction of Hindu philosophy of morals, and such a reconstruction is both desirable and possible in Hindu thought.

Notes

1. *Mbh. Śān. P.* CX. 11; cf. ibid XCI. 5
2. *M.S.* II. 6-8; IV. 178, VII. 46; *Āpast. D.S.* I. 7. 20. 7-8.
3. *Āpast. D.S.* I. 1.1. 1-3.
4. See *History* (1973), vol. III, pp. 825-826; 856 ff.
5. *M.S.* I. 85-86; VIII. 41.
6. *Gaut. D.S.* XI. 20.
7. *Yājñ. S.* I. 343; II. 192; also see *History*, vol. III, pp. 859-863.
8. *M.S.* IV. 1-2; VI. 1, 38, 88, 93-97.
9. *Mbh. Śān P.* LXI. 2-7.
10. *Āpast. D.S.* II. 9. 21. 1, 8 ff., 18 ff.; *Gaut. D.S.* III. 2, 11 ff., 26 ff.
11. *M.S.* VI. 39 ff.
12. *Mbh. Śān P.* VII. 36 ff.; IX. 4 ff., 12 ff.
13. *Āpast. D.S.* I. 2.5. 9 to I. 2.8. 30.
14. *M.S.* VI. 8, 44-48.
15. *M.S.* III. 77-78; *Mbh. Śān. P.* VIII. 6 ff., 13 ff.; XII. 11 ff.
16. *Gaut. D.S.* III. 36.
17. *M.S.* IV. 138 ff.
18. Ibid, I. 87 ff.; X. 74 ff., 100, 121-123; *B.G.* XVIII. 41 ff.
19. *M.S.* X. 95-100.
20. *Mbh. Anuś. P.* chs. XXVIII to XXX; especially XXVIII. 4, 27, 28; XXX. 5-7.
21. *History* (1974), vol. II, pp. 23-24.
22. *Ṛg. Veda* X. 90.
23. *B.G.* IV. 13.
24. Ibid III. 33; XVIII. 41.

25. Ibid III. 35, XVIII. 45-47.
26. *M.S.* X. 97.
27. *B.G.* III. 21-25.
28. *History*, vol. II., pp. 25 ff.
29. *M.S.* IV. 210 ff.
30. Ibid X. 25-30.
31. *Śatapatha Brāhmaṇa* II. 2.2.6.
32. *M.S.* I. 93-96; IX. 316-319; XI. 83-84.
33. *Mbh. Śān. P.* LVI, 12-13; LX. 40-42; *Anuś. P.* XXX. 4-6; XXXII. 25 ff; XXXIII. 4-6; LXXVI. 4, 13 etc.
34. *M.S.* VIII. 270-272; IX. 248.
35. Ibid IV. 165-169.
36. *Gaut. D.S.* VIII. 12-13.
37. *M.S.* II. 135; *Āpast D.S.* I. 4.14. 25.
38. *M.S.* IX. 319.
39. Ibid II. 157-172; III. 128 ff.; *Mbh. Śān. P.* XXXVII. 34 ff.
40. *Āpast. D.S.* I. 3.9. 9-11; *Gaut. D.S.* XII. 4-6.
41. *Rāmāyaṇa, Uttara Kāṇda*, ch. 24, (1978, p. 603).
42. *Ś.B., Br.S.* 1.3. 34-38; ref. to *Gaut. D.S.* XII. 4-5.
43. *M.S.* X. 122-123.
44. *Viṣṇu Purāṇa*, bk. VI, ch. 2, (1972, pp. 491-492).
45. *M.S.* VIII. 415-417.
46. Ibid VIII. 413-414.
47. Ibid IV. 80; *Āpast. D.S.* I. 11.31.22.
48. *Āpast. D.S.* II. 1.2. 8-9.
49. *M.S.* X. 50 ff.
50. Ibid III. 92; *Āpast. D.S.* II. 4. 9.5.
51. *M.S.* XI. 131-132; *Āpast. D.S.* I. 9. 25.13.
52. *M.S.* XI. 54; *Āpast. D.S.* I. 9. 24.7, 24-25.
53. *M.S.* XI. 127-131.
54. Ibid VIII. 359, 362 ff.; 374 ff.; *Apast. D.S.* II. 10.27. 8-9; *Gaut. D.S.* XII. 2-3
55. *M.S.* VIII. 270-272; *Āpast. D.S.* II. 10.27. 14-16.
56. *M.S.* VIII. 279-283; *Gaut. D.S.* XII. 1
57. *Gaut. D.S.* XII. 15-16.
58. *Āpast. D.S.* II. 2.3.4.
59. Ibid II. 4.9. 10-11.
60. *M.S.* III. 116.
61. Ibid X. 124.
62. *Mbh. Āraṇ. P.* CLXXVII. 16 ff; CCVI. 11-13
63. *M.S.* VIII. 14-18, 82-85, 127-128.
64. *Ibid* VII. 14 ff., 20-22,; *Mbh. Śān. P.* XV. 2 ff.
65. *M.S.* VII. 35; VIII. 172; X. 96; *Arthaśāstra*, bk. I., ch. 3, (1967, p. 7).
66. *M.S.* VIII. 285 ff.
67. Ibid VIII. 126-129.
68. *Āpast. D.S.* II. 11. 29.1.
69. *M.S.* VIII. 335-336.

70. Ibid VIII. 267 ff., 359, 366 ff.
71. Ibid XI. 55-59.
72. Ibid VIII. 4-7.
73. Ibid VIII. 314-315; XI. 99-101.
74. Ibid VIII. 321 ff.; IX. 270 ff., 292.
75. Ibid VIII. 345-346.
76. *Arthaśāstra*, bk. III, ch. 17, (1967, pp. 219-220)
77. Ibid, bk. III, ch. 19, (pp. 222-223); bk. IV, ch. II, (pp. 259-261).
78. Ibid, bk. IV, ch. 8, (p. 252).
79. *Mbh. Śān. P.* XXIX. 58-59.
80. *Śatapatha Brāhmaṇa* XIV. 1.1.31.
81. *M.S.* IX. 18.
82. *Āpast. D.S.* I. 9.24.5; *Gaut. D.S.* XXII. 17.
83. *Aitareya Brāhmaṇa* VIII. 13-18, quoted in Cromwell Crawford, op.cit., p.43.
84. *Women in the Vedic Age* (1952), p. 69.
85. *Evolution of Morals in the Epics* (1959), pp. 35 ff., 46 ff., 63 ff.
86. *M.S.* III. 20-35.
87. Ibid III. 37-40; 173-175; IX. 120-125; 138 ff.
88. Ibid IX. 32-44; *Gaut. D.S.* XVIII. 11-14.
89. *M.S.* IX. 59-63; *Gaut. D.S.* XVIII. 4-11.
90. *M.S.* IX. 64-65.
91. *Ibid* XI. 104-105.
92. *Gaut. D.S.* XVIII. 21-23.
93. *Yoga Vāsiṣṭha, Vairāgya Khaṇḍa*; chs. XII and XXII, (1978, vol. I, pp. 45 ff., 77 ff.).
94. *M.S.* IX. 13-18; cf. *Mbh. Anuś. P.* XXXVIII. 11 ff., XXXIX. 4 ff., etc.
95. *M.S.* V. 147-149; IX. 2-3; *Yājñ. S.* I. 85.
96. *M.S.* V. 155; IX. 29; cf. *Mbh. Anuś. P.* XLVI. 12.
97. *Rāmāyaṇa, Uttara Kāṇḍa*, ch. XV (1978, p. 592).
98. *M.S.* V. 153, 166.
99. Ibid V. 156-158; IX. 75.
100. *Ṛg. Veda* X. 85, quoted in *Women in the Vedic Age* (1952), p. 17.
101. *M.S.* VIII. 359; XI. 191.
102. *Mbh. Śān. P.* CCLVIII. 34-38.
103. *M.S.* VIII. 359, 364-366.
104. *Āpast. D.S.* II. 10.26. 21-24.
105. Ibid II. 10. 27.1; *Yājñ. S.* I.72; *Mbh. Śān. P.* XXXVI. 18, 26-27.
106. *M.S.* XI. 189.
107. Ibid V. 130; *Yājñ. S.* I. 71-72.
108. *M.S.* III. 52; VIII. 29; IX. 192-196.
109. *Arthaśāstra*, bk. III, chs. 2 to 4, (pp. 174 ff).
110. *M.S.* III. 55-61; IX. 95
111. *Mbh. Śān. P.* CCLVIII. 35.
112. *M.S.* IX. 27-28.
113. *M.S.* IX. 72-79; *Āpast. D.S.* I. 10.28.19.
114. *M.S.* II. 145; cf. *Vasiṣṭha Dharmasūtra* XIII. 48; *Mbh. Śān. P.* CIX. 15-16; *Anuś. P.* CVIII. 14-15.

115. *Āpast. D.S.* I. 10.28.9.
116. *Mbh. Śān. P.* CCLVIII. 24 ff.
117. *M.S.* IX. 45.
118. Ibid IX. 95-96; 101-102.
119. *Āpast. D.S.* II. 6. 14. 16-19.
120. *M.S.* III. 60.
121. Ibid XI. 7-10.
122. Ibid II. 227.
123. Ibid II. 225-237; cf. *Mbh. Śān. P.* CIX. 3 ff., 17-18.
124. *M.S.* III. 114-118.
125. Ibid VIII. 27-29.
126. *M.S.* III. 77-80; VI. 89-90; *Mbh. Śān. P.* XI. 15 ff.; XII. 6 ff.
127. *Taittirīya Saṁhitā* VI. 3.10.5, quoted in M. Hiriyanna, *Indian Conception of Values* (1960) p. 151.
128. *M.S.* VI. 35-37; *Mbh. Śān. P.* XXV. 6; XXVIII. 54; CCLXI. 15; CCLXXXI. 9-11.
129. *B.G.* III. 9-13; *M.S.* III. 115-118.
130. *Comparative Ethics in Hindu and Buddhist Traditions* (1974), pp. 45 ff.
131. *Mbh. Śān. P.* XXI. 11; LX. 7-8 etc.
132. Ibid, *Anuś. P.* CXXIX. 16-19.
133. *Āpast. D.S.* II. 3.6. 5 to II. 3.7.17.
134. *Ibid* II. 2.4. 13, 19-20; *M.S.* III. 112.
135. *Yājñ. S.* III. 226.
136. *Mitākṣarā* on ibid.
137. *M.S.* XI. 73; *Āpast. D.S.* I. 9.24. 10-11.
138. *M.S.* XI. 190.

Chapter IV

LIBERATION-CENTRIC MORALITY OF THE TRADITION OF KNOWLEDGE

I. Morality of Liberation (Mokṣa) Opposed Both to the Ritualistic and Social Moralities

We have discussed in our earlier chapters the ritualistic and social moralities of the Vedic-Dharmaśāstric tradition. The two moralities are intimately related and together form the way of action (*karma-mārga*). Hinduism contains another very important religio-philosophical tradition, that of the quest of liberation. The tradition of liberation incorporates in it both the way of knowledge (*jñāna-mārga*) and the way of turning-away-from-the world (*nivṛtti-mārga*), as expressed in the creed of world renunciation (*saṁnyāsa*). Liberation is expected to be realized through the metaphysical knowledge (*jñāna*) which in its turn necessarily implies a turning away from the world. The goal of liberation and the morality associated with it have been developed in conscious contradistinction to the first or Vedic-Dharmaśāstric tradition. As we know, both religio-moral conduct (*dharma*) and knowledge (*darśana*) are generally valued in Hinduism as means of achieving human goal(s). While the ritualistic morality of the Vedic tradition is mostly recommended as a means of achieving prosperity here and heaven hereafter, its social morality is formulated with the specific goal of preserving the stability of the social order. Presumably, if the goal changed, the morality would change too.

In the beginning itself Upaniṣads declared the Vedic sacrifices as totally irrelevant for the realization of liberation (*mokṣa*):

"Frail indeed are those rafts of sacrifices, conducted by eighteen persons, upon which rests the inferior work; therefore they are destructible. Fools who rejoice in them as the highest good fall victim again and again to old age and death."[1]

Not only did the Upaniṣadic seers condemn Vedic sacrifices, they also affirmed even philanthropic or humanitarian works as equally irrelevant to the quest of liberation, because the mortal cannot lead one to the Immortal.[2] At the same time, having declared the futility of mundane pursuits as a means of realizing liberation, Yājñavalkya, the most prominent Upaniṣadic seer, did not give up all actions, and even claimed the prize of cows.[3] In fact, Upaniṣads, *Bhagavadgītā* and *Brahma Sūtra* recommend a synthesis of the way of action with the way of knowledge.[4] They emphasize that the ritualistic and social duties must not be abandoned, and contend that the performance of duties can be continued along with the practice of the way of knowledge.[5]

On the other hand, Advaita Vedāntins categorically deny the usefulness of the path of action for a seeker of liberation, as well as the desirability or even the possibility of an active life for a man of liberation. Sāṁkhyas likewise condemn Vedic ritualism and affirm that the knowledge of the metaphysical truth alone can liberate a man from the bondage of transmigratory existence. This search for liberation is generally understood as *nivṛtti-mārga* and contrasted to the *pravṛtti-mārga* of the Vedic-Dharmaśāstric tradition. *Pravṛtti* means inclination towards the external world or the outgoing tendency of the senses and mind. Both the ritualistic and social moralities, as developed in the Dharmaśāstras, express the *pravṛtti-mārga* at its best, in that they affirm the values of this world which is both real and worthwhile for them. On the other hand, liberation (*mokṣa*) is generally conceived as a transcendent state, totally unrelated to the three Dharmaśāstric values (*trivarga*) of righteousness (*dharma*, conceived often in ritualistic terms), prosperity (*artha*) and pleasure (*kāma*). While the pursuance of the three values requires the direction of the human mind outwards, the search for liberation requires a complete breaking away of the mind from the outer world and its direction towards the innermost reality of self, culminating in the total absorption of the former (mind) into the latter (self). This is the *nivṛtti-mārga* which seeks to forcefully curb the outgoing tendency of the human mind and is supposed to be the *sine qua non* of self-realization or *mokṣa*. It is contended by Śaṁkara that the pursuit of the three goals (*trivarga*) and that of liberation are entirely unrelated, and the teachings regarding the way of knowledge and that of action are meant for two distinct classes of persons. It is so because the two, knowledge and action, are mutually opposed, so that a man cannot simultaneously devote himself to both.[6]

The tradition of liberation or *nivṛtti-mārga* is, of course, primarily concerned with man's quest of liberation (*mokṣa*). Man is constantly exhorted to seek his individual liberation and not worry about his other socio-moral obligations. It is even asserted that a man need not wait to take up the quest of liberation till he has reached the last stage of renunciation (*saṁnyāsa-āśrama*); instead, he can take up renunciation whenever the desire for liberation is aroused in his heart.[7] In contrast, the philosophy and world-view associated with the *pravṛtti-mārga* of Vedas and Dharmaśāstras, as we have seen, is socio-centric and stresses that a man must repay all his debts and fulfil all his obligations before commencing the quest for his salvation.[8] The tradition of liberation is also world-and-life-negating, in that it conceives liberation (*mokṣa*) as a state of transcendent being and consciousness, totally unrelated to this world and its values which are viewed as hindrances in a man's search for liberation. This is again in sharp contrast to the world-and-life-affirming ethos of the earlier or Vedic tradition, with its three values, pertaining to the life-in-the-world.

II. *Two Concepts of Liberation as Developed in the Systems of Philosophy (Darśanas)*

Just as in other traditions of Hinduism, morality in the tradition of liberation or the way of knowledge (*jñāna-mārga*) is determined by its concept of the supreme goal, liberation. Of the six orthodox systems of philosophy (*darśanas*), all, but *Mīmāṁsā*, affirm liberation as the ultimate goal of human life. They all agree that liberation is a transcendent state of being, unlike either this world or heaven. They also agree that the way of action (largely conceived as ritualistic acts) cannot be of any use in man's quest of liberation. At the same time, they conceive liberation quite differently in consonance with their respective metaphysical viewpoints. The five orthodox systems of philosophy which affirm the goal of liberation may be divided into two broad categories, Vedānta and the rest, i.e. Nyāya, Vaiśeṣika, Sāṁkhya and Yoga. The last four are grouped together by us because they uphold a more or less similar concept of liberation which is very different from that of the Vedānta. Thus, we have two concepts of liberation, the Vedāntic and the Sāṁkhyan, and these two concepts in their turn have given rise to two rather different outlooks or attitudes towards the world, life and morality. Gradually, the two concepts of liberation merged together, resulting in the development of a uniform but negative morality in the tradition of liberation. We think that the two viewpoints were initially developed independently, and so their ethoses are quite different, even though they do not any more exist as separate systems of thought and morality.

(i) The Vedāntic concept of liberation is metaphysical or even mystical and cannot be appreciated without a prior understanding of the Vedāntic religio-philosophy (*darśana*). The Upaniṣads, as we know, subscribe to a monistic world-view, according to which there is only one nondual Absolute which is both the source, ground and Inner-controller of the world (*Brahman*),[9] as well as the innermost Self of man (*Ātman*).[10] The very immanence of *Ātman-Brahman* in the world implies its transcendent being, for only a truly transcendent reality can be thus immanent in all.[11] That is why, the Upaniṣadic seers are never tired of proclaiming the transcendence of *Brahman* by means of the use of negation of all determinate descriptions of It (*Neti-neti*).[12]

In the original Vedānta, the individual self is essentially the same as *Brahman*, and its individual being is just a transient product of the association of the Pure-consciousness with individuating factors, such as intelligence, mind, vital breath etc.[13] Now, if the essence of the individual self is the supreme Self, the individual existence becomes rather illusory, or at best an undesirable state of imperfection; and the ultimate goal of human life becomes the realization of one's identity with the supreme Self. This Vedāntic liberation (*mokṣa*) is a state of unitive experience which transcends the duality of the knower and the known.[14] In that state, the individual self does not know the absolute Self, but rather 'becomes' that Self, and that becoming is to be understood in terms of self-transcendence.

There is a suggestion of some existential distinction between the individual self and the transcendent Self in the famous Upaniṣadic simile of two birds. But even there it is clearly stated that when the individual self realizes its true nature as identical with the transcendent Witness-consciousness, it has no more any consciousness of individuality.[15] The same Upaniṣad has also used the simile of the rivers merging into the sea to express the state of liberation as merger of the individual self into *Brahman*.[16]

This understanding of unitive experience in terms of self-transcendence is in the best tradition of mysticism and is comparable to the Sūfī concept of *fanā* or self-naughting. This is no negative experience, as is clear from several Vedāntic passages which describe the state of liberation or mystical union as characterized by a sense of freedom, peace and even exhilaration.[17] Significantly, the above concept of liberation does not refer to the theory of karma and transmigratory existence, as liberation is conceived in the Upaniṣads mostly as mystico-unitive experience which can be realized here and now.

(ii) The second concept of liberation comes from Sāṁkhya and it is shared in its broad outline by the remaining three systems of philosophy, i.e. Nyāya, Vaiśeṣika and Yoga. Tradition groups the six systems of philosophy as orthodox, that is, based on the Vedas, and contrasts them with the heterodox systems of Buddhism and Jainism. Probably there was no such clear-cut distinction in the beginning. Kumārila included Sāṁkhya, Yoga, Pāśupata and Pañcarātra systems, along with Buddhism, in the category of philosophies opposed to Vedas (*Veda-viruddha*).[18] There is a strong possibility that Sāṁkhya and Yoga originated in some non-Vedic tradition. At the same time, excepting Vedānta, Sāṁkhya is the most important system of orthodox philosophy. It has had far-reaching influence on the entire Hindu thinking. R. Garbe has rightly remarked that the entire Indian literature has been saturated with the doctrines of Sāṁkhya.[19]

As ably argued by Prof. G.C. Pande, Sāṁkhya is an atheistic, pluralistic and pessimistic philosophy and expresses an entirely different ethos from that of the Vedic-Vedāntic tradition. In his own words,

"Independence from Vedic revelation, complete pessimism about natural life, atheism and rejection of Vedic ritualism, all these features of the Sāṁkhyan doctrine attest its origin among the non-Vedic ascetics and mendicants, called the *Śramaṇas*..... Historically, thus, Sāṁkhya and Vedānta are quite independent and were often hostile. They enshrine quite different types of cultural *Weltanschauung*. This remains true in spite of the fact that the Vedānta borrowed a lot from Sāṁkhya and attempts were made from time to time to create synthetic systems."[20]

As is well-known, Sāṁkhya-Yoga affirm two ultimate realities —the *puruṣa* (self) and the *prakṛti* (nature). According to this view, the self is a transcendent pure-consciousness and it is the nature which is the real subject of all our experiences and the agent of all our actions.[21] Sāṁkhya naively argues for the plurality of selves on the basis of differences in the temperaments, capacities and external circumstances of various living beings.[22] It seems to us that the Sāṁkhya philosophy contains a basic self-inconsistency, as the plurality of selves, transmigratory existence and the law of karma cannot be justified on the basis of the Sāṁkhyan hypothesis of a totally transcendent self. And yet, not only Sāṁkhyas, but most Hindu thinkers and all religious texts have affirmed both beliefs. A typical example is provided by the *Bhagavadgītā* which believes in both, the transmigratory existence, implying the plurality of selves,[23] and the transcendent nature of the self.[24]

Sāṁkhyas conceive liberation in self-centric terms. Their concept of liberation is derived from their concept of the self which is an ultimate, transcendent reality and which, like the monads of Leibniz, is self-sufficient and alone or unrelated to the world and other selves. The self's involvement in the transmigratory existence is considered its bondage, and its liberation consists in getting rid of this false involvement and realizing its original pure nature or aloneness.[25]

The Nyāya-Vaiśeṣika concept of liberation is closer to the *kaivalya* of Sāṁkhya, rather than to the Vedāntic *mokṣa*. The self, in Nyāya, is unique to each individual, and there are innumerable individual souls. Liberation means the realization by the soul of its original pure nature; and the liberated self exists as a pure substance without any qualifying attributes, including consciousness. Thus, in all of these philosophies, excepting Vedānta, liberation consists in the realization of the self's original nature and has no reference to a Divine Being.

(iii) Śaṁkara's Advaita was the first step towards an amalgamation of the two approaches, the Sāṁkhyan and the Vedāntic. Being a true Advaitin, Śaṁkara cannot accept the Sāṁkhya doctrine of a plurality of selves and firmly believes in the individual selves being identical with the supreme Self. He argues in a convincing manner that since all selves are identical with the Pure-consciousness or universal Self, the separate identity of the individual self and its distinction from other selves are illusory, or at best empirical.[26] Śaṁkara is also fully aware of the implications of the Upaniṣadic identification of the *Ātman* with *Brahman* which means that the ultimate Reality of Vedānta is a universal and transcendent one, and not one's individual self. To quote Śaṁkara,

"Indeed distinct from the agent who is the content of 'I', the real Self is the Witness of the idea of 'I', which exists in all creatures,......which is one, unchanging, eternal and all-pervading Consciousness....... It is the Self of all, It is beyond all rejection and acceptance, for all mutable and impermanent things culminate in *Puruṣa* as their ultimate limit."[27]

If the individual self is essentially identical with the universal Self, then its bondage consists only in its apparent separate existence and its liberation would mean its merger into the universal Consciousness. Śaṁkara often explains liberation in the familiar terminology of the Upaniṣadic seers, as the merger of the individual consciousness into the universal Consciousness.[28]

So far Śaṁkara seems to be very close to the spirit of the original Vedānta. But either he is not always self-consistent, or the nature of the metaphysical truth is such that it defies all logical descriptions. Thus it happens that Śaṁkara mostly understands liberation as Self-realization, and explains the latter in terms largely reminiscent of the Sāṁkhya philosophy.[29]

The reason for this rather inconsistent approach lies in Śaṁkara's understanding of the Absolute (*Ātman-Brahman*) exclusively in terms of the Self (*Ātman*). According to him, no man can deny his own self,[30] and if it is asserted that the reality behind the universe is the same as the Self within, then the being of the Absolute also does not require any proof.[31] Perhaps because of the very certitude of the being of one's inner Self, Śaṁkara always prefers the word *Ātman* to describe the ultimate Reality. Even when the context is definitely cosmic, he still chooses to call the Absolute *Ātman* or Self.[32]

Śaṁkara further seeks to understand and explain the *Ātman* in a subjective context, as the presupposition of all our experiences and knowledge.[33] Of course, the Upaniṣads have described the Self in exactly these terms; but their understanding of the Absolute is saved from the subjective bias by their constant equation between *Ātman* and *Brahman.* On the other hand, even though Śaṁkara is equally convinced of the universality and transcendence of the *Ātman,* his choice of the term *Ātman* to denote the Absolute and the subjective context in which the reality of the *Ātman* is mostly understood by him give the impression that it is the inner Self, and not *Brahman,* that is being discussed. In his own words,

"The non-attainment of the Self is but the ignorance of It. Hence knowledge of the Self is Its attainment...... Here there is no difference between the person attaining and the object attained."[34]

In all such passages Śaṁkara has still not departed from the original Vedāntic vision. But there is a subtle, perhaps unconscious, shift from the Vedāntic position in his discussions. Liberation is no longer conceived as merger of the individual self into the universal Divine Being, but as the realization of one's Self. This subtle change in emphasis was destined to transform the entire post-Śaṁkara Advaita, and even popular Hinduism to a certain extent.

III. The Self-centric Approach of the Philosophies of Liberation and Its Influence on Morality

(i) The general philosophic approach and the concept of liberation in all the classical systems of philosophy, except Mīmāṁsā, is to a certain extent self-centric. But R. C. Zaehner is entirely off the mark when he indiscriminately groups together Sāṁkhya and Vedānta under the category of soul-centric mysticism.[35] While the Sāṁkhya liberation can be understood only in terms of a soul-centric approach, the *mokṣa* of neither in Upaniṣadic Vedānta, nor even that of the Advaita of Śaṁkara, can thus be understood as soul-centric. The individual soul is never the object or goal of seeking, or the referent of mystical experience in the classical Vedānta.

We have argued in our second section for the essential difference between the Vedic-Vedāntic approach and the Sāṁkhya one. And yet, the Sāṁkhya ideas have so much influenced and conditioned the Vedāntic writers, that the post-Śaṁkara Advaita Vedānta appears to be some kind of subjective idealism. To a certain extent, all major philosophic systems share one faith, best described in the words of Prof. N. K. Devaraja:

"Release in these systems consists, not in the establishment of a relationship with a being external to the self, but in the realization of the essential nature of one's own self." And,

"Our conclusion is that the classical systems of Indian philosophy conceived the ultimate goal of man's existence as being intrinsic to him; it consists, according to them, in the realization or attainment of a perfection which is inherent in our own being."[36]

It is this introverted vision which has brought all philosophies close to each other. The Sāṁkhya upholds the individual self (*puruṣa*) as the ultimate reality and the referent of the concept of liberation, while the Vedānta asserts that it is the supreme universal Self that is realized in the state of liberation. Yet both conceive their respective realities as within us, i.e. our very self. Both Sāṁkhya and Vedānta further affirm that this inner reality is realized through introverted contemplation.

Ninian Smart has made some very interesting observations in this context. According to him, a meditational approach in religion is mostly associated with a belief in the plurality of selves. It implies that the self that is realized in introverted contemplation or meditation is the individual self. On the other hand, a devotional approach presupposes a personal Lord who is also the Creator God. When the devotional and meditational approaches are combined, we have the concept of the Absolute who is both the Creator and the inner Self.[37] If we apply these observations to the various classical systems of philosophy, we would find that the Sāṁkhya-Yoga self consistently affirm the plurality of selves and a meditational approach to the religious goal. But the Vedānta emphatically affirms an all-comprehending Absolute, and yet recommends the way of meditation as the means of realizing one's identity with the Absolute.[38] It is this emphasis on meditation or introverted contemplation that led to the greater self-centricity of later Advaita Vedānta. (It was only when the devotional approach was emphasized in the *Bhakti* tradition that a more balanced and comprehensive religio-philosophical approach could be developed. Perhaps due to this exclusive preference for introverted contemplation, the later Advaitins were led to interpret the Absolute more and more in terms of the subject self. Thus, Advaita Vedānta has an inherent tendency towards self-centricism which has only been strengthened by the influence of Sāṁkhya ideas. As a result, even Śaṁkara often describes the Vedāntic vision in a way that appears soul-centric:

"Without action, a non-agent and one without a second, I, the universal Self, make the world go round like a king who is only a witness or like the loadstone which moves iron by its proximity only."[39]

The tendency of understanding both the supreme Reality and liberation in terms of the subjective self increased in post-Śaṁkara Advaita. Later Advaitic writers do not even bother to refer to the cosmic or universal nature of the Self, and frankly describe liberation or the mystical experience of ultimate identity in subjective terms. Later minor Upaniṣads are full of such supposedly mystical declarations, as the following:

"I am 'I' (the Self). I am also another (the not-Self). I am *Brahman*. I am the source (of all things)......... I am the Supreme. I am...... I am all."[40]

Such passages can be multiplied indefinitely from the works of Advaita writers like Prakāśātman, Madhusūdana Sarasvatī, Citsukha, Śrīharṣa etc. The true unitive experience denies the individual self in order to affirm the sole reality of the 'Divine'. Here the process seems to be reversed, and the man of realization seems to repeatedly sing the glory of his own self.[41] This apparently soul-centric understanding of liberation brings post-Śaṁkara Advaita very close to the subjective idealism of Buddhist Vijñānavāda variety. The teacher tells his disciple in the *Aṣṭāvakra Saṁhitā*:

"It is through your ignorance alone that the universe exists. In reality you are one. There is no individual self or supreme Self other than you."[42]

There is another closely related reason for the later transformation of the Vedānta into a self-centric philosophy. The Vedānta not only asserts the essential identity of the individual self and the universal Self; it also uses the same term *ātman* for both. And there is no way we can tell which self is being talked about in a given context. This has caused certain confusion in the Vedāntic approach from very early times.

It is not that the Upaniṣadic seers are entirely free from blame for the above confusion. They often indulge in quite self-centric statements which are open to misinterpretation due to their vague use of the concept of self. The *Bṛhadāraṇyaka Upaniṣad* declares that one loves others, not for their sake, but for the sake of the Self. The husband loves the wife, or the wife loves the husband, or the parent loves the son, but in all such love the real object of love is not the wife, husband, or son, but the Self.[43] Obviously, the Upaniṣad means the universal Self here which is common to all, the ultimate Reality behind all distinctions of name and form. But the Upaniṣad uses the term *ātman*; and as pointed out by R. C. Zaehner at some place, there are no capital letters in the Sanskrit language, so that it is difficult to know as to which self is being discussed in a given context. Such assertions are always liable to be misunderstood as referring to the subjective self. Commenting on the above passage, Vidyāraṇya says:

"A wife shows affection for her husband when she desires his company......

"Her love is not for the husband's sake, but for her own. Similarly, the husband's love also is for his own satisfaction and not for hers.

"Thus, even in the mutual love between husband and wife the incentive is one's own desire for happiness."[44]

In the same context he further says:

" 'May I never perish, may I ever exist', is the desire seen in all. So love for the self is quite evident."[45]

That the term self is understood here as the individual self is obvious, but what is even more surprising is the extreme egoistic and hedonistic tone of the entire explanation. The above observations of Vidyāraṇya are not even psychologically true, what to say of their spiritual or moral worth. The word *svārtha* (for one's own sake) is liberally used by Vidyāraṇya, suggesting that one's own interests come first and foremost. The self whose interests are so dear to man can but be the subject self and not the universal Self, common to all. To quote Vidyāraṇya again:

"A son is dearer than wealth, the body dearer than the son, the sense organs dearer than the body and the self is supremely dear than life and mind."[46]

The context of body and senses leaves no doubt as to which self is being referred here. How and why this unfortunate transformation in the meaning of the concept of *ātman* took place is difficult to say. But there is no doubt that it has had very important negative ramifications for morality.

(ii) This philosophical soul-centricism seems to have penetrated popular Hindu thought quite early. A verse of the *Mahābhārata* advises that a person may be sacrificed for the sake of the family, the family may be sacrificed for the sake of the village and the village for the sake of the country, and concludes that for the sake of the *ātman* the whole earth can be sacrificed.[47] (The advice was given by Kṛṣṇa to Dhṛtarāṣṭra and concerned the need to sacrifice Duryodhana to save the kingdom.) Both the context of the advice and the manner of its presentation leave no doubt as to which self is being talked about here. This passage of the Epic is a classical example of the confusion in the Indian mind between the two senses of the term *ātman*, and the dangerous implications of this confusion for Hindu morality.

It is generally contended in reply to any charge of soul-centricism that the interest of the self for which all else must be sacrificed is not any material or selfish interest of the individual, but the spiritual interest of liberation (*mokṣa*) which is a transcendent and in a way an impersonal goal. But the above passages from *the Pañcadaśī* and *Mahābhārata* are not talking about liberation. They simply seem to be saying that the interests of the individual self are the governing consideration in all human actions. Moreover, even if they mean that all relations and obligations must be sacrificed for the sake of individual's liberation, it would hardly make a relevant difference to social morality. Does it make any great difference whether you sacrifice the interests of the entire earth for your selfish (in the materialistic or hedonistic sense) interests, or for the sake of your personal salvation? This kind of pseudo-philosophical individualism definitely undermines the values of social morality.

The soul-centric ideas of popular religious texts are founded on certain vaguely formulated ontological beliefs, regarding the nature of bondage, the nature of the soul, the plurality of souls, the duality of the soul and body and the causes of bondage and liberation. Above all, this popular tradition believes in the law of karma and transmigratory existence and conceives liberation primarily in terms of freedom from the cycle of rebirths. The law of karma is responsible for the extreme individualism of this approach. According to Manu:

"Living being is born alone, he dies alone, he suffers the good and bad fruits of his accumulated merits and demerits alone."[48]

Since man alone is responsible for his destiny, and since each man acts and suffers alone, no one else is responsible for his sufferings, joys or final destiny, no one can directly and effectively help him. In this context, the story of Vālmīki's early life as a robber is revealing. Once Dharma and other gods asked Vālmīki, in order to enlighten him, whether his family members, for whose sake he was committing so many crimes, would share with him the sin accruing from his criminal deeds. When Vālmīki asked this question from his wife and parents, they flatly refused, saying that every man's sins and merits are his own and cannot be shared by others. Disillusioned thus, Vālmīki abandoned his mode of life, as well as his family, and set upon the search for his liberation. The individualism implied in the above story has become very deep rooted in the Indian psyche. The *Mahābhārata* advises that if a man desires liberation, he should renounce the world and should not let himself be bothered by such thoughts as, 'how would my dependents be sustained, if I renounce them?'. Such a man should not worry about others, as no one is responsible for the fate of others. He should remember that whether he lives or dies (worrying about others), others would suffer only what they deserve. Knowing this, he should understand that he can in no way help others; and therefore, he should devote himself whole-heartedly to the pursuit of his liberation.[49]

From Manu to Kabīr, all Hindu saints and philosophers have emphasized the fact that man dies alone and after he is dead, no one else, except his own merits and demerits, accompanies him to the other world.[50] Kabīr repeatedly sings how all relatives leave and forget a man when he is dead, thus emphasizing the essentially lonely character of man's journey through transmigratory existence (*saṁsāra*). Of course, all Hindus also believe in the transference of merit, and the virtue of compassion; but these ideas are generally overshadowed by the strong universal belief in the law of karma. The latter has resulted in an attitude of detachment towards the sufferings of others which are mostly seen as results of their own past actions, and hence as what they themselves deserve. (This does not hold true for the devotional saints like Kabīr and Nānak. Even though they often emphasize the aloneness of man, their main concern is devotion to the Lord which makes all the difference to their mental attitude and values. We shall have occasion to discuss them in our next chapter *infra.*)

Though in the present-day Hindu society the desire for liberation is no longer a relevant factor in man's religio-moral conduct, the self-centric approach which is intimately associated with the quest of liberation is even now quite evident in Hindu thought and conduct. It is so, because while most Hindus do not take the supra-mundane values and goals of the tradition of liberation seriously, they all firmly believe in the law of karma which has been an integral part of the later Hindu concept of liberation. And this law of karma is a thoroughly individualistic theory which engenders a similarly individualistic or self-centric approach in socio-moral matters.

IV. World-and-Life-Negation in the Tradition of Liberation

For the Sāṁkhya-Yoga the world is real, while for the Advaita Vedānta it is empirically real, but ontologically false. Both agree that the soul's connection with it is transient and false, a product of the cosmic ignorance (*avidyā*) or non-discrimination (*aviveka*) between the self and the not-self or nature. Śaṁkara adds that not only the bondage of the self, but the entire world of name and form (including man's empirical personality) is false, a projection of the *māyā* or *avidyā*.[51] At the same time, *avidyā* remains a cosmic entity for Śaṁkara which is rather to be understood as a power of *Brahman*.[52] On the other hand, later Advaita works either declare *avidyā* as belonging to the self (*jīva*), or just dispense with it, and simply assert the world-diversity to be a false projection (*vivarta*) or play (*vilāsa*) of the mind (*citta* or *manas*).[53] This makes the world a creation of the individual self or even mind, and as such totally unreal.

While the Advaitins declared the world to be false, the Sāṁkhyas understood it as full of suffering. Popular treatises accepted both the ideas. They argued rhetorically for the transitoriness, painfulness, undesirability and even the unreality of the world. The transience of life and objects of desire, the undesirability of old age, disease and death were constantly harped upon. Persistent attempts were made to paint the life-in-the world in the darkest colours. Morbidly exaggerated versions of the supposedly filthy nature of human body, old age and its miseries were given in order to create repulsion for them in the mind of the listeners:

"This body which is composed of intestines, muscles etc. and is subject to change...... comes into being in this world simply to undergo pain. What thing more palpably fruitless, pain-giving and degraded could be conceived of than this body...?"[54]

The woman suffered most at the hands of these fanatical advocates of *nivṛtti* or turning-away-from-the world, as she was seen to be the centre of man's lust for worldly pleasures. Such writers excelled in rejecting the desirability of woman through a morbid dissection of her body.[55] This world-and-life-negation leading to a turning-away-of-the-mind-from-the world (*nivṛtti-mārga*) had necessarily to negate all that the creed of an active life-in-the world (*pravṛtti-mārga*) stood for.[56] Though this creed could find some support in the Vedāntic dictum that 'the Immortal cannot be realized through the mortal', the morbid way in which life's sufferings and transitoriness were argued suggests the influence of some non-Vedic tradition. If we were to undertake a comparative study of the Buddhist and later Vedāntic thought on this subject, we would find a marked similarity between the two. Later Vedāntins seem to follow Buddhist thinkers both in the negative conclusions (regarding the reality and the worth of the world) and the dialectical reasoning applied to reach those conclusions.[57]

Once this tradition gained popularity, it exercised a profound influence on the Hindu psyche. Albert Schweitzer and other critics have argued that the world-and-life-negation found in Hindu philosophy cuts at the very roots of morality. You cannot possibly engage yourself in meaningful moral action in a false and meaningless world.[58] Prof. S. Radhakrishnan has given a detailed reply to the above criticism by arguing first, that Hinduism has world-and-life-affirmation also in equal measure; and secondly, that other religions also contain world-and-life-negation.[59] His arguments are well-documented and conclusive; but they still do not prove that the world-and-life-negation of the tradition of liberation does not negatively affect Hindu morality.

V. The Creed of Renunciation Integrally Related to the Way of Knowledge

The creed of renunciation follows from some generally agreed contentions of the philosophies of liberation. Life-in-the world is understood in this tradition to be a state of bondage, a result of ignorance of the true nature of one's self; while the self is conceived as a transcendent consciousness, unrelated to the world of diversity. We would concentrate here on the Advaita views on the relation between knowledge and action, first, because they have been most influential in shaping up the Hindu attitude towards life-in-the world, and secondly, because they are most consistently presented.

(i) According to the Advaita Vedānta, the way of action (and social morality) is of no use in a man's quest for liberation. It is so because work is useful only in the context of temporal goals, such as achieving or producing something new; but it can have no use in the realization of the *Ātman* which is our very Self.[60] The only obstruction in the realization of Self is our ignorance of our real nature. This ignorance can be destroyed only by its opposite, i.e. knowledge of one's true nature, and not by action, since action is in no way contradictory to ignorance.[61] Rather, action belongs to the domain of ignorance, as it presupposes the reality of the world and attributes agency and individuality to the Self, which are both illusory products of the cosmic ignorance (*avidyā*).[62] Śaṁkara, therefore, contends that,

"(Renunciation of works) is necessary, for *mokṣa* consists in the realization of the immutability of one's Self...... Hence the conclusion that devotion to knowledge should be practised through renunciation of action."[63]

The conclusion that renunciation of action is mandatory for a seeker of liberation does not necessarily follow from the contention that the way of works cannot lead to liberation, unless you also believe that action should be undertaken only if it is conducive to some personal end. Advaitins seem to think so:

"No one engages in any activity in matters towards which he is indifferent. Why should the one desirous of liberation act, seeing that he is indifferent to the three worlds?"[64]

It seems that the creed of renunciation was very closely related to the self-centric approach of the philosophies of liberation. It was not very popular at the time of the Upaniṣads, when most of the teachers of the knowledge of *Brahman* were householders. Later Upaniṣads recommended the way of renunciation only as an alternative means of liberation, saying that some have attained immortality through renunciation.[65] It was only gradually that the creed of renunciation gained wide acceptance under the influence of the heterodox traditions of Jainism and Buddhism. At first renunciation (*saṁnyāsa*) was accepted as the fourth stage of life. And then it was boldly affirmed that since the renunciation of the world is a pre-requisite for any quest for liberation, a man can renounce the world whenever a desire to do the same arises in his mind, even though he may still be a student.[66]

(ii) Advaitins are equally positive regarding the uselessness or undesirability of the way of action for a man who is liberated-while-living (*jīvan-mukta*). Sāṁkhya, Yoga and Advaita Vedānta believe that even though the knowledge of the ultimate Truth liberates a man here and now, it does not terminate the present life; so that there is always a period when a man of knowledge continues to live due to the force of his past actions (*prārabdha-karma*). Such a man is known as one who is liberated-while-living,[67] and is naturally the paradigm of human perfection. According to the Upaniṣads, renunciation of, and complete detachment towards, the world of diversity and desires become natural for such a man:

"Wishing for this world (Self) alone, the monks renounce their homes......... The knowers of *Brahman* of olden times, it is said, did not wish for offspring, because they thought, 'what shall we do with offspring, we who have attained this Self, this world?'"[68]

Śaṁkara affirms liberation to be a transcendent state of being or a state of disembodiedness which is totally unrelated to the mundane world of time, distinctions and action. Taking this transcendent nature of liberation as his point of departure, Śaṁkara gives several related arguments in support of the advisability of a life of renunciation of all actions in the world for a knower of *Brahman*.

First, all action (or morality) presupposes the reality of the world diversity, as well as the being of the empirical subject or agent of actions. Now, both, the world and the empirical self, are supposed to be the products of the cosmic ignorance (*avidyā*) in Advaita Vedānta. It is further asserted by Śaṁkara and others that this *avidyā* is destroyed (sublated) by the knowledge of *Brahman*, and with the destruction of the ignorance both, the world and the agent of actions, are realized as illusory. Śaṁkara concludes from the above that engagement in action is not possible for a knower of *Brahman*, who is thus convinced of the illusory nature of everything.[69] Secondly, all action presupposes the attribution of agency and other qualifications to the Self, while metaphysical knowledge reveals the Self to be actionless and transcendent. A man who has realized his unconditional identity with the transcendent Self cannot, therefore, engage himself in worldly activities.[70] Śaṁkara concludes that:

"All dualistic dealings, brought about by unreal ignorance, are sublated by right knowledge."[71]

Śaṁkara's third argument against the possibility of the performance of actions by a knower of *Brahman* is not a metaphysical one, and refers to the psychology of a liberated man. Such a man feels a profound gratification and sense of fulfilment. Since all action is *exhypothesi* taken up for the fulfilment of some personal desire or the other, no action is possible for such a man (except that done for the bare maintenance of the body). Śaṁkara believes that the renunciation of the world of actions is a spontaneous act on the part of a knower of *Brahman* and needs no extraneous justification.[72]

This last argument, which directly refers to the psychology of the man of realization, is the most misleading of all. It denies completely the possibility of action with motives other than the purely selfish ones. This argument deliberately neglects to take cognizance of the *Bhagavadgītā*'s ideal of desireless performance of one's duties. It is implied in all such arguments that a man must above all look after his spiritual welfare; and as it is served best by renouncing the world and all its obligations, he must do so. A seeker of liberation must renounce the world (and indirectly all his duties towards his fellow beings), since his supreme goal, liberation, cannot be achieved through a life of action (and morality). A man who has realized his liberation here and now (*jīvan-mukta*) must also renounce the world, since he has no personal desires which can motivate him to take up a life of action. It seems to us that this way of thinking regards a man's personal interest as his primary concern. Whether a man engages in worldly activities or desists therefrom depends upon whether he desires mundane objects or liberation. The goal may be different, but it has to be a personal goal.

VI. Ethical Discipline As a Means of Liberation

Even though the creed of renunciation implies a certain devaluation of the way of works and morality (*karma-mārga*), at no place have the Hindu thinkers undermined morality. Morality is mostly understood in this tradition in the context of liberation, and it is unanimously agreed that a high level of self-discipline and purity of heart are a pre-requisite of even one's undertaking the quest for liberation. According to the *Kaṭha Upaniṣad*,

"He, who has not first turned away from wickedness, who is not tranquil and subdued and whose mind is not at peace, cannot attain the *Ātman*."[73]

The aim of the ethical discipline, suggested in the Upaniṣads, is total transformation or spiritualization of man's empirical personality. "When all desires that dwell in the heart fall away", says the same Upaniṣad, "then the mortal becomes immortal and here attains *Brahman*."[74] Here desires signify all lower tendencies of the mind and passions which must be transcended or conquered before one can aspire for the unitive experience. The *Muṇḍaka Upaniṣad* even contends that the practice of cardinal moral virtues is a direct means of the realization of the supreme Self:

"This *Ātman*, resplendent and pure, whom the sinless *saṁnyāsins* behold as residing within the body, is attained by unceasing practice of truthfulness, austerity, right knowledge and continence."[75]

Nyāya, Vaiśeṣika, Sāṁkhya and Yoga not only regard ethical discipline as a pre-requisite of acquiring knowledge, but also affirm the two to be mutually complementary. All the popular religious texts contend that one cannot hope for liberation without first achieving moral perfection which is generally conceived as consisting in the control of the senses and passions and the practice of such virtues as non-violence and forgiveness.[76]

Both Sāṁkhya and Advaita Vedānta regard the *avidyā* or primeval ignorance as the cause of man's bondage. But while Śaṁkara conceives *avidyā* mainly as contradictory to knowledge, for Sāṁkhya-Yoga it represents man's entire mental set-up and includes not only positive mis-apprehension (*avidyā*), but also egoism (*asmitā*), desire (*rāga*), aversion (*dveṣa*) and fear or clinging to life (*abhiniveśa*).[77] Sāṁkhya also believes that the discriminatory knowledge (*viveka*) which liberates the soul from transmigratory existence is achieved through the practice of strict ethical discipline. The chief virtues valued by Sāṁkhya and Yoga are *vairāgya* (complete detachment) and *viveka* (discriminatory knowledge of the self and the not-self). In addition, one must undergo primary ethical discipline which aims at the purification of the (lower) self. It consists of the well-known rules of ethical discipline, called *yamas* (i.e. truth, non-violence, non-stealing, sense-control and non-acceptance of gifts) and *niyamas* (i.e. purification of the body and mind, contentment, austerity, study of scriptures and devotion to God).[78] Both sets of virtues are more or less negative and pertain to self-culture. Other-regarding virtues find no place in the above list.

Here Yoga offers some positive suggestions. It observes that certain evil propensities of the mind like egoism, attachment, aversion etc. obstruct the task of self-discipline. It advises that the best way to curb them is not to suppress them forcefully, but to counter them by the development of positive feelings that are directly opposed to them. The *Yoga Sūtras* advise the development of four great positive feelings, viz. friendliness towards all (*maitrī*), compassion towards the suffering (*karuṇā*), happiness at the good fortune of others (*muditā*), and detachment towards evil persons (*upekṣā*).[79] Yoga shares the conception of the four positive feelings with Buddhism. The *Yoga Vāsiṣṭha*, an Advaita work, also advocates the practice of these four virtues. According to it, the mind has two kinds of tendencies (*vāsanās*), pure and impure, and the latter can be mastered by the assiduous practice of the four positive virtues.[80] These four virtues are as positive and other-regarding as can ever be conceived. But unfortunately, these feelings are generally valued as aids to self-discipline and do not provide a motive for acts of mercy or active help of others. What is more, these positive feelings are to be transcended, along with all the negative or impure tendencies or feelings, in the state of *samādhi*, which is the culmination of yogic discipline. The aim is the gradual control of the senses and the mind, resulting in the severing of all contact of the mind with the outer world and the cessation of all modes of the mind (*citta-vṛtti-nirodha*).[81] The state of trance (*samādhi*) is a mystical experience of transcendence of all thought processes, as well as the consciousness of individuality. The way to this transcendent experience is through the practice of yogic discipline (*abhyāsa*) and complete detachment (*vairāgya*).[82] The usual yogic discipline, consisting of control of breath, deliberate withdrawal of the senses and mind from the outer world, meditation (*dhyāna*) and finally deep trance (*samādhi*), is accepted by all other schools of philosophy and Hindu texts as a means of self-purification.[83] It is to be noted here that the yogic discipline is fully self-centred and aims at directing the mind away from the world and even from one's inner thoughts. When a yogin sits to practise yoga, he simply cuts himself off from the entire world. The universal acceptance of yogic discipline as a means to man's spiritual goal is responsible for much of the self-centredness in the Hindu ethos.

According to Śaṁkara, the search for liberation (or the inquiry about *Brahman*) can be commenced only after one has acquired complete self-purification through the practice of four cardinal virtues, viz. discrimination between the Self and the not-Self (*viveka*), dispassion or turning-away-from-the world (*vairāgya*), the [group of six virtues viz. calmness (*śama*), self-control (*dama*), withdrawal from sense objects (*uparati*), forbearance or bearing all the vicissitudes of life with absolute indifference (*titikṣā*), faith in the teacher and scriptures (*śraddhā*) and constant concentration of the self on *Brahman* (*samādhāna*)] and intense yearning for freedom (*mumukṣutva*).[84]

Śaṁkara also accepts the worth of moral action or the selfless performance of one's duties, but regards it only as an indirect means (*ārādupakāraka*) of liberation. The practice of moral virtues and moral conduct are useful for achieving self-purification which is a necessary condition for acquiring the knowledge of Self which, in its turn, is the true means of liberation.[85] This approach in a way devaluates moral conduct by declaring it to be of secondary importance; but it also makes it a pre-condition of any quest for liberation, and hence mandatory for a seeker thereof. In his minor works Śaṁkara even acknowledges the usefulness of the way of yogic concentration, leading to supra-conscious trance (*samādhi*) as a means of liberation.[86]

Both, the list of virtues given by Śaṁkara and the *yamas* and *niyamas* given in the *Yoga Sūtras*, are generally accepted by all the philosophies of liberation. According to the later Advaita writers, the mind's affective inclinations (*vāsanās*) and conative tendencies (*saṁkalpas*) are the cause of the soul's (apparent) bondage; and therefore the metaphysical knowledge of the true nature of the self alone is not sufficient, and must be supplemented by a very strict control of the mind and all its affective-conative tendencies. The aim of the ethical discipline is the complete restraint of all inclinations or tendencies of the mind (*vāsanākṣaya*), leading to a total destruction of the mind (*manonāśa*). A complete destruction of the mind and its various tendencies also constitutes an integral part of the state of liberation.[87] In a way, the later Advaitic works seem to give much greater importance to ethical discipline as a means of Self-realization than was perhaps given by Śaṁkara. At the same time, the discipline advocated in the later Vedāntic works is quite negative and self-centred.

Complete detachment (*vairāgya*) is the key virtue or attitude which pervades and determines the entire morality of these philosophies of liberation. The seeker of personal liberation is only interested in acquiring mastery over his lower self. In order to do so, he turns his back away from his fellow beings. A man cannot engage himself in meaningful moral activity in a frame of mind of absolute detachment. (The detachment (*anāśakti*) advocated by the *Bhagavadgītā* is quite different from the detachment or dispassion (*vairāgya*) advocated by the philosophies of liberation.)

VII. The Morality of a Liberated Man and the Ideal of Human Perfection

Most of the philosophies of this tradition can be termed 'leap' philosophies, to borrow a significant phrase from Karl H. Potter;

that is, they affirm a marked transition from the state of a seeker of liberation to that of a liberated-man-while-living (*jīvan-mukta*). Now, this liberated man is also the paradigm of human perfection, so that the morality practised by him would truly represent the moral values and norms of the tradition of liberation.

Both Sāṁkhya and Yoga have acknowledged the state of liberation-while-living. But their descriptions of a liberated man are mostly confined to the elucidation of the state of trance (*samādhi*) which transcends all empirical experience. Presumably, no man stays in the trance throughout his life. The question is—how does a man of realization behave when he is not lost in trance? An answer to this question can be found only in the Vedānta. And since Vedānta is the central philosophy of Hinduism, the Vedāntic concept of a man-of-liberation (*jīvan-mukta*) is very important for a balanced evaluation of Hindu morality.

(i) According to the Vedānta, complete detachment towards, and transcendence of, all worldly concerns and distinctions (and by implication of all moral norms) characterize a knower of *Brahman* or a liberated man. The Upaniṣads have affirmed the futility of the life-in-the world for the knowers of *Brahman* thus:

"He (the knower of *Brahman*) is not overcome by these two thoughts, 'For this I did an evil act and for this I did a good deed.' He overcomes both. Things done or not done do not afflict him.

"This is the eternal glory of *Brahman*; it neither increases, nor decreases through work. Therefore, one should know the nature of that alone. Knowing it one is not touched by evil actions..."[88]

Such descriptions of the liberated man, mostly made from the mystical point of view, are sometimes amenable to the criticism that the man of realization is expected to be amoral or beyond ethical distinctions, or that he is given a licence for self-indulgence.[89] But such observations are made by deliberately neglecting the unanimous emphasis on the total mastery over one's lower self and all its desires and passions as the pre-requisite of even one's undertaking the quest for liberation.

Having asserted the transcendence of all worldly norms by a knower of *Brahman*, the *Bṛhadāraṇyaka Upaniṣad* goes on to explain its meaning:

"Therefore he who knows it as such becomes self-controlled, calm, withdrawn into himself, patient and collected. He sees the

Self in his own Self, he sees all as the Self. Evil does not overcome him, but he overcomes all evil. He becomes sinless, taintless, free from doubts..."[90]

The man of liberation has left the evil temptations far behind and in their absence there is no possibility of his indulging in evil. As so aptly put by Śaṁkara, a person who has fallen into a ditch in the darkness does no more fall into it after sunrise.[91] Sureśvara expresses the same idea more forcefully:

"If a man who has known this truth of oneness acts according to his wishes, then where is the difference between a knower of truth and a dog?"[92]

Here the knowledge of *Brahman* does not mean some kind of intellectual knowledge; rather, it is a mystico-unitive experience which involves a total transformation of the personality of the knower of *Brahman*. Interestingly, later Vedāntins do not believe in a marked transition from the state of the seeker to that of the knower of *Brahman*. They seem to believe that the knower of *Brahman* or a liberated-man-while-living (*jīvan-mukta*) is as much prone to evil temptations as a seeker. They, therefore, prescribe an identical ethical discipline for both, a seeker of liberation and a man who is liberated. This discipline mainly consists of yogic concentration, aiming at the complete restraint of all the affective-conative tendencies of the mind and the final destruction of the mind (see section VI *supra*). It means that they envisage no stage at which a man so transcends his empirical personality that no residue of evil propensities of the mind is left in him. This stand seems to deny the classical concept of *jīvan-mukti*.

But theory apart, the later position is much more realistic and seeks to give morality its due. Even Śaṁkara has acknowledged in his *Viveka-cūḍāmaṇi* that vigil and effort are needed to keep the mind disciplined, even after achieving the supreme unitive experience:

"Even after the truth has been realized, there remains that strong beginningless obstinate impression, that one is the agent and experiencer which is the cause of one's transmigration. It has to be carefully removed by living in a state of constant identification with the supreme Self. Sages call that liberation which is the attenuation of *vāsanās* (tendencies or impressions) here and now."[93]

"There is no greater danger for a knower of *Brahman* (*jñānin*) than carelessness about his real nature. From this comes delusion, then egoism, this is followed by bondage and this carries misery...

"As sledge, even if removed, does not stay away for a moment, but covers the water again, similarly, *māyā* also covers even a wise man who is averse to meditation."[94]

Śaṁkara here seems to contradict his own stand in his philosophical commentaries. It may express his personal view, as unhampered by philosophical necessity. It means that all the Advaitins recognize the possibility of a knower of *Brahman* becoming a prey to his lower tendencies or mundane temptations, and recommend constant vigilance and practice of strict self-discipline. Such a view could have provided a much needed emphasis on morality in the Vedānta; but instead, it led the Vedāntins to the extreme position of dread of the involvement of the knower in the world. Most of the moral virtues advocated in this tradition aim at individual self-culture or self-mastery. Certain inter-personal virtues like non-violence and forgiveness are also recognized; but even they are valued mostly as a means of protecting the self from passions or involvements in the world.

(ii) To a certain extent, all the classical systems of philosophy share one vision of human perfection, which is best described in the words of Prof. N.K. Devaraja:

"The classical schools of Indian thought present us with a plurality of ontologies. And yet the moral and religious implications of these ontologies are surprisingly similar. Every system upholds the ideal of passionless sage, though each of them gives its own reasons for pursuing that ideal. This leads us to note the most important result of the attainment of metaphysical knowledge and destruction of ignorance, viz. the eradication of passions, consequent upon the liquidation of the empirical self or the ego-sense... Common conclusion of the systems is that the person aspiring to reach the goal of ultimate release should cultivate complete detachment towards the pleasures and pains, victories and defeats, of the embodied spatio-temporal existence."[95]

Prof. Devaraja suggests that the "intuition of the ideal life as consisting in detachment towards the vicissitudes of earthly existence" came first and the various ontologies were developed afterwards to provide the *raison d'etre* of such an ideal.[96] But we feel that both, the ideal of absolute detachment and the transcendentalist ontologies, are derived from the mystical experience of the early seers and thinkers. Almost all religio-mystical experience has a transcendent core. It is necessarily ineffable and its most important feature is the experience of transcendence of, or freedom from, all mundane distinctions and limitations. The ideal of absolute detachment is naturally derived from this experience of transcendence. While the various ontologies differ, the core of mystical experience seems to be common to all Indian philosophies of liberation, and so is the ideal of perfection. A perfect man is universally understood as one who has totally transcended all worldly distinctions, norms and concerns. Śaṁkara has given an eloquent description of a man-of-liberation (*jīvan-mukta*) as follows:

"The sage living alone enjoys the sense objects, being the very embodiment of desirelessness, always satisfied with his Self and himself present as the all.

"Sometimes a fool, sometimes a sage, sometimes possessed of regal splendour, sometimes wandering, sometimes behaving like a motionless python, sometimes wearing a benign expression, sometimes honoured, sometimes insulted, sometimes unknown, thus lives the man of realization, ever happy with the supreme bliss.

"Though without riches, yet ever content; though helpless, yet very powerful, though not enjoying the sense objects, yet eternally satisfied, though without an exemplar, yet looking upon all with an eye of equality.

"Though doing, yet inactive, though experiencing the fruits of past actions, yet untouched by them, though possessed of a body, yet without identification with it; though limited, yet omnipresent is he.

"Neither pleasure, nor pain, nor good, nor evil ever touches the knower of *Brahman* who always lives without the body idea......

"The man of realization lives unmoved in the body, like a witness, free from mental oscillations like the point of the potter's wheel.

"He neither directs the sense organs to their objects, nor detaches them from them, but stays like an unconcerned spectator. And he has not the least regard for the fruits of actions, his mind being thoroughly inebriated with drinking the undiluted elixir of the bliss of *Ātman*."[97]

The central idea here is the total transcendence of all mundane interests or concerns by the mystic saint and the resulting attitude of absolute detachment towards the world and all it stands for. The possibility of moral actions by a knower of *Brahman* is not denied; but the level of detachment (*vairāgya*) and the perception of the worthlessness of all mundane distinctions and concerns by the liberated-man-while-living are such that any meaningful moral action would be a psychological impossibility for him. Later Advaita works compete with each other in portraying the supreme state of Self-realization in more and more negative terms. And such descriptions are in sharp contrast with those of unitive experience found in the early Vedānta. See,

"That is the real supreme state wherein all determinate tendencies (*saṁkalpas*) are at rest, which resembles the state of a stone, and which is neither waking nor sleeping."[98]

A minor Upaniṣad, *Nārada-Parivrājaka*, gives the mode of life of an ideal ascetic thus:

"He is a *muni* who is devoid of love and hate, who regards equally a clod of earth, stone or gold, who does no injury to any living creature and is freed from all......

"He should be alone and desireless. He should not converse with anybody... An ascetic who plays the part of the dumb, the eunuch, the lone, the blind, the deaf and the idiot is emancipated through the above six means."[99]

The ascetic is advised in later Vedāntic works not to perceive sense objects or persons, especially women, and never to respond to outer stimuli, and generally to behave as if in sleep. He is further advised to generally withdraw himself from the world and even to avoid speaking to others, lest the respect shown to him by them may divert him from his goal.[100] The *Yoga Vāsiṣṭha* enumerates seven stages of knowledge through which a seeker of liberation becomes progressively absorbed in his own consciousness and cut off from the world diversity, till at last he is totally lost to the outer world.[101]

The obsession of these ancient lovers of liberation with the need to stay free from all involvements must have precluded all possibility of their practising inter-personal morality. If you are so much afraid of others, lest any contact with them bind you to this world, you can hardly bother about your obligations towards them. This morbid concern often led the later Vedāntins to very negative and often amoral conclusions:

"There is no attachment or aversion in the one for whom the ocean of the world has dried up. His look is vacant, his action purposeless and his senses inoperative."[102] And,

"In the wise one, whose worldly life is exhausted and who has transcended the limitations of human nature, there is neither compassion, nor any desire to harm, neither any humility, nor insolence, neither wonder, nor mental disturbance."[103]

Though such works still say that a liberated man may work or perform his worldly duties, it is made clear that being supremely detached, the purposes and results of his actions have no interest for him. This absolute detachment makes his actions mechanical and morally meaningless, as is evident from the following passage:

"Devoid of the feelings of 'I' and 'mine', knowing for certain that nothing is, and with all his inner desires set at rest, the man of knowledge does not act, though he may be acting."[104]

Such descriptions of human perfection in terms of absolute detachment towards and transcendence of all worldly relations and concerns are found in almost all works of philosophy. But while the ideal of complete withdrawal from the world is very much in consonance with the metaphysics of Sāṁkhya-Yoga, it is not so easily reconciled with the Vedāntic vision of an all-comprehending Absolute. Significantly, there is a marked change in tone and emphasis in the descriptions of a man of liberation in the works of post-Śaṁkara Advaitins from those of the Upaniṣads and Śaṁkara's works. This change reflects the change in the Advaitic philosophy itself, especially its concept of liberation (*mokṣa*) which came gradually to be conceived in terms of Sāṁkhya *kaivalya* or realization by the soul of its transcendent aloneness.

The entire approach engenders extreme individualism. Excepting the theistic Vedānta, all Indian philosophies believe the individual to be the supreme arbiter of his destiny. If a man is wholly responsible for, and necessarily reaps the fruits of, his actions, then he alone can realize his spiritual upliftment and final liberation through sustained personal effort. Even a theistic work like the *Bhagavadgitā* subscribes to the above view:

"Let a man raise himself by himself, let him not lower himself. He alone is the friend of himself, and he alone is the enemy of himself.

"To him who has conquered himself by himself, his own self is the friend of himself; but to him who has not conquered himself, his own self is like his enemy."[105]

Self-reliance in one's spiritual quest expresses an individualistic approach to morality; it also expresses faith in the possibility of one's achieving a total mastery over one's passions and inclinations, or freedom of will. The *Yoga Vāsiṣṭha* argues for freedom of will in a very forceful manner. According to it, man has in him both morally good and evil inclinations, and it is in his power to overcome the evil tendencies by a deliberate exercise of morally good feelings and inclinations (*vāsanās*). It assures us that if one tries, one can achieve anything, especially in the field of self-mastery:

"It is our good exertions that are attended by good results, as the bad ones are followed by bad consequences. Chance is a mere meaningless word."[106]

And,

"This is the long and short of scriptures that diligence preserves our minds from all evils by employing them to whatever is good and right."[107]

At the same time, even though we have distinguished between earlier and later versions of the Advaitic concept of liberation and human perfection, the difference between the two is not one of kind, but one of degree only. The main difference between the two sets of views lies in their emphasis and not in their content.

VIII. Some Positive Suggestions for Morality in Vedānta

There were some thinkers within the tradition of liberation who did not fully subscribe to the above view. In his *Pañcadaśī*, Vidyāraṇya ridicules those who say that a knower of *Brahman* is incapable of performing actions, saying that they seem to equate the knowledge of *Brahman* with the disease of consumption.[108] Unitive vision, being a spiritual experience, exalts and spiritualizes one's entire personality and cannot result in a negative outcome, i.e. the destruction of all one's capacities. When questioned about the ideal of *Jaḍa* Bharata who, having realized *Brahman*, behaved like an imbecile, Vidyāraṇya comments:

"*Jaḍa* Bharata and others never gave up food and sleep, nor were like sticks or stones. It was because they were afraid of forming attachment that they behaved as if they were completely disinterested."[109]

Here lies the crux of the whole issue. Advaitins practised absolute detachment and inaction for fear of involvement in the world, and not because of any metaphysical necessity. But so long as they were afraid of getting involved, they could not have been enlightened, as enlightenment or Self-realization means total fearlessness (*abhaya*). Vidyāraṇya, therefore, concludes that a man of realization can perform his duties well, as there is nothing in the knowledge of the Self which clashes with the performance of one's duties. He assures us that a life of action can in no way affect adversely either the knowledge or the mental peace of a liberated man.[110] He adds that having no desires or needs for himself, the enlightened man acts for the welfare of others. Vidyāraṇya recognizes an obligation on the part of the knower towards the ignorant:

"It is proper that the wise man, when with the ignorant, should act in accordance with their actions, as a loving father acts according to the wishes of his children....

"With the ignorant the wise man should behave in such a way as will enable them to have realization. In this world he has no other duty, except awakening the ignorant."[111]

The classical texts of Vedānta are of the same opinion, the *Vedāntasāra* makes it clear that a life of action is quite possible for a man of liberation, as the supreme knowledge results in the sublimation or exaltation of one's empirical personality, and not in its destruction.[112] If the knower of *Brahman* does not act, it is because he does not have any motive for performing actions. The only possible motive for action, worthy of a knower of Self, is fellow-feeling or compassion (*karuṇā*). The worth of compassion as a motive for action is recognized by the Advaitins like Śaṁkara:

"There are good souls, calm and magnanimous, who do good to others, as does the spring, and who, having themselves crossed this dreadful ocean of birth and death, help others also to cross the same without any motive whatsoever.

"It is the very nature of the magnanimous to move of their own accord towards removing others' troubles."[113]

There is another significant positive suggestion for morality in Vedānta. As we know, the *Chāndogya Upaniṣad* sharply distinguishes the stage of the man who is established in *Brahman* from the first three stages. Similarly, Śaṁkara has emphatically affirmed that not only is *Brahman* beyond all class (*varṇa*) distinctions, the man who is identified with Him also transcends the distinctions and limitations of class (caste).[114] This implies that the class distinctions pertain only to the field of ignorance, and are transcended once the knowledge of the ultimate Reality is achieved. That is why, a renunciant or man of knowledge is usually called *varṇātita* (beyond all *varṇas*) in Vedāntic works. The renunciant is also advised not to bother about the caste of the family from which he begs his food. The idea is quite cogent for challenging the justifiability of the practice of caste distinctions which merely pertain to the world of ignorance.

The Vedāntic thinkers did not care to emphasize the value of compassion; nor did they ever try to develop the practical or moral implications of the Vedāntic vision of one Self in all. It is the task of a future Hindu thinker to develop or interpret the Vedāntic ontology in such a way that it would provide a convincing justification for a morality of universal compassion. It is not to deny that the Vedāntic ontology of the transcendent Self contains suggestions that could well be interpreted in a self-centric manner. But it also contains ideas which can be understood better in a cosmic or universal context. The tradition of liberation is not so relevant in the present-day Hindu society, but Vedānta is very much so. And an understanding of Vedānta, whether in self-centric terms or in more positive ones, has always been a potent factor in determining the moral philosophy of Hinduism.

NOTES

1. *Muṇḍaka Up.* I. 2.7, also 8-9.
2. Ibid I. 2.10-12; *Bṛhad. Up.* II. 4.2.
3. *Bṛhad. Up.* III. 1. 1-2; IV. 1.1.
4. *Iśāvāsya* 1, 2, 11; *Br.S.* III. 4. 26-27; *B.G.* IV. 41-42; V. 3-4 etc.

5. *B.G.* IV. 41-42; V. 7-13; XVIII. 45-48.
6. *Ś.B.*, *B.G.*, introd. to ch. III., IV. 4, 16; introd. to ch. V.
7. Ibid, introd. to ch. III.
8. *M.S.* VI. 35-36; *Mbh. Śān. P.* XXV. 6; CCLXI. 15-16.
9. *Chān. Up.* III. 14.1; VI. 8.4; *Taittirīya Up.* III. 1.1; *Bṛhad. Up.* II. 1.20; III. 7.3 ff.
10. *Chān. Up.* VI. 8.I; *Bṛhad. Up.* IV. 4.3; IV. 4.25.
11. See writer's *The Roots of World Religions* (1982), pp. 131 ff., 162 ff.
12. *Bṛhad. Up.* II. 3.6; III. 9.26; IV. 2.4.
13. Ibid IV. 4. 5-6; IV. 4.22.
14. Ibid II. 4. 12-14.
15. *Muṇḍaka Up.* III. 1. 1-3.
16. Ibid III. 2. 8-9; cf. *Kaṭhā Up.* II. 1.15; *Bṛhad. Up.* II. 4.14.
17. *Muṇḍaka Up.* II. 2.8; *Bṛhad. Up.* I. 4.10.
18. *Tantra-vārttika* I. 3.4, quoted in S. Radhakrishnan, *Indian Philosophy* (1956), vol. II. p. 21.
19. R. Garbe, essay on Sāṁkhya in the *Encyclopaedia of Religion and Ethics*, ed. by J. Hastings (1954), vol. XI, p. 189.
20. *Foundations of Indian Culture,* vol. II, *Spiritual Vision and Symbolic Forms in Ancient India* (1984), p. 90.
21. *Sāṁkhya Kārikā* 19-20.
22. Ibid 18.
23. *B.G.* II. 12 ff., 20 ff.
24. Ibid II. 18 ff., III. 27-28.
25. *Sāṁkhya Kārikā* 61-62; *Yoga Sūtra* IV. 33.
26. *Ś.B.*, *Bṛhad. Up.* II. 1.20.
27. *S.B.*, *Br.S.* I. 1.4.
28. *Ś.B.*, *Bṛhad. Up.* II. 4.12.
29. *Ś.B.*, *Br.S.* I. 1.4; *Ś.B.*, *Bṛhad. Up.*, introd. to III. 3.1.
30. *Ś.B.*, *Br.S.* I. 1.4.
31. Ibid I. 1.1.
32. Ibid I. 1.4; I. 2.2, 12; I. 4.6; *Ś.B.*, *Aitareya Up.* I. 1.1.
33. *Ś.B.*, *Br.S.* II. 2.31; II. 3.7; *Ś.B.*, *Kena Up.* I. 1-2.
34. *Ś.B.*, *Bṛhad. Up.* I. 4.7.
35. *Mysticism Sacred and Profane* (1973), pp. 150, 158, 164, 180 ff.
36. *The Mind and Spirit of India* (1967), pp. 223, 225.
37. Ninian Smart, *Doctrine and Argument in Indian Philosophy* (1964), pp. 130 ff.
38. *Bṛhad. Up.* II. 4.5.
39. *Upadeśa-sāhasrī* II. 17.80.
40. *Maitreya Up.* ch. III, (*Thirty Minor Upaniṣads.* 1979, p. 28).
41. *Ātmabodha Up.*, (op. cit, pp. 38-40); *Aṣṭāvakra Saṁhitā* II. 6.14.
42. *Aṣṭāvakra Saṁhitā* XV. 16; cf. ibid I. 16.
43. *Bṛhad. Up.* II. 4.5.
44. *Pañcadaśī* XII. 7-9 and following.
45. Ibid XII. 31.
46. Ibid XII. 60.
47. *Mbh. Udyoga Parva* CXXVI. 48.

48. *M.S.* IV. 240.
49. *Mbh. Śān. P.* CCLXXVII. 15 ff.
50. *M.S.* IV. 238-243; *The Bījak of Kabīr* (1986), pp. 71, 88 etc.
51. *Ś.B., Br.S.* II. 1.9, 14, 27.
52. Ibid. I. 4.9;II. 1.3. For an excellent interpretation of Śaṁkara's Advaita in this context, see R.P. Singh, *The Vedānta of Śaṁkara—A Metaphysics of Value* (1949), pp. 292 ff., 371 ff. etc.
53. *Laghu Yoga Vāsiṣṭha* (1980), pp. 59 ff., 241 ff.; *Yoga Vāsiṣṭha, Utpatti Khaṇḍa*, ch.s III-IV, (1978, vol. I, pp. 232 ff.); ch. XIII, (pp. 281 ff.).
54. *Laghu Yoga Vāsiṣṭha*, pp. 18-19; cf. *Yoga Vāsiṣṭha, Vairāgya Khaṇḍa*, chs. XII to XXII, (vol. I, pp. 45 ff.).
55. *Laghu Yoga Vāsiṣṭha*, p. 21; *Yoga Vāsiṣṭha, Vairāgya Khaṇḍa*, ch. XXI, (pp. 77-79).
56. "When the Self is known, things other than it are realized as evils, being full of defects, such as transitoriness, painfulenss and impurity, while the Self is contrary to them." *Ś.B., Bṛhad. Up.* I. 4.7; cf., *Ś.B., Br.S.* 1.3.19; II. 1.22; III. 4.16.
57. See N.K. Devaraja, op, cit., pp. 140 ff.
58. Albert Schweitzer, *Indian Thought and Its Development* (1980), p. 60.
59. *Eastern Religions and Western Thought* (1958), pp. 67 ff.
60. *S.B., Br.S.*, I.1.4; *Ś.B., Bṛhad. Up.*, introd. to III. 3.1.
61. *Ś.B., Bṛhad. Up.*, I. 3.1; introd. to III. 3.1; *Naiṣkarmya-siddhi* I. 24, 34-35, 54-55.
62. *Ś.B., Br.S.* I. 1.4; *Ś.B., Bṛhad. Up.* II. 4.14; *Ś.B., Chān. Up.* II. 23.1; *Ś.B., B.G.* II. 69.
63. *Ś.B., B.G.* XVIII, 55; cf "Why should, therefore, one perform actions when the result is known to be disembodiedness which cannot be produced by actions?" *Upadeśa-sāhasrī* II. 15.17.
64. *Upadeśa-sāhasrī* II. 18.231.
65. *Kaivalya Up.* 2., *Mahānārāyaṇa Up.* XII. 14.
66. *Jābāla Up.* 4; cf. "Finding the world worthless, the seekers after the truth renounce the world, even before marriage, feeling the supermost sense of detachment within themselves." *Bṛhaspati Smṛti*, both quoted in *Ś.B., B.G.*, introd. to ch. III.
67. *Sāṁkhya Kārikā* 68; *Viveka-cūḍāmaṇi* 550-551 *Pañcadaśī* II. 99, 102; VI. 287-288; VII. 166, 263.
68. *Bṛhad. Up.* IV. 4.22.
69. *Ś.B., Br.S.* I.1.4; II. 1.14, 20; *Ś.B., Bṛhad. Up.* II. 4.14.
70. *Ś.B., Br.S.*, introd.; I. 1.4; *Ś.B., Bṛhad. Up.* II. 1.20; II. 4.13; III. 9.28; *Ś.B., B.G.* XVIII. 66.
71. *Ś.B., Br.S.* II. 1.22.
72. *Ś.B., Aitareya Up.* I. 1.1.
73. *Kaṭha Up.* I. 2.24.
74. Ibid II. 3.14; cf. *Bṛhad. Up.* IV. 4.7; *Viveka-cūḍāmaṇi* 317.
75. *Muṇḍaka Up.* III. 1.5.
76. *M.S.* VI. 60.
77. *Yoga Sūtra* II. 3-9.

78. Ibid II. 30-45.
79. *Yoga Sūtra* I. 33.
80. *Yoga Vāsiṣṭha, Mumukṣu Khaṇḍa*, ch. IX, (1976, vol. I, pp. 159-160).
81. *Yoga Sūtra*, I. 1-3; I. 50-51; *Laghu Yoga Vāsiṣṭha* (1980), pp. 59-60, 193, 198. 309 ff.
82. *Yoga Sūtra* I. 12-16.
83. *B.G.* VI. 10 ff.; Madhusūdana, *Bhagavadgītā Bhāṣya* VI. 15, 32.
84. *Ś.B.*, *Br.S.* I. 1.1; *Viveka-cūḍāmaṇi* 17-27.
85. *Ś.B.*, *B.G.*, introd. to III.4; *Naiṣkarmya-siddhi* I. 47-51.
86. *Viveka-cūḍāmaṇi* 353-356.
87. *Yoga Vāsiṣṭha, Utpatti Khaṇḍa*, ch. CXI-CXII, (1978, vol. II, pp. 335 ff.; 341 ff.).
88. *Bṛhad. Up.* IV. 4. 22-23.
89. Albert Schweitzer, op, cit., p. 44-45, 62.
90. *Bṛhad. Up.* IV. 4.23.
91. *Ś.B.*, *Aitareya Up.* I. 1.1.; *Ś.B.*, *Chān Up.* II. 23.1.
92. *Naiṣkaramya-siddhi* IV. 62.
93. *Viveka-cūḍāmaṇi* 267.
94. Ibid 322, 324.
95. Op. cit. (1967) pp. 225-226.
96. Ibid, p. 226.
97. *Viveka-cūḍāmaṇi* 541-546, 551-552.
98. *Maitreya Up.*, ch. II, (*Thirty Minor Upaniṣads*, p. 29).
99. *Nārada-Parivrājaka Up.*, ch. III, (op. cit., pp. 140-142).
100. Ibid ch. III, (op. cit., p. 139); *Aṣṭāvakra Saṁhitā* XVIII. 87.
101. *Yoga Vāsiṣṭha, Utapatti Khaṇḍa*, ch. CXVIII, (1978, vol. II, pp. 373 ff.).
102. *Aṣṭāvakra Saṁhitā* XVII. 9.
103. Ibid XVII. 16.
104. Ibid XVII. 19.
105. *B.G.* VI. 5-6.
106. *Yoga Vāsiṣṭha, Mumukṣu Khaṇḍa*, ch. V, (vol. I, pp. 143 ff.).
107. Ibid, *Mumukṣu Khaṇḍa*, ch. VII, (vol. I, p. 151).
108. *Pañcadaśī* VI. 271.
109. Ibid VI. 273.
110. Ibid VII. 281-283.
111. Ibid VII. 287, 290.
112. *Vedānta-sāra* 218-226 (1978, pp. 118 ff.).
113. *Viveka-cūḍāmaṇi* 37-38.
114. *Chān Up.* II. 23.1; *Ś.B.*, *Br.S.* introd.; I. 1.4.

Chapter V

THEO-CENTRIC MORALITY OF DEVOTIONAL SECTS

I. Development of Bhakti Tradition

We have used the word *bhakti* (devotion) to characterize the Theo-centric tradition, instead of the usual term theistic, as the latter term is usually understood in a rather narrow context. In fact, the entire Vedānta is Theo-centric; but we mean here specifically those schools of Vedānta which regard devotion to one Lord, and not knowledge, as the supreme means of liberation.

We have earlier discussed two main traditions of Vedic-Hindu 'religio-culture', viz. the ritualistic, polytheistic and world-and-life-affirming tradition of Vedas and Dharmaśāstras and the rather self-centric and world-and-life-negating tradition of the philosophies of liberation. A third tradition, the theistic-devotional one has flourished in Hinduism, alongside the above two traditions, since about two centuries before Christ. Like the philosophies of liberation, the devotional approach is critical of the violence and externality of the Vedic ritualism and puts greater emphasis on inner attitude than on external conformation. But unlike the former (the tradition of liberation), it is much more positive and world-and-life-affirming. And it recommends the practice of socio-moral virtues of a very high order. It is also markedly different from the popular polytheism on two counts. First, it advocates one-pointed devotion to one supreme God and does not concern itself with innumerable gods of the polytheistic tradition. Secondly, it asserts that this devotion to one God should be without any ulterior motive, as opposed to the polytheistic tradition wherein different gods are always worshipped with specific personal desires. Even more significant contribution of the theistic-devotional (*Bhakti*) tradition lies in its reaffirmation of the vision of one Self (*Ātman*) or the Divine Lord (*Īśvara*) indwelling all living beings. Its advocacy of a positive morality and rejection of the relevance of caste distinctions are both derived from the above vision.

The most important texts of Hindu theism are *Śvetāśvatara Upaniṣad*, *Bhagavadgītā*, *Bhāgavata* and *Viṣṇu* Purāṇas and *Bhakti Sūtras* of Nārada and Śāṇḍilya. In addition, there is a very vast literature, known as Āgamas, written both in Sanskrit and Tamil, as also the Tamil collections of the songs of Vaiṣṇava *bhakta* saints (*Āḷvārs*) and Śaiva *bhakta* saints (*Nāyanārs*). Significantly, the two main theistic sects of Śaivism and Vaiṣṇavism had their beginnings in South India. There was a prolonged controversy whether the *Āgamas*, the main texts of the *Bhakti* tradition, were to be regarded as orthodox or heterodox. The controversy itself is suggestive of the possible non-Aryan (Dravida?) influence on the development of the theistic sects. One of the Śaiva sects, Vīra-Śaivism was openly anti-establishment and anti-brāhmaṇa and put forward quite unorthodox ideas and practices. But on the whole, the entire theistic-devotional tradition is basically Vedāntic in its philosophic approach.

At a very early stage the theistic-devotional movement got divided into two main traditions of Vaiṣṇavism and Śaivism. Both these traditions or sects developed side by side, sometimes confronting each other, but mostly coexisting peacefully. Within each tradition there were further divisions as a result of the twin processes of the synthesis of several concepts into new ones and diversification due to sectarian differences. Since these sects developed and thrived during a very long period of Indian history (from about 2nd century B.C. to 17th century A.D.), it is but natural that there would be differences in the philosophy and moral approach of different sects, as also in the same sect during different periods of its history.

The various sects seem to have had two parallel sources, which may explain their diversity and certain inconsistencies in them. For example, Vaiṣṇavism is based on the Vedāntic texts listed above, as well as on the Pañcarātra Saṁhitās (which are regarded as un-Vedic by the Vedic scholars)[1] and the works of Tamil saints (*Āḷvārs*), called Prabandhas (first to seventh century A.D.). By about the 10th century, various concepts were synthesized and a definite philosophic position was developed in a strict Vedāntic terminology. The age of the Tamil *bhakta* saints was followed by the age of Vaiṣṇava *ācāryas* or teachers, like Rāmānuja, Vallabha and others (between twelfth to sixteenth century). Interestingly, all of them, except Caitanya, hailed from the South. The *Bhakti* movement spread from the South to the central and western India. Then it gave rise to several poet-saints of very high spiritual calibre, as Jñāneśvara, Nāmadeva, Tukārāma and Ekanātha. The Vaiṣṇava theistic-devotional movement reached its peak in the North only in the fifteenth and sixteenth centuries, when it produced such saints as Kabīr, Nānak and Tulasīdāsa. The experiences and teachings of these Vaiṣṇava *bhakta* saints, from the *Āḷvārs* of Tamil region in the early centuries of the Christian era to the poet-saints of Maharashtra and North India, express whatever is best and most profound in Hindu religion. Since the period during which they lived and wrote covers the acme of Aryan culture, as well as its decline, we can assume that they did not have much influence on the politico-social conditions of the sub-continent. But they always interested themselves in the masses, for whom they provided the much needed spiritual guidance and succour.

Śaivism has had a similarly chequered history. It also flourished in the South among the Tamil-speaking people first. It owes its origins to *Śvetāśvatara Upaniṣad*, some Purāṇas and Śaiva Āgamas (which are considered non-Vedic or un-orthodox by the Vedic scholars), several works known as Śaiva Siddhānta, as also the works of Tamil Śaiva saints (*nāyanārs*), whose songs are highly respected in the South. At first, some of the Śaiva sects like Vīra-Śaivism maintained their separate identity and even expressed their antagonism to the Vedic 'religio-culture'. The two devotional traditions, Vaiṣṇavism and Śaivism were also antagonistic to each other for quite some time for sectarian reasons. But their constant interaction and the underlying affinity of their religious experience gradually brought them closer. Also, whatever their origins, almost all the theistic-devotional sects in their present form are a unique product of the Vedāntic philosophy and the devotional approach in religion.

II. Vedāntic Theism: The Concepts of God, Liberation and Devotion

In spite of all the divergence of sources and sectarian differences, the various devotional sects, excepting that of Madhva, affirm a markedly Vedāntic or monistic concept of the 'Divine' and His relation to the soul and the world.

(i) The concept of God in the *Bhakti* tradition is developed in the Vedāntic framework. According to the *Śvetāśvatara Upaniṣad*, the Divine Absolute is the Creator of the world, and 'is' also in some sense the creation.[2] For the theistic-Vedānta, there is no contradiction involved in affirming the Absolute to be both the Creator and the creation. The *Bhagavadgītā* affirms the transcendence of the Creator to the creation.[3] At the same time, the Divine Being is the all-in-all, the source, ground and Self or Inner-controller of the entire creation and all individual selves.[4] The *Viṣṇu Purāṇa* affirms that the entire world is both pervaded by and exists in the Lord, who is also the Witness-consciousness or the Self of all.[5] Even the comparatively independent Śaiva texts describe the 'Divine' as the *Sthala* which means the source, stay, support and end of the entire creation. Rāmānuja insists that in the final analysis the Absolute 'is' all this, the ultimate referent of, or the reality behind, all names and forms.[6]

At the same time, the various teachers (*ācāryas*) of theistic Vedānta were opposed to the extreme monism (*Advaita*) and illusionism (*māyāvāda*) of Śaṁkara. They sought to develop a Vedāntic world-view and concept of God which would be much more satisfying from the religious point of view than that of Śaṁkara. According to this later theistic-devotional philosophy, the relation between the Creator and the creatures (individual souls) is such that the latter are absolutely dependent on Him, but still enjoy their separate individual existence. The world is seen as a meaningful creation of the Lord. The world and the souls have the Divine Being as their Self or Inner-controller and are instrumental to His will.[7]

The Absolute of theistic-devotional sects is also a personal God. All the philosophers of theistic Vedānta take up issue with Śaṁkara on his concept of an indeterminate Absolute and proclaim their God to be a perfect Person with innumerable auspicious qualities.[8] He is everything, the all-comprehending Absolute, the transcendent Creator and Destroyer and the beloved Master and Friend, who is kind towards all His creatures, but more so towards His devotees.

(ii) This new perception of the relation between the individual soul and the ultimate Self has resulted in the emergence of a new concept of liberation. *Mokṣa* is neither the realization by the soul of its total aloofness and transcendence (*kaivalya*), nor its complete merger into *Brahman*; rather, it is the realization by the soul of its essential 'creatureliness' or dependence on the Lord. This concept of absolute dependence or 'creatureliness' of the soul (*kārpaṇya*) emphasizes the volitional nature of the soul. Liberation is therefore conceived not as a mere cognitive experience (*jñāna*), as in the philosophies of liberation, but as freedom from all passions and sin, as also knowing, loving and serving (or attaining) God.

(iii) It is unanimously agreed in this tradition that the supreme goal of liberation is achieved neither through knowledge (*jñāna*), nor through rituals (*karma*), but only through true devotion (*bhakti*). Devotion is defined by Nārada as 'of the nature of supreme love of God'. Nārada explains that this love is not of the nature of lust, because it is of the form of renunciation and complete unification with the object of love and concomitant indifference towards everything opposed to it. It is the total response of the creature to the Creator, comprising all one's cognitive and conative tendencies. Devotion is thus one-pointed and whole hearted love of God.[9] The *Bhāgavata Purāṇa* contends that this devotion must be desireless, one-pointed and spontaneous like an instinct and devoid of any extraneous motives. Ideal devotion is the total response of the creature to the Creator. It includes the knowledge of the true nature of the soul as essentially dependent upon the Lord (*jñāna*), dispassion or detachment towards the world (*vairāgya*), as also complete self-surrender to and unmotivated love of the Lord (*bhakti*).[10] According to Rāmānuja:

"The means for attaining *Brahman* is *parā-bhakti*. This *parā-bhakti* is of the nature of devotion which, in its turn, is aided by one's performance of one's duties, after a due understanding of the nature of supreme Reality through the scriptures."[11]

A very important feature of the ideal devotion is the absence of any ulterior motive. All religious texts distinguish several kinds of devotees and put those who approach God with specific requests as much lower than those who love God for His own sake.[12] For Nārada, love of God is its own reward, that is, it is an end-in-itself.[13] It is in sharp contrast with the ritualistic-polytheistic tradition's emphasis on personal desire as the natural motive for the performance of all rituals. This devotion is both a means and an integral part of liberation (*mokṣa*). The latter is conceived in theistic Vedānta as a state of perfection in which the soul enjoys the bliss of serving the Lord.

As against the ritualistic tradition's insistence on the self-efficacy of Vedic rituals, or of all actions in general, and the self-reliance implied in the way of knowledge, the theistic tradition insists on man's incapacity to emancipate himself on his own and the need of God's grace. To quote Nārada again:

"And also because God dislikes the reliance on one's own unaided self-effort and likes the complete feeling of misery due to the consciousness of one's helplessness in independently working out one's salvation, *bhakti* is greater."[14]

The concept of man's 'creatureliness' (*kārpaṇya*) in the *Bhakti* tradition is comparable to the creature-consciousness, considered to be the essence of all religious experience by Rudolf Otto.[15] But since the entire idea is developed in a Vedāntic context, there is much less emphasis here on man's sinfulness and God's *Tremendum* than in the Semitic religions, though both are recognized. Instead, the ideal religious attitude is conceived as that of total self-surrender (*prapātti*) which is understood as a profound religious feeling of one's helplessness and total dependence (*kārpaṇya*) on the Lord. It also includes complete trust in Him and the desire to do the will of God.[16] The idea here is that a man cannot emancipate himself without the grace of God and that grace is available to all, but first of all to those who surrender themselves fully to God.

The *Bhagavadgītā* gives a very exalted and yet simple and nonsectarian version of true devotion. Lord Kṛṣṇa advises Arjuna:

"Fix thy mind on Me, be devoted to Me, sacrifice to Me, bow down to Me. Thus steadied, with Me as thy supreme goal, thou shalt reach Myself, the Self."[17]

III. The Vision of God's Indwelling All and a Positive Morality Based on It

(i) The vision of 'Divine' (*Ātman-Brahman*) indwelling all living beings is the most basic vision of Hinduism. The Upaniṣads affirm it, so does the *Bhagavadgītā*. The beauty of the latter's views lies in its theistic understanding of the Vedāntic vision. See,

"The Self abiding in all beings, and all beings abiding in the Self sees he whose self has been made steadfast by yoga, (and) who everywhere sees the same.

"He who sees Me everywhere and sees everything in Me, he does not abandon Me, nor do I abandon him...

"Whoso intent on unity worships Me who abide in all beings, that yogin dwells in Me".[18]

While no other religio-philosophical tradition has cared to develop the practical implications of this vision, two very positive and morally relevant conclusions are derived from it in the theistic-devotional tradition: First, in view of the essential divinity of all beings, distinctions of caste or social class are irrelevant, especially before God. Second, the worship of God has no spirituo-moral worth, unless it is accompanied by a practical realization of Him in all creatures.

From the moral point of view, the most important aspect of the tradition of devotion (*bhakti*) is its universality. As against the Vedic religion which was traditionally meant for the males of three 'upper' classes only, in the *Bhakti* tradition the right to worship and love one supreme God and receive His universal grace is open to all human beings, including those who belong to the lowermost rung of social hierarchy (*cāṇḍālas*) and non-Aryans (*asuras*).[19] It is repeatedly asserted that all, irrespective of their caste or sex, are freed from mundane existence by hearing and reciting God's names and qualities. No external qualification is required for practising devotion to God which is essentially a matter of inner feelings or attitude. According to Nārada,

"In them (the devotees) there is no distinction based on caste or culture, beauty or birth, wealth or profession and the like."[20]

Śāṇḍilya agrees with the above:

"All persons, even down to the lowest born, have equal right to follow the path of devotion. They are filled with the presence of God."[21]

It is unanimously affirmed that in view of the essential divinity of all, distinctions of caste and class are irrelevant, especially in the context of devotion to the Lord. The *Bhāgavata Purāṇa* affirms:

"I rather consider a *śvapaca* (one who eats dog's meat, i.e. a man of very low caste), who has dedicated his mind, his riches, his life and all unto the Lord, as worthier in point of virtue than a brāhmaṇa who does not worship God."[22]

This was not mere rhetoric, but an ideal that was sought to be practised in everyday life. It is the miracle of the *Bhakti* tradition that in a caste-ridden society it could confer sainthood on persons who belonged to the so-called lower castes, or were even non-Hindus. Among the *Āḷvār* saints of the South quite a few hailed from 'lower' castes, while one was a reformed robber. Of the Maharashtra saints, Nāmadeva and Tukārāma, the paradigms of mystico-unitive experience, were a tailor and a farmer respectively. In the north, Kabīr was a Muslim, so were many others like Dādu, Rasakhān and Rahīm, who were accepted and venerated by the Hindu masses. Raidāsa, a cobbler, declares, "Caste is no consideration; that man is God's own who worships Him." Kabīr says that it is needless to ask a saint his caste, for Hindus of all castes and Muslims have alike achieved that End which is beyond all distinctions.[23] It was this perception of the worth of every human being who is devoted to God and is of righteous conduct which led to the undermining of caste distinctions among the followers of the *Bhakti* tradition. Inasmuch as they constituted a very large portion of the society, the deprecation of caste distinctions by them must have favourably influenced the society's attitude towards the so-called lower castes.

Not only does the theistic-devotional tradition value individuals who are devoted to God, but it also regards every human being, nay, every living being as sacred; a living manifestation of the 'Divine'. The Lord says in the *Bhāgavata Purāṇa*:

"Knowing Me to be residing in the hearts of all living beings, it naturally behoves every person to serve others with gifts, honour and equal regard, as they would unto Me."

And,

"*Īśvara* (God) is present in all beings. Thinking in this way, one should bow down before all creatures."[24]

Prahlāda advises his *asura* (non-Aryan) friends:

"Direct your whole-hearted devotion to the lord Śrī Hari, who is the soul of all created beings, by considering everybody else as your own Self."[25]

In the entire theistic-devotional tradition devotion to God is conceived in such a way that it necessarily includes love and compassion for one's suffering fellow-beings. The theistic texts repeatedly exhort men to recognize the Lord indwelling all hearts and model one's behaviour according to this vision. This vision negates all practical distinctions between the high and the low, the good and the bad, as all are equally divine and should be respected as such.[26] According to Guru Nānak, all human beings are born out of one *Nūr* (Glory) and are servants of one God (*Khudā*), even though they may be professing different faiths; and therefore it is useless to categorize them as either good or bad.

The *Bhāgavata Purāṇa* distinguishes three types of devotees. The highest are those who perceive all creatures as permeated by the Divine Self. Then come those devotees who distinguish between God, His devotees, common men and men of evil character, and entertain towards them different attitudes of love, piety, indifference etc. And the lowest are those who worship God in images, but are not considerate towards others.[27] The Lord further says in the same text:

"I am always residing in the heart of every creature as his soul. By disregarding My existence, a person would merely waste his time worshipping My idols etc."[28]

The *Bhakti* tradition believes in individual souls as existentially different both from other souls and God; and yet the perception of the basic divinity and unity of all living beings is perhaps more genuine and intense in this tradition than even in the Advaita Vedānta. Nowhere in Hinduism is this vision of one Self in all presented so forcefully and its practical implications accepted so honestly as in the *Bhakti* tradition. Perhaps it is so because this vision is affirmed in it, not at the theoretical level, but at the experiential level. God's indwelling all and the perception of all as divine are an integral part of the God experience that is sought to be achieved through devotion. The *Viṣṇu Purāṇa* presents the concept of God (*Vāsudeva*) as the all-in-all, and goes on to derive a very high moral code from this vision. According to it, since the Divine Being resides in the hearts of all beings, He is the Object of all sacrifices, worship and even violence, so that if one hurts others, in fact one hurts God Himself.[29]

(ii) Both the philosophy of theistic Vedānta and its conception of devotion are such that the practice of morality becomes an integral part of a man's religion. The *bhakta* saints boldly assert that it becomes meaningless to affirm the vision of one Self in all at the theoretical level only and not to practise it at the socio-moral level. Devotion to the Lord is understood as directed to the 'One' who resides in the hearts of all creatures. The entire universe and all living beings are sanctified by the Divine presence. As a result, the love of man is seen for the first time in Hindu thought as integrally related to the love of God. The emphasis everywhere is not on mere theoretical assertion, but on actually living, feeling and acting according to the vision of one Self in all. The Lord says in the *Bhāgavata Purāṇa*:

"Understanding that I reside in all bodies, the person who always meditates upon Me is surely delivered from the evil habits of malice, haughtiness, entertaining disregard for others and foolishness."[30]

Moral virtue and conduct are essential to a man's quest for liberation, and thus become desirable. Moral discipline is unanimously accepted as a pre-requisite for devotion (*bhakti*). According to the *Bhāgavata Purāṇa*,

"When the mind is free from the impurities caused by the consciousness of individuality and passions, such as lust and covetousness, ... then the individual (*jīva*), with the aid of the knowledge of the self, dispassion and devotion, beholds the supreme Soul."[31]

The theistic-devotional texts assert that devotion necessarily means redemption or freedom from sin or sinful tendencies. It is repeatedly affirmed that devotion destroys all sins; or that the Lord enters the heart of a devotee and cleanses it of all sinful tendencies. Thus, freedom from sin or victory over one's flesh is at once a pre-requisite for and a result of true devotion.[32] Other religious texts of this tradition similarly derive a simple positive morality from man's love of God:

"That man is a true devotee of God, who never hurts any living being (*jīva*), who serves the teachers, brāhmaṇas and other elders, ... who is concerned about the welfare of all living beings as his own children, and whose mind is free of all baser passions."[33]

Virtues like universal kindness, friendliness and love are constantly exhorted in the *Bhakti* tradition, while they have found relatively much less mention in the previous two traditions. At the same time, the virtues of self-culture like self-control, forbearance and equanimity, so highly valued in the tradition of liberation, are given a new dimension in the theistic-devotional tradition by integrating them with inter-personal morality and religion. Lord Kṛṣṇa describes a true devotee as:

"Those ... who having restrained all the senses, are always equanimous and intent on the welfare of all beings, they reach Myself."[34]

And,

"...He, who hates no single being, who is friendly and compassionate to all, who is free from attachment and egoism, to whom pain and pleasure are equal, who is enduring, ever content and balanced in mind, self-controlled and possessed of firm conviction..., is dear to Me."[35]

All the *bhakta* saints of medieval India affirm an intimate connection between the love of God and the love of men, a concept immortalized in the sayings of Christ. Narasī Mehatā (13th century) defines a true devotee (Vaiṣṇava) as one who knows and feels for the sufferings of others, who is ever willing to do good to others and who is free from such evil passions as egoism, anger, greed and hypocrisy. This devotional song was a favourite of Mahatma Gandhi and expresses truly the spirit of *Bhakti* tradition.

An important reason for this recognition of the worth of morality is the perception of devotion as a process of asymptotic approximation to God. Most of the philosophies of liberation hypothesize that the stage of knowledge and freedom (*jivan-mukti*) implies a complete break from the stage of ignorance and bondage, so that there is no possibility of evil and no necessity for moral discipline, once the liberating experience is realized. Though there is nothing wrong in the above stand from the mystical point of view, the theistic stand, that there can be no point of time which can be said to demarcate a complete victory over the flesh and a total transcendence of the body and mind, seems to be much more sensible and meaningful from the moral point of view. As we have seen, devotion is conceived in this tradition both as a means and as an end, but mostly as an end. And inasmuch as a moral way of life is an integral part of the devotional attitude, it never becomes irrelevant. That is, one is expected to follow moral norms and practise rigorous ethical discipline throughout one's life. It is very significant that Nārada emphasizes ethical discipline in the very beginning of his short treatise on devotion:

"For otherwise there is the risk of fall."[36]

No one is, therefore, exempt from moral norms and obligations. True, a devotee of God or saint exists on a higher level of spirituo-moral experience, and is therefore revered in the Bhakti tradition as equal to God. But even such saints are described, not in the classical Vedāntic terminology of transcendence of all distinctions, but in that of compassion and love for all beings. According to the *Bhāgavata Purāṇa*, the devotees of Viṣṇu always live for the welfare of mankind and roam about the world at will to extend their mercy towards the unfortunate ones.[37] Of course, mercy towards mankind chiefly refers here to the saint's duty of enlightening the ignorant and suffering mankind, or sharing with others his own inner experiences and knowledge, an ideal shared by all Indian traditions. And yet, the devotee saints of the *Bhakti* tradition were compassionate and concerned about the masses in a way that was quite unprecedented in the history of Hindu India.

IV. *The Ambivalent Attitude of the Bhakti Tradition Towards World and Life*

Most of the works of the *Bhakti* tradition are not very philosophical in their approach and often express different and self-inconsistent points of view. Thus, most works simultaneously advocate the performance of one's duties in the world and hail the virtue of total dispassion (*vairāgya*), without noticing their essential incompatibility.

(i) Broadly speaking, the theistic-devotional sects have a positive or affirmative attitude towards the world and life. The *Bhagavadgītā* affirms the world to be a meaningful creation of the Lord, and adds that it is the Lord's will that the wheel of creation should be kept rotating by all men performing their respective duties.[38] What is more, the performance of duty, when undertaken in a spirit of devotion and self-surrender, is glorified as a form of worship:

"Whatever thou doest, whatever thou eatest, whatever thou sacrificest, whatever thou givest, in whatever austerity thou engagest, do it as an offering to Me.

"......Equipped in mind with the yoga of renunciation, and liberated, thou shalt come to Me."[39]

The *Bhagavadgītā's* theistic world-view and moral approach made two significant contributions to Hindu morality. First, the *Gītā's* advocacy of action-in-the-world helped in restoring the balance in Hindu religio-moral approach which is often tilted in favour of world-renunciation. Secondly, its advocacy of desireless action provided a much needed corrective to the excessive emphasis in the Vedic tradition on desire being the sole motive of undertaking all actions.

If duties can be performed in a way so that they are not the cause of man's involvement in the world, but rather become a direct means of God-realization, then there is no reason why one should give up life-in-the world. True devotion to God consists in the recognition of the divinity of all, and not in denying the reality of the world. It also consists in a genuine spirit of self-surrender to the Lord, and not in outer acts, or their renunciation. According to Nārada,

"On the attainment of *bhakti*, or even for the attainment of it, life in the society need not be shunned, but only the fruits of all social actions are to be surrendered to the Lord, while such activities may be continued."[40]

The *Bhāgavata Purāṇa* contends that a householder who performs his duties in the right frame of mind is delivered from transmigratory existence through the grace of God. It adds that a liberated man can and must continue performing his worldly duties:

"No creature can do anything independently of God......We execute the wishes of the Lord......A person who has conquered his senses and passions meets with no harm, even when leading a life of the householder."[41]

During the middle ages there were Vaiṣṇava sects, specially the *Puṣṭi Saṁpradāya* of Vallabha, which encouraged their disciples to live a life of comfort and luxuries. Such sects came very close to the original Vedic 'religio-culture'.

In practical life too there is a marked affirmation of the world and all its values in the theistic-devotional sects. The celebration of religious festivals has formed an integral part of worship since the early middle ages. They are invariably occasions for lavish spending, festivities and enjoyment of rich food. Even for daily worship in the temples, the images are bedecked with rich jewellery and offered very rich food which is later on often sold outside temples. Wasteful expenditure and even vulgar display of wealth are welcomed on the occasion of religious festivals. The temples and *maṭhas* (seats of religious authority) have long been centres of concentration of enormous wealth and corruption. Excepting a few norms regarding purity of body and food, no other restraints are observed by present-day devotees of the *Bhakti* tradition. They are all householders who live in the society and follow their religion alongwith the other pursuits of life.

(ii) On the other hand, since the very beginning of the *Bhakt* movement importance of dispassion or detachment (*vairāgya*) towards the world has been recognised. Dispassion was seen as a natural result of the total absorption of the devotee in his devotion for the Divine Lord. According to the *Bhāgavata Purāṇa*, devotion (*bhakti*) should always be combined with knowledge (*jñāna*) and dispassion (*vairāgya*); and God-realization results only when these three are combined.[42] To quote Nārada again:

"But that state of supreme love and immortality is made possible only by giving up the objective reality of the world, as it appears to the ego-centric intellect and senses, and the consequent renunciation of attachment."[43]

Thus, we find the advocates of the path of devotion (*bhakti-mārga*) speaking the same language as that of the followers of the path of knowledge and renunciation (*jñāna-mārga* or *nivṛtti-mārga*):

"A person endeavouring to conquer his heart should keep company with none and should forsake his abode. Thereafter, becoming a mendicant and living alone at a solitary place, he should maintain his life ... by begging."[44]

And,

"Though blessed with the best of understanding, he (the ascetic-devotee) should show and behave himself as an insane boy... and an idiot. He should act in compliance with the whims of the people around."[45]

The *Bhāgavata Purāṇa* gives a detailed account of the sage Bharata who, adopting the life-style of a python (*ajagara-vṛtti*), remained totally inactive and unconcerned about the circumstances of his life, not to say anything about others.[46] There are some passages in which not only attachment to one's kinsmen, but even looking after the welfare of one's dependents is decried as detrimental to the interests of true devotion.[47] Renunciation of home and all one's relations is often lauded as true devotion.

All mysticism is naturally transcendentalist in its approach. In all mystical or true religious experience, attachment to God necessarily means freedom from attachment to, or involvement in, the world. The intenser the God-experience, the greater are the chances of the devotee-saint's forgetfulness of the world around him. This forgetfulness of the world was deliberately encouraged in the *Bhakti* tradition. The classical texts of the *Bhakti* tradition generally understand devotion as consisting of the following nine marks or aspects (*navadhā Bhakti*): hearing narrations of the glorious deeds (*līlā*) and excellences of Viṣṇu (God), chanting His name and reciting hymns in praise of Him, remembering Him continuously, serving Him, worshipping Him, paying obeisance to Him, practising servitude to Him, being a friend to Him, and making total self-surrender to Him.[48] The emphasis in the above version of devotion is largely on the inner spirit of devotion which is to be strengthened by certain practices. At the same time, devotion (*bhakti*) was considered in this tradition to be an all-time, all-absorbing occupation, involving the application of the triad of man's body, mind and speech. The devotee was encouraged to devote all his mind and time to the remembrance of the Lord.

From the very beginning, devotion to God was conceived in terms of being overwhelmed by emotions, shedding tears, experiencing and expressing ecstasy. *Kīrtana* or singing praises of God, accompanied by music and dancing, was accepted as an important aspect of the ninefold devotion. Gradually, singing, dancing and (hysterical) weeping in the remembrance of the Divine Beloved became an integral part of true devotion, especially in the school of Caitanya.

Detachment towards the world is associated with this kind of mysticism. It is natural, though not necessary, for a mystic devotee to remain absorbed in the bliss of his inner experiences, so much so that, in the words of Nārada, even a casual forgetting of God results in the anguish of separation.[49] Such an absorption, in its turn, would result in a corresponding forgetfulness of the world.

(iii) A perusal of the devotional literature in various Indian languages would suggest the presence of some tension between the above two tendencies in the devotional tradition. In the North we have a clear-cut division between the *Saguṇa* and *Nirguṇa bhakti* cults which profess devotion to a qualified Absolute or personal God and a transcendent, indeterminate Absolute respectively. The devotees of the first cult uphold a rather down-to-earth philosophy and conceive devotion largely in terms of image worship and observance of other rituals, so that they come quite close to the spirit of the polytheistic-ritualistic tradition of the Vedas. The devotees of the second (*Nirguṇa*) cult are much more other-worldly and esoteric in their approach to both religion and morality, and hence are closer to the spirit of the tradition of liberation. Such a clear-cut division is not made in other regions of the country. But it seems that a determinate concept of God is closely related to a realistic world-view and a rather less emotional form of devotion. On the other hand, a concept of the 'Divine' as a transcendent and all-comprehending Reality is often associated with the practice of an intenser form of devotion which may lead to mystico-unitive experience. Such an experience, in its turn, makes one supremely detached to all worldly concerns and norms.[50]

We would take a slight diversion here in order to study two characteristic instances of the above two opposing tendencies in the Bhakti tradition.

Tulasīdāsa (16th century) is the greatest exponent of *Saguṇa bhakti* or devotion to a qualified Absolute in Northern India. The works of Tulasīdāsa seek to present an integral way of life in which true religion and moral conduct are inseparably bound together. Tulasīdāsa's Rāma is a personal God who is extremely kind and compassionate towards all His creatures, and even more so towards His devotees.[51] He affirms the transcendence of God to the creature and contends that the proper response of the creature to the Creator is one of devotion of the nature of servitude (*dāsya bhakti*) which is open to all.[52] The world is perceived as a meaningful creation of the Lord and the fulfilment of one's socio-moral duties is strongly recommended. Being an orthodox person, Tulasīdāsa supports the caste system and even advises the worship of brāhmaṇas.[53] But being a saint of the devotional tradition, Tulasīdāsa is equally sure that the purity of a man's heart and his sincere devotion, and not his caste, alone can endear a man to the Lord. Moral conduct and the practice of moral virtues, such as equanimity, kindness towards all and freedom from evil passions like anger, conceit etc., are seen as an integral part of true devotion. A saint is one who is at once a paradigm of true selfless devotion to the Lord and an epitome of all moral virtues.[54] Thus, Tulasīdāsa's religio-moral philosophy is extremely world-and-life-affirming, and comes very close to the Vedic-Dharma-śāstric tradition.

Kabīr (15th century) was probably a senior contemporary of Tulasīdāsa. But he expresses an entirely different world-view and ethos which seems to be derived from his concept of the 'Divine' as *nirguṇa* (indeterminate or transcendent). The most recurring theme of Kabīr's songs concerns the Divine Being (Rāma) who dwells in all hearts, while men foolishly search for Him in mosques and temples.[55] No kind of ritual can be of any use in man's quest for the Creator who is within himself. This profound conviction of God's indwelling all beings led Kabīr to a total condemnation of all rituals, whether Hindu or Muslim ones.[56] It will be interesting to observe here that the followers of the *Saguṇa bhakti* tradition advocate and practise a large number of rituals, usually related to idol worship. On the other hand, saints like Kabīr and Guru Nānak who belong to the *Nirguṇa bhakti* tradition affirm the in-dwelling of God and categorically reject all rituals as irrelevant in one's quest for God.

The assertion of the need for the inwardization of man's consciousness in order to find the 'Divine' is closely related to a world-view and approach that sees the world as foreign to the nature of the soul and seeks to mentally transcend it. Kabīr's songs repeatedly assert the transitoriness of the world and the futility of man's lonely journey through transmigratory existence.[57] His transcendent mystical experience thus led him to a rather negative world-view and attitude towards the world and society. That is why, we do not find in him that positive emphasis on socio-moral virtues which is so prominent in Tulasīdāsa. Of course, Kabīr does recommend the practice of moral virtues as kindness, freedom from evil passions etc.[58] They are necessary in view of the fact that man's heart is a temple of God and therefore must be kept clean and pure. But his main concern is inward purity and not outward actions, or even social morality.

There may or may not be a direct relation (as suggested by us) between a man's concept of God and his religio-moral philosophy and approach. The determining factor in the world-view and moral approach of most of the *Bhakti* saints seems to be the quality and intensity of their devotion. World-and-life-negation is not generally explicitly asserted in the *Bhakti* tradition. But when intense one-pointed devotion or love for the Divine Being is practised, it often results in other-worldliness and a tendency to belittle and condemn the world as an obstruction in one's quest for the Divine Beloved. We have innumerable legends in the Hindu folklore of the intense other-worldliness and forgetfulness of the mystic saints of the middle ages. These stories prove that those who were advanced on the path of God experience often became incapable of paying proper attention to mundane matters and performing their worldly duties.

Middle ages gave birth to a large number of genuine devotional mystics who were extremely pure in heart and intensely in love with God. But very few people are capable of sustaining an intense religious emotion all through life. Religion, for the majority, mainly consists in the assertion of some beliefs and the practice of certain rituals. Though the *Bhakti* tradition put much greater emphasis on inner spirit than on outer rituals, it also offered rituals of its own as accessories to inner devotion.

V. Bhakti Rituals Overshadow the Spirit of Devotion

Middle ages saw the proliferation of devotional rituals which gradually overshadowed the basic spirit of devotion. In the beginning, image worship was not so common, and so meditation (*dhyāna*) on God's form (*rūpa*) was advised. The detailed descriptions of the physical appearance of Lord Viṣṇu, with various jewels decorating His body and various objects in His four hands, as well as of His heavenly abode, Vaikuṇṭha and his consort, Lakṣmī were frequently given in the texts for the devotees to meditate upon. With the increase in the popularity of image worship, there was even greater emphasis on the Lord's physical appearance. Devotion came to be mainly conceived as consisting of serving the idol(s) through various specified rituals. These rituals are very elaborate and 'physicalistic' in some of the theistic-devotional sects. Thus, in the sect of Vallabha, called *Puṣṭi Saṁpradāya*, the entire worship of God (i.e. His image) is divided into eight parts. There are specific instructions as to when to get up, how to wash oneself, and then how to approach the image of God, clean the place where the image is kept, request God to get up and put Him (His image) on the proper seat, then give Him a bath and offer Him morning breakfast ! There are also instructions regarding what to offer for breakfast, noon and evening meals. In between the meals there are other rituals to be enacted, till at night the God (His image) is put to sleep.[59] The whole series of rituals is followed to the letter in most of the Vaiṣṇava temples. Idol worship and all its associated rituals are practised in Hindu homes also. And in many cases these rituals take up the best part of the day of the devotee.

In Rāmānuja's school devotion consists of sixteen aspects, out of which seven are concerned with ethical discipline, practice of moral virtues and proper religious attitude. The remaining nine consist of purely ritualistic observances. The list of sixteen aspects of devotion is headed by the requirement of food being pure and of a kind that is not prohibited. Then come the stamping of one's body with the insignia of Viṣṇu, putting a specific number and pattern of lines on one's forehead with specified coloured muds and sandal, reciting *mantras*, drinking water which has been used to wash the feet of the image, eating food offered to the image, serving the devotees of God, keeping fast on every eleventh day of the lunar calendar and putting basil (*tulasi*) leaves on the image.[60]

Listening to the narratives of God is an important aspect of devotion. The intensity and purity of one's piety are to be judged by one's capacity of taking interest in, and being emotionally overwhelmed by, the stories of God's incarnations on earth.[61]

We would not like to sit on judgment on the religious merit or otherwise of a particular religious ritual. But we are within our rights to evaluate the moral ramifications of a particular religious practice. Take for example, the ritualistic listening to the stories of the exploits (*līlā*) of the Divine Being in any of His several incarnations on earth. Many of these stories directly undermine basic moral values, or are at best amoral in their import. A ritualistic listening to such stories can hardly be instrumental to a higher religious experience. Rather, it engenders an amoral approach to life and related socio-moral issues. The rituals of image worship are particularly amoral; and it can be presumed that in a life in which they form the central concern, moral concerns and values can have only a secondary place. It is in the very nature of rituals that they tend to proliferate and occupy the centre of stage in a man's life. Once a man or a society starts performing rituals, the latter gradually undermine or overshadow that very inner spirit which they are supposed to symbolise or express. The proliferation of rituals in a society definitely undermines the moral point of view. The moral qualifications of a priest who performs elaborate ritualistic worship (*pūjā*) in a temple are never questioned by the Hindu devotees. Even the devotees, who visit temples or perform ritualistic worship at home, hardly ever consider their own moral conduct as relevant for their religious activities. The amoral nature of rituals thus tends to permeate the society's entire approach to life and morality.

At first glance it may appear that the Hindu theistic-devotional tradition was much purer in the beginning and the multiplication of devotional rituals and Purāṇic mythology, as also a renewed emphasis on caste distinctions, are the results of the decadent middle ages. This is true to a certain extent. However, it is an over-simplification of the facts. The *Bhāgavata Purāṇa*, which gives such an exalted version of the vision of one Self, is quite a late work. Kabīr, Nānak and many others of the mystico-devotional tradition belong to late middle ages; and yet they express whatever is most sublime and exalted in the *Bhakti* tradition. On the other hand, though elaborate rituals are relatively a later growth, the mythology which forms the rationale for these rituals is very old. Later middle ages saw both the proliferation of rituals and a reaffirmation of the inner spirit of devotion as the essence of all religion by certain *Bhakta* saints.

The emphasis on external observances, instead of inner purity, grew in later middle ages. Gradually the Vaiṣṇavas became more particular about the kind of food they ate, the manner of its cooking and the person who cooked it, than about any other religious feeling or activity. Not only the food cooked by śūdras was uneatable, for many Vaiṣṇavas the food cooked by anybody else (except perhaps near relations) was a taboo. Both Vaiṣṇavas and Śaivas grew very particular about caste distinctions and the untouchability of certain castes. Both the externalistic rituals and the emphasis on caste, with its related custom of untouchability, are typical marks of an age of degeneration. They would not have mattered to us so much, but for the fact that both practices are more or less common even now.

The *Bhakti* tradition thus comprises several philosophical beliefs, moments of religious experience and religio-moral attitudes. They give it richness and depth, and are also responsible for its decay and staleness later on. The most important contributions of the *Bhakti* tradition to morality are its renewed emphasis on God's indwelling all which means the equal worth or the divinity of all beings and its perception of a very high level of morality as integral to genuine devotion.

Notes

1. *Br.S.* II. 2.42-45.
2. *Śvetāśvatara Up.* IV. 3-4.
3. *B.G.* VII. 24-25; IX.4, 11; XV. 17-18.
4. Ibid VIII. 22; IX. 17-18; X. 20.
5. *Viṣṇu Purāṇa*, bk. I, ch. 2, (1972, pp. 7-8).
6. Rāmānuja ,*Vedārtha-saṁgraha* 11-15; 81-95, (1978, pp. 14 ff., 65 ff.).
7. Ibid 47-49, (pp. 41-43); cf. *Viṣṇu Purāṇa*, bk. VI. ch. 5, (p. 503).
8. *Śrī Bhāṣya, Vedānta Sūtra* I. 1.1.
9. *Nārada Bhakti Sūtra* 2, 7-10.
10. *Bhāg. P.*, bk. III, ch. 25, (1973, vol. I, pp. 244-247).
11. *Vedārtha-saṁgraha* 238, (p. 185).
12. *B.G.* VII. 16-18.
13. *Op. cit.* 30, 67.
14. Ibid 27.
15. *The Idea of the Holy* (1959), pp. 23-24.
16. Rāmānuja, *Bhagavadgītā Bhāṣya*, introd. to ch. VII.
17. *B.G.* IX. 34.
18. Ibid VI. 29-31.
19. *Bhāg. P.*, bk, III, ch. 33, (vol. I, p. 279); bk. VI, ch. 16, (p. 597), bk VII, ch. 7, (p. 647); bk. XI., ch. 14, (vol. II, p. 419).
20. Op. cit. 72.
21. *Śāṇḍilya Bhakti Sūtra* 78.
22. *Bhāg. P.*, bk. VII, ch. 9, (vol. I, p. 656).

23. *Poems of Kabīr* (1972), pp. 21-22.
24. *Bhāg. P.*, bk. III, ch. 29, (vol. I, pp 264-265).
25. Ibid, bk. VII, ch. 7, (vol. I, p. 647).
26. Ibid, Bk. XI, ch. 29, (vol. II, pp. 475-476).
27. Ibid, bk. XI, ch. 2, (vol. II, p. 376).
28. Ibid, bk. III, ch. 29, (vol. I, p. 264).
29. *Viṣṇu Pūraṇa*, bk. III, ch. 8, (p. 234).
30. *Bhāg. P.*, bk. XI, ch. 29, (vol. II, p. 475)
31. Ibid, bk. III, ch. 25, (vol. I, p. 244).
32. Ibid, bk. III, ch. 5, (vol. I, p. 150); bk, VI, ch. 1, (p. 531), bk. XI, ch. 14, (vol. II, pp. 417-418); bk. XII, ch. 3, (p. 500).
33. *Viṣṇu Purāṇa*, bk. III, ch. 8, (p. 234).
34. *B.G.* XII. 4.
35. Ibid XII. 13-14.
36. Op. cit. 12-13.
37. *Bhāg. P.*, bk. III, ch.s 4-5, (vol. I, pp. 144 ff.).
38. *B.G.* II. 47 ff.; III, 10 ff; V. 7 ff.
39. Ibid. IX. 27-28.
40. Op. cit. 62.
41. *Bhāg. P.*, bk. V, ch. 1, (vol. I, p. 434)
42. Ibid, bk. III, ch. 25, (vol. I, pp. 244-247); bk. V, ch. 5, (pp. 447-450)
43. Op. cit. 35.
44. *Bhāg. P.*, bk. VII, ch. 15, (vol. I, p. 691).
45. Ibid, bk. VII, ch. 13, (p, 680).
46. Ibid, bk. V, ch. s 5 and 9, (vol. I, pp. 450-451; 461-462).
47. Ibid bk. VII, ch. 6, (vol. I, pp. 638-639); bk. XI ch. 17, (vol. II, p. 430).
48. Ibid, bk. VII, ch. 5, (vol. I, p. 634) *Bhakti Ratnāvalī*, ch. III (1979, pp. 143 ff.)
49. Op. cit. 19.
50. See author's, *The Roots of World Religions* (1982), pp. 132 ff., 156 ff. 161 ff.
51. *Rāma-carita-mānasa, Uttara Kāṇḍa* 86-87.
52. Ibid, *Araṇya Kāṇḍa* 16, 35-36, *Uttara Kāṇḍa* 45-46.
53. Ibid, *Araṇya Kāṇḍa* 16, 34; *Uttara Kāṇḍa* 45.
54. Ibid, *Ayodhyā Kāṇḍa* 128-131; *Uttara Kāṇḍa* 38, 46.
55. *Poems of Kabīr* (1972), pp. 21. 64-65, 82-83.
56. *The Bījak of Kabīr* (1986), pp. 42, 46-47, 54-55, 64, 69, 74-75, 85, 87-88; *Poems of Kabīr*, pp. 62-63.
57. *The Bījak of Kabīr*, pp. 60-61, 68-69.
58. *Poems of Kabīr*, pp. 47, 65, 78.
59. See R.G. Bhandarkar, *Vaiṣṇavism, Śaivism and Minor Religious Systems* (1965), pp. 80-81.
60. See ibid, p. 55.
61. *Bhāg. P.*, bk. I, ch.s 1-3, (vol. I, pp. 3, 6, 10); bk. III, ch. 13, (p. 190). etc.

CHAPTER VI

UNIVERSAL MORALITY AND THE IDEAL OF HUMAN PERFECTION

I. An Essentially Moral Approach: Some Observations

(i) *Dharma* or righteousness is perhaps the most basic concept of Hindu thought. Man is constantly exhorted to act righteously, or according to *dharma.* He is assured that both his life and eschatological destiny are determined by the moral quality of his conduct. As we know, the world order is conceived in the Hindu thought as a moral order which is vaguely understood as *ṛta, dharma* or *satya.* The *Bṛhadāraṇyaka Upaniṣad* equates *dharma* with truth and ultimate reality. *Dharma* represents the moral order of the universe which ensures the victory of righteousness over evil, so that even a weak man hopes to defeat a strong man through righteousness (*dharma*).[1] It is naively assumed that *dharma* (righteousness) or *satya* (truth) always wins in the end. This faith characterizes the Indian ethos so well that the Indian Government has accepted the phrase, *satyameva jayate* (truth alone triumphs), as the motif on the national emblem. (See chapter I, section IV *supra.*)

At first the term *dharma* mainly referred to ritualistic duties. Gradually the concept of *dharma* became more comprehensive and came to mean all the duties of a man, both ritualistic and socio-moral. Though the ritualistic meaning of *dharma* has continued alongside, it is now primarily a moral term. The term *dharma* now comprehends all one ought to do (duty) and all one ought to be (virtue). The concepts of duty and virtue are two distinct concepts of ethics and have been treated separately in Western thought. At the same time, thinkers like Kant have emphasized their intimate relation when they have understood duty in terms of good-will or respect for the moral law. Virtue finds its fulfilment when it is expressed in moral act, and duty is an empty word unless performed with a virtuous frame of mind. Hindu moral thought does not make any distinction between virtue and duty, because character and conduct are integrally related. What one ought to do (duty) and what one ought to be (virtue) are two sides of the same coin. Thus, *dharma*, by comprehending the two most basic concepts of morality, becomes an invaluable and unique concept of ethics.

That one should perform one's duties with perseverance and alertness and should never slacken in their performance is the constant refrain of Hindu religious texts. The manner in which the advice to follow *dharma* or righteousness is repeated over and over again in the Dharmaśāstras and other texts expresses the genuine moral concern of the Hindu thinkers. Manu advises man:

"Let him, untired, follow the conduct of the virtuous men..."

"When the performance of an act gladdens his heart (conscience), let him perform it with diligence; but let him avoid the opposite."[2]

And,

"Let him always delight in truthfulness, (obedience to) the sacred law, conduct worthy of an Aryan and purity..."[3]

The *Tirukkuṛāḷ* (9th century) is an ancient Tamil text which expresses a rather different religio-moral perspective than that of the Sanskrit texts. But its emphasis on the need to follow the path of righteousness is very similar to that of the Dharmaśāstras. See,

"Strive with ceaseless effort to work your way along the path of righteousness, as far as you can, in all aspects of conduct."[4]

Manu gives two reasons for his plea to follow *dharma.* The first is a very simple argument, acceptable to all religions, but presented in the Vedāntic terminology. It says that man should not delude himself by thinking that he can sin in private, as the inner Self (*Ātman*) or the 'Divine' indwelling all hearts is the witness of all his acts and thoughts.[5] The second argument of Manu is a more specific one and is based on the law of karma. Manu is a firm believer in the inexorable necessity with which the fruits of a man's moral actions (*karmas*) follow him both here and hereafter. Manu believes that evil deeds necessarily result in suffering for, or the destruction of, the evil doer.[6] A man's good deeds are equally sure to bring happiness to him here and secure heaven or a better birth for him hereafter. According to Manu, *dharma* (merit earned through righteous conduct) is a man's best friend, as it alone accompanies him throughout his transmigratory existence.[7] The law of karma guarantees that a man cannot escape the fruits of his past actions, and thereby provides a very strong motive for following the path of righteousness. Manu repeatedly exhorts man to think of the possible fruits of his actions, and then diligently follow the path of *dharma.* The desire for, or the fear of, the fruits of one's action is not a very commendable motive for moral action; in fact it reduces the moral worth of an action. Yet, this natural desire of man has been exploited by the authors of popular religious texts for a good end, i.e. providing an incentive for righteous conduct.[8] And an objective appraisal of the Hindu society through the ages would suggest that this pragmatic and rather un-ethical incentive for ethical conduct has mostly been effective.

(ii) Traditionally, *dharma* or moral duty has been divided into two broad categories: the specific or class duties that are incumbent on man by virtue of his class and role or stage of life (*varṇāśrama dharma*) and the duties common to all men, irrespective of their class or other contingent circumstances (*sādhāraṇa dharma*). While the former mainly refer to man, not as an individual, but as a member of a particular class, the latter apply to man in his capacity as an individual or a moral agent in his own right.

S.K. Maitra contends that universal duties formed the basis for performing special or caste duties, and that whenever there was an occasion for conflict between the two kinds of duties, general or universal duties were given priority over caste duties.[9] Now, we do not find any ancient thinker categorically affirming the priority or supremacy of universal duties over caste duties, though such sentiments have been voiced from time to time. Yudhiṣṭhira argued that truthfulness, magnanimity, forgiveness, good character, non-violence and compassion are supposedly the characteristics of a brāhmaṇa; but if they are exhibited by a śūdra, and are not present in a brāhmaṇa, then that śūdra is not a śūdra, and that brāhmaṇa is not a brāhmaṇa.[10] But it should be remembered that Yudhiṣṭhira's stand was not vindicated in the *Mahābhārata.* We think that caste duties were generally given preference to universal duties. The most obvious example is that of the universal duty of non-violence. At first, *ahiṁsā* was regarded as the special virtue of the brāhmaṇas and recluses only. The *Mahābhārata* abounds in passages declaring that non-violence and its allied virtues were meant for the brāhmaṇas only, whereas fighting wars, awarding punishments (*daṇḍa*), protecting the weak and practice of charity were the chief duties of kṣatriyas. Yudhiṣṭhira tried time and again to escape from the burden of his kingly duties, but was conclusively told that non-violence, friendliness to all and world-renunciation were the duties of brāhmaṇas and not of kṣatriyas.[11] Nor were the masses, vaiṣyas and śūdras, expected to practise non-violence. A man's apprecia-tion of the ideal of non-violence was not allowed to interfere in his caste duties, as is proved by the story of Dharmavyādha, the meat-seller sage. While instructing the brāhmaṇa, Dharma-vyādha gave a detailed apologetic explanation for the violence practised by him in the pursuit of his caste profession, saying that violence is an integral part of everyday life. He also admitted, at the same time, that a poor śūdra like him had no choice but to sell meat,[12] suggesting that violence practised by him in his profession was not a matter of free choice.

Arjuna, like Yudhiṣṭhira, was unwilling to fight, as the war was bound to result in tremendous loss of life and wide-spread suffering. Lord Kṛṣṇa's main argument in persuading Arjuna to wage the war was that, being a kṣatriya it was his bounden duty to do so. As we have seen (vide chapter III, section II *supra*), the *Bhagavadgītā* strongly advocates that all members of the society must perform their respective class duties, and no one should ever think of exchanging his class duty (*sva-dharma*), howsoever lowly that may be, for a better duty of another.[13] The Dharma-śāstras and the *Bhagavadgītā* have given separate sets of duties for the four differentc lasses (*varṇas*), and there is hardly any duty or virtue which is common to all the four lists. It seems that no other moral excellence was generally expected from śūdras and women, their only (compulsory) duty being the service of the three 'upper' classes[14] and their husbands respectively.[15]

And yet, this is only one side of the coin. We have emphasized it only to counter any sweeping generalization regarding the primacy of universal duties in Hindu morality. We think that on the whole, the Hindu thinkers put greater stress on the performance of caste duties by all men; as from their rather limited perspective they thought that a stable and harmonious social order could be achieved only if all men adhered to their respective caste (*varṇa*) duties. At the same time, all Hindu thinkers have persistently recommended the practice of universal moral virtues by all persons, irrespective of their caste or sex. Characteristically, when a Hindu author is considering universal duties, he exalts them as the highest, thus giving the impression that according to him, universal virtues have greater religio-moral worth and must be given priority over caste duties. But when the same author discusses caste duties, he advocates them with equal enthusiasm and conviction. Still, there is no denying the fact that certain universal virtues are uniformly commended by most Hindu thinkers.

II. Universal Virtues (Sādhāraṇa dharma)

As we have seen, the concept of *dharma* comprehends both virtue and duty. Certain moral terms like non-violence, truthfulness, forgiveness etc. are understood as denoting both virtues and duties.

(i) Morality is not the prime concern of the Upaniṣadic seers; yet it forms an important part of all their discussions, both as a pre-requisite of acquiring metaphysical knowledge of *Brahman* and as something which is expected from all human beings. Significantly, the morality prescribed in the Upaniṣads has no reference to class distinctions. Unlike the Brāhmaṇic writers, the Upaniṣadic seers seem to judge the worth of man on the basis of his moral conduct, rather than his caste. The example of Satyakāma may be cited here, who was highly admired for his truthfulness, even though he was a śūdra.[16] Whenever morality is discussed in the Upaniṣads, it is always conceived as universal morality, that is, a morality which is applicable to all men. The famous parting instructions of the teacher to the disciple (i.e. speak the truth, practise *dharma* and magnanimity and serve your teachers and parents) are an example of a very simple but positive code of conduct, obviously meant for the householders of all classes.[17] The *Chāndogya Upaniṣad* has compared the entire life of a man to a sacrifice and moral virtues of austerity, alms-giving, uprightness, non-violence and truthfulness to the gifts to the priests at the end of the sacrifice.[18] The comparison of man's entire life to a sacrifice sanctifies it and also signifies that the practice of moral virtues is expected from all men at every stage of life. It also indirectly negates the worth of Vedic rituals, since living righteously itself is a great sacrifice (*yajña*). Interestingly, it also negates the need to renounce the world, as righteous life is a worthy one and there is no reason to renounce it. The *Bṛhadāraṇyaka Upaniṣad* recommends three cardinal virtues in the story of Prajāpati's instructions to the three classes of creatures—gods, men and demons. He uttered a monosyllable—*da*—three times, and the gods understood it to mean that Prajāpati was asking them to control themselves; men understood it as an exhortation to be magnanimous; and the demons understood it as a command to be compassionate. The Upaniṣad concludes:

"That very thing is repeated by the heavenly voice in the form of thunder, as Da, Da, Da, which means control yourselves (*dāmyata*), give (*datta*) and be compassionate (*dayadhvam*). Therefore one should learn these three, self-control, giving and mercy."[19]

(ii) The authors of Dharmaśāstras were mainly interested in the social organization, and hence their primary emphasis was on class (*varṇa*) duties. At the same time, all of them have recognized certain virtues or duties (*dharma*) which are applicable to, or expected from, all men. Manu lists ten virtues which he calls the characteristics (*lakṣaṇa*) of *dharma* and which should be practised by men belonging to the three 'upper' classes in all stages of life. They are forbearance (*dhṛti*), forgiveness (*kṣamā*), self-discipline (*dama*), non-appropriation of others' wealth (*asteya*), cleanliness (*śauca*), control of senses (*indriya-nigraha*), intelligence (*dhī*), knowledge (*vidyā*), truth (*satya*) and non-anger (*akrodha*).[20] On another occasion he lists non-violence (*ahiṁsā*), truth, non-appropriation of others' wealth, cleanliness and control of senses as the duties of all the four classes (*varṇas*).[21] While the first passage limits the practice of universal virtues to the three upper classes, the second understands universal morality in its true perspective, as referring equally to all men. The two lists can be combined into a more balanced and comprehensive list of universal virtues. Though Manu's main concern is the preservation of the social order, his list of universal virtues surprisingly consists mainly of virtues of self-culture and lacks those of interpersonal morality.

Manu also offers some moral maxims or guiding principles of human conduct. In a way, they express his own moral point of view or the Vedic-Dharmaśāstric ethos much better than the above lists of universal virtues. *Dharma* is declared as the guiding principle of all human conduct. At the same time, the other two goals or values of *artha* (prosperity) and *kāma* (desire fulfilment) are not to be rejected. The latter two are to be pursued under the guidance of the principle of righteousness. Manu thus advises man:

"Let him say what is true, let him say what is pleasing, let him utter no disagreeable truth, and let him utter no agreeable falsehood, that is the eternal law."[22]

"Let him avoid (the acquisition of) wealth and (the gratification of his) desires, if they are opposed to the sacred law, and even lawful acts which may cause pain in the future, or are offensive to men."[23]

"There is no sin in eating meat, in (drinking) liquor and in carnal intercourse, for that is the natural way of created beings; but abstention brings great rewards."[24]

The above norms of conduct are set forth from a pragmatic point of view. They are supposedly meant for the three 'upper' classes. But their very simplicity suggests that they are meant as universal norms of morality, and therein lies their worth. They are not commonplace, only they are not impracticably idealistic.

Generally, the ancient Hindu concept of universal morality comes to us in the form of an extremely unsystematic enumeration of certain moral virtues which are asserted to be applicable to all men. Significantly, most of these universal virtues pertain to individual self-culture. It seems that the universal virtues are mostly understood by Hindu thinkers as complementary to the performance of caste duties. They are concerned with the inner spirit of man, while caste duties are concerned with the external acts. They are, therefore, aptly called *ātma-guṇa* (qualities of the soul) by Gautama, meaning that they should characterize the inner self of a righteous man (man of *dharma*), whatever his outer way of life or profession. Gautama lists eight excellences of the soul (*ātma-guṇa*)—kindness towards all (*dayā sarva-bhūteṣu*), forbearance (*kṣānti*), non-hostility (*anasūyā*), cleanliness (*śauca*), quietude (*anāyāsa*), doing good acts or behaving auspiciously (*maṅgalam*), not asking for favours or freedom from avarice (*akārpaṇya*) and freedom from covetousness (*aspṛhā*). He adds that mere fulfilment of religious duties is useless, unless it is accompanied by the practice of these universal virtues.[25] Thus, Gautama's list of moral virtues, unlike that of Manu, contains several inter-personal virtues, as kindness, non-hostility and good conduct.

Two other lists of moral virtues come from Yājñavalkya. The first includes non-injury (*ahiṁsā*), purity (*śauca*), control of the senses (*indriya-nigraha*), charity (*dāna*), mercy (*dayā*), self-restraint (*dama*) and forbearance (*kṣānti*).[26] The second list consists of the virtues of patience (*dhṛti*), absence of pride (*ārjavam*), intelligence (*dhī*), absence of anger (*akrodha*), spiritual knowledge (*vidyā*), modesty (*hrī*), non-appropriation of others' property (*asteya*) and restraint of senses (*indriya-nigraha*). This second list of moral excellence is accompanied by a most profound advice that a man should not treat another in a way in which he would not like to be treated himself.[27]

(iii) Moral discipline and moral conduct are equally important for the thinkers of philosophic systems. But their treatment of moral matters are not any more systematic than that of the authors of Dharmaśāstras or other religious texts. Praśastapāda enumerates faith in spiritual truth, non-violence, seeking the good of creatures, truthfulness, non-appropriation of others' property, sexual continence, purity of motive, abstaining from anger, personal cleanliness, eating purifying substances, devotion to the deity, fasting and non-neglect of religious duties as the duties of all men.[28] The inclusion of non-injury and seeking the good of the creatures provides some saving grace to this otherwise unimaginative and confusing list of moral duties or virtues.

Vātsyāyana's discussion of moral virtues and vices is relatively more positive and comprehensive, but even this lacks clear classification or analysis. His treatment of the subject has been discussed in detail by S.K. Maitra and Cromwell Crawford,[29] and so we would only give a summary of his views here. According to Vātsyāyana, cruelty, theft, forbidden sexual indulgence, speaking untruth and speaking ill of others, hostility and ill-will towards others, covetousness and irreverence are the main moral vices or sources of moral evil. As against them, universal virtues that constitute moral perfection are: charity (*dāna*), helping the distressed (*paritrāṇa*), serving the elders (*paricāraṇa*), speaking truth (*satya*), speaking with a view to good (*hita-vacana*), agreeableness of speech (*priya vacana*), reciting the Vedas (*svādhyāya*), kindness (*dayā*), indifference to material well-being (*aspṛhā*) and piety (*śraddhā*).[30] The above list contains several inter-personal virtues of a high moral order, such as charity, kindness and even helping others. (At the same time, we should not read too much meaning in the word *paritrāṇa*, which probably did not mean actively helping the distressed.)

The well known *yamas* and *niyamas* of the *Yoga Sūtras*[31] are normative rules of conduct which are meant to be practised by all persons. They present a rather limited concept of morality, both in its vision and scope. They mainly aim at individual self-culture, and do not contain any positive inter-personal virtues or norms. (See chapter IV, section VI *supra.*) As we have seen earlier, the *Yoga Sūtras* also suggest four highly positive moral virtues, viz. friendship towards all (*maitri*), mercy towards the suffering (*karuṇā*), gladness at the good of others (*muditā*) and indifference towards evil persons (*upekṣā*).[32] They are very positive interpersonal virtues or feelings. But unfortunately they were mostly understood as aids for self-discipline, and were not generally meant for active practice. Any future attempt at the reconstruction of a Hindu philosophy of morals must give them more specific content and also assign to them a more central place in its concept of moral perfection.

(iv) We find such lists of ideal moral virtues throughout the Sanskrit literature, especially in the Epics and Purāṇas. All such lists show want of any systematic thinking and even suggest that their authors had other priorities and were quite casual about the task of providing a universal ideal of human perfection.

The greatest and most fascinating source of Hindu morality, both as taught and as lived, are the two Epics. Though both the Epics are committed to a caste-oriented social organization and strongly advocate the performance of class (caste) duties by all, their admiration is reserved for truly moral virtues. Typically, all discussions of moral perfection in the Epics are highly unsystematic, repetitive and sometimes even mutually inconsistent. Only a very careful and comparative perusal of the various descriptions of human perfection, given in the Epics and other religious texts, can give us a general idea of the virtues that were admired most.

We quote here a typical enumeration of virtues comprising moral perfection from the *Bhagavadgītā*:

"Fearlessness, purity of heart, steadfastness in knowledge and yoga, magnanimity, self-restraint, study of scriptures, austerity, uprightness, non-violence, truth, absence of anger, renunciation, serenity, absence of enmity, compassion for creatures, non-covetousness, gentleness, modesty, absence of fickleness, energy, forgiveness, fortitude, purity, absence of hatred, absence of pride these belong to one born of divine nature."[33]

The *Mahābhārata* offers innumerable such lists of moral excellences or ideal universal virtues, often out of all context, and always without any attempt at a clear formulation of the moral point of view. We would quote here a few at random. One such list enumerates forgiveness, patience, non-violence, equableness towards all creatures, truthfulness, simplicity, control of the senses, dexterity, gentleness, sense of propriety, non-miserliness or magnanimity, non-anger, contentment, not paying any attention to the defects of others, non-greed, compassion, not asking for favours and speaking gently and pleasantly.[34] On another occasion, it gives detachment towards sense objects, self-control, being equable in happiness and suffering, truthfulness, magnanimity, kindness, dutifulness, patience, non-violence, doing good to others, always adhering to the path of *dharma*, as also freedom from desire, anger, attachment, avarice and egoism as the characteristics of an ideal man of high moral character (*sādhu*) or a man of *dharma*.[35] The vices that lead to sin are enumerated as attachment (*rāga*), aversion (*dveṣa*), delusion (*moha*), greed (*lobha*), as also egoism, anger, languidness, enmity and ignorance.[36] These are the sources of sin or evil which are rightly perceived as within our own selves. Sin, thus, consists in succumbing to one's lower tendencies, and moral perfection naturally means victory over them.

Purāṇas give similarly long lists of virtues in which genuine moral qualities like truthfulness, kindness, charity, forgiveness, dutifulness, asceticism, self-control and contentment are juxtaposed with such amoral qualities as sharpness of intellect and beauty.[37]

Another Hindu text which considers morality in its true universal perspective, i.e. as applicable to all persons, is the Tamil work, *Tirukkuṟāḷ*. It offers a large number of moral axioms which are universal in application and highly positive in nature. Though there is no systematic thinking behind them, the axioms have immense practical value from the point of view of inter-personal morality. More importantly, righteousness (*dharma*) is conceived in the above text in terms of non-violence, compassion and fellow-feeling. We quote here a few verses:

"Those who follow the principle of universal love and are adorned with mercy towards all living creatures are called godly."

"Imagine thyself before those more powerful than thou art, when about to treat harshly those more weak than thyself."

"To suffer patiently and cause no pain and to cause no injury to others constitute *tapas* or penance."

"It is the considered belief of the sages of spotless purity that even when out of malice evil is done to a person, he ought not to do in return anything evil."

"Whatever is known to be bitter pain by his own experience should not be done to others."

"Share your meal with the needy. Protect every living being. This is the chief of moral precepts."[38]

This popular Hindu morality is a unique admixture of the norms and virtues, affirmed by all the previous religio-philosophical traditions of India. It is un-systematic and often includes self-contradictory elements. It is highly dogmatic also and contains very reactionary ideas, such as the idealization of *satī* (the widow who burns herself). But it has some very positive ideas also. First, though it accepts the traditional emphasis on caste duties, it puts much greater stress on the practice of certain basic moral virtues by all human beings, irrespective of caste and other considerations. Purāṇas and Epics are mainly concerned with the narration of stories about legendary heroes and heroines who were necessarily the epitomes of all moral virtues and righteousness. These heroes have earned the admiration of Hindu masses for centuries, not because they performed their respective caste duties, which of course they did, but because they personified certain universal virtues, such as truth (Hariścandra), magnanimity (Karṇa) and dutifulness towards parents (Śravaṇakumāra). What is more, the virtues exemplified by them are expected to be practised by all men. That is to say, the morality advocated in the Epics and Purāṇas is mostly a universal morality, meant for all human beings.[39]

Secondly, this popular morality generally affirms a more intimate relation between the religious quest and moral conduct than the two earlier traditions of the way of rituals (*karma-kāṇḍa*) and the way of knowledge (*jñāna-mārga*). The *Mahābhārata* declares the virtues of kindness, forgiveness, non-violence, quiescence, truthfulness, absence of enmity, anger and ego, forbearance and withdrawal from mundane actions as the means of the realization of *Brahman*.[40] The *Bhakti* treatises are all the more eloquent in their praise of such virtues as non-violence and kindness and declare that the Lord is propitiated by the practice of such virtues.[41] Both the *Bhagavadgītā* and the *Bhāgavata Purāṇa* declare that to consider all creatures as oneself constitutes true devotion to God. By linking morality with devotion to God[42] the *Bhakti* tradition has given it prestige and a new meaning. In a country where religion holds the central place in a man's life, the assertion of the moral way of life as an integral part of religious quest provides the most effective incentive for pursuing a moral way of life.

It is obvious from the above discussion that though Hindu thinkers have recognized, admired and recommended the entire spectrum of spirituo-moral virtues, they have never attempted their classification or systematic enumeration. While some virtues are common to all such lists, others are expected from different classes of persons, such as renunciants and householders.

Various religio-moral perfections, admired by the ancient Hindus, can be divided into two classes, viz. virtues of self-culture and inter-personal virtues. Self-control, withdrawal of the senses and mind from the outer world, patience, forgiveness and forbearance etc. are the virtues of self-culture which were originally conceived as the characteristic virtues of renunciants. Fulfilling all one's socio-moral obligations, magnanimity and kindness are the chief virtues of social (inter-personal) morality, mainly expected from householders. At the same time, this classification is often misleading for various reasons. First, even though the various virtues of self-culture have been originally developed in the context of the quest for liberation, most of these virtues (with the exception of a few extreme ones) are expected from all men, though in varying degrees of rigour. Secondly, most of the virtues of self-culture, like forgiveness, non-violence and kindness, can be meaningfully practised in a social context only, and cannot possibly be exercised by a renunciant who has totally cut himself off from the world. That makes them more or less inter-personal virtues. Thirdly, the virtues which would definitely be classified as inter-personal ones, like kindness, forgiveness and doing good to others, are often conceived in such a way that they become passive qualities of the soul which are nurtured for the sake of self-purification, or as an indirect means of liberation. This highly vague and un-systematic approach made the amalgamation of the two traditional moralities easier, leading to a general synthetic Hindu morality.

III. The Ideal of Human Perfection and Some Cardinal Virtues

Like Hindu philosophy, Hindu morality is a very complex and composite one. The Hindu concept of human perfection, thus, actually comprises several rather heterogeneous concepts of moral excellence. We are already familiar with two such concepts, viz. the ideal of manliness, self-assertion and world-and-life-affirmation and the ideal of world-renunciation and transcendence of all mundane desires and passions. Gradually there has emerged a third synthetic concept of human perfection that generally comprehends all the virtues and values of the previous two traditional ideals.

(i) In the first or Vedic-Dharmaśāstric tradition, an ideal man is expected to personify three main virtues of truth (*satya*), charity (*dāna*), and duty (*dharma*). Truth is the one virtue that is unanimously included in all descriptions of human perfection. Truth also expresses the ontological moral order that governs the world, so that a moral agent acts from the faith that truth always prevails, or the truthful or righteous cause always triumphs in the end. We shall have occasion to consider it later.

The virtues (duties) of charity and dutifulness are more typical of the first or Brāhmaṇical tradition. As we know, this tradition expresses a very positive and world-and-life-affirming ethos and its concept of a perfect man refers mainly to a householder. A man is expected to earn wealth so that he can practise charity. The virtue or duty of charity is further associated with the affirmation of a man's indebtedness to various sections of society and his responsibility towards the maintenance of those of his fellow beings who cannot maintain themselves, such as travellers, teachers, mendicants and student-celibates, as well as his dependents and old relations. This charity is generally conceived on a very wide canvas. It does not merely mean giving some token gift to brāhmaṇas; rather it consists in actually sharing one's food and wealth with all living beings (*saṁvibhāga*).[43] The *Bhāgavata Purāṇa* goes as far as to say that the embodied beings can lay claim to only as much wealth as is enough to fill their belly and keep their body and soul together. Those who want more are pilferers. It adds that a householder should look upon all beings as his sons, as there is very little difference between his children and other beings.[44] The *Mahābhārata* even advises man to put aside one-third portion of his income for such philanthropic works, as digging wells, planting trees etc. According to the Epic, the only right use of wealth is providing for the poor and the destitute, apart from which its accumulation is detestable.[45]

The most important constituent of this first ideal is devotion to duty (*dharma*). An ideal man (or householder) is expected to exercise full control over his senses and mind, never to pursue self-interest at the cost of others, to pay his debts to the teachers and parents, to procreate and look after all his dependents, as also to perform all his caste duties. It is an ideal of manliness, personal effort, doing one's duties against heavy odds and willingly sacrificing everything, even one's life, for the sake of *dharma*. The ideal man is not one who devotes himself to the pursuit of his salvation, but one who accepts his obligations and fulfils them with perseverance and forbearance. Personal sufferings and trials do not deter him from the path of duty. Moreover, this ideal of human perfection is conceived in a social context. Its most valued virtues are inter-personal ones.

The concept is developed at two levels, first, as an ideal which is both universally applicable and within the reach of common man and second, as an extreme example of human perfection. Tulādhāra and Dharmavyādha are presented in the *Mahābhārata* as ideal householders. These men did not perform any great deeds, but were still the pillars of society and were admired and respected for their dutifulness and inner poise. The ideal of *dharma* in this tradition is thus not an unattainable ideal, but one to be realized by common man in everyday life. The ideal of conduct presented in the Dharmaśāstras and other religious texts reminds us of the rule of the mean of Aristotle. The ideal or good conduct is generally defined as *śīla* which is explained as acting in a way (through body, speech and mind), so as not to cause any injury to any person, and being kind and magnanimous towards others. Simply stated, *śīla* is that conduct for which one need not feel ashamed before others.[46] The ideal of *śīla* is closely associated with the ideal of social culture (*śiṣṭācāra*). Even a casual reader of Sanskrit literature would be impressed by the very high level of social culture maintained at all levels by different legendary characters.

The above idea was at first conceived in a simple pragmatic context. But the folklore and possibly the hightened moral sensitivity of the Hindus of post-Buddhist era gave it a new dimension. The greatest heroes of Hindu folklore are those who sacrificed everything for the sake of the standards of moral conduct they had set for themselves. We may recall here the discussion of moral virtues by W.M. Urban. He distinguishes three kinds of virtues, the objective, the inter-personal and the subjective. It is his contention that the virtues of the first two types, though essential for morality, are limited in their conception and scope; and it is in the field of subjective morality alone that one can achieve heights of moral perfection, inconceivable in other contexts.[47] His views are vindicated by a study of Indian folklore.

Karṇa is the legendary paradigm of the virtue of charity. It is said that he was born with a protective shield and earrings which were part of his body, and that he was invincible as long as he was wearing them. Yet, he willingly tore them off his body and gave them to Indra who begged for them in order to ensure that Karṇa could not kill his (Indra's) son, Arjuna. Karṇa hated Arjuna and his honour demanded that he should defeat

Arjuna who had insulted and humiliated him time and again. Karṇa also knew that deprived of his protective armour, he would not be able to achieve his life's ambition. And yet, he gave them to Indra, because he could not refuse anything asked of him.[48] Likewise, King Śivi cut his body up and gave it in bargain to a vulture in order to save a little pigeon who asked for his protection. And King Dadhīci gave his bones so that a weapon could be forged out of them which alone could destroy the enemies of gods. The *Mahābhārata* recounts the story of an otter, one half of whose body was golden. It so happened that during a severe draught a brāhmaṇa's family was starving. One day the brāhmaṇa could manage a small quantity of food which was divided into four portions for the four members of the family. Just then a guest came to their door demanding to be fed. All members of the family gave their share of food to the guest, knowing fully well that without it they would not be able to survive. The otter rolled over the few grains of the left over food and found that that part of his body had turned golden. When the same otter came to the great sacrifice (*yajña*) of Yudhiṣṭhira, he found that it was ineffective in transforming the remaining part of his body, as he had hoped.[49] The story clearly implies that the sacrifice by the brāhmaṇa family was far greater than that of the great king Yudhiṣṭhira.

Keeping one's promise at all costs and protecting a person who has taken refuge with oneself are other highly cherished values of this tradition. Thus, Rāma willingly surrendered his legitimate right to his father's kingdom and went to the forest, just to honour a promise given by his father to his stepmother. Similarly, Hariścandra gave up his entire kingdom and even sold himself and his wife to keep his promise to a brāhmaṇa. During the middle ages many a Rajput king sacrificed his entire army and kingdom to protect someone who had taken refuge with him. Such sacrifices do seem disproportionate and even irrational, and yet there is a certain grandeur in these immense sacrifices, willingly undertaken for the sake of one's ideal, which expresses a very high level of moral perfection.

(ii) The second traditional ideal of human perfection belongs to the tradition of world-renunciation. As we have seen (vide chapter IV, sections I and II *supra*), this tradition affirms the self as a transcendent pure-consciousness and the world as transient and full of suffering. It is rightly observed by the thinkers of this tradition that it is not the world, but man's desire for mundane objects that binds him to the transmigratory existence. The sufferings of this world affect that person most who forgets the essentially transcendent nature of his inner self and identifies himself with his body and mind. It is, therefore, advised that in order to avoid all sufferings, a man must transcend his ego or empirical personality and become totally detached to the vicissitudes of life. A man of knowledge or one who has achieved perfection in this life (*jīvan-mukti*) is expected to be totally detached towards the outside world and equable or composed towards all beings and under all circumstances. Most of the virtues of this tradition can be summed up under the two heads of dispassion (*vairāgya*) and equanimity (*samabhāva*).

Characteristically, this ideal of a passionless sage is also developed by Hindu thinkers at two levels. While the philosophers of the tradition of liberation, especially the post-Śaṁkara Advaitins, present the ideal of a liberated man in an extreme form, the same concept is put forward in a milder version by the religious texts, especially the *Bhagavadgītā*. (See chapter IV, section VII *supra*.) We would concentrate here on the ideal of a passionless sage, as found in the religious texts, as we feel that the ideas in these texts have exercised much greater influence on the Hindu mind than the more esoteric views of the philosophic schools. According to the *Bhagavadgītā*:

"When a man, satisfied in the Self alone, by himself completely casts off all the desires of the mind, then he is said to be one of steady knowledge (*sthitaprajña*).

"He, whose heart is not distressed in calamities, from whom all longing for pleasure is departed, who is free from attachment, fear and wrath, is called a sage, or a man of steady knowledge.

"Whoso without attachment anywhere, in meeting with anything, good or bad, neither rejoices, nor loathes, his knowledge becomes steady."[50]

And,

"The same in honour and disgrace, the same towards friends and enemies, abandoning all undertakings, he is said to have crossed beyond the qualities of nature (*guṇātīta*)".[51]

A perfect man is also supposed to possess the knowledge of ultimate truth which is variously understood as discriminative knowledge (*viveka-jñāna*) or the knowledge of the Self (*Ātma-jñāna*) in different schools of philosophy. But in all of them it has transcendentalist implications and provides the *raison d'etre* of the creed of renunciation.

A sense of complete freedom from all restraints, involvements, miseries and obligations also characterizes the renunciant. It involves keeping oneself away from the rest of the world and all one's fellow beings. Yudhiṣṭhira describes this attitude as that of a person who stands on a hill top and perceives the people in the plains in a detached way.[52] A renunciant really transcends this world and all its limitations and distinctions (including caste rules).[53] Theoretically, all Vedāntic works concede the possibility of action for a man of renunciation. But the detachment which is expected from a renunciant is so complete that any act that he may possibly perform would be mechanical and even amoral. Moral actions presuppose moral distinctions and owning of the responsibility for one's actions, and both seem to be denied in this ideal, as is evident from the following passage of *Bhagavadgītā*:

" 'I do nothing at all', thus would the knower of truth think, remaining steadfast, though seeing, hearing, touching...... remembering that senses move among sense objects."[54]

In its more extreme form, the ideal expresses not only a rejection of all socio-moral obligations, but also of all norms of conduct. *Jaḍa* Bharat, who did absolutely nothing and remained prostrate in his own filth, is often cited as the paradigm of absolute detachment.[55]

Certain moral virtues, such as control of the senses (*indriya-nigraha*) and total self-control (*dama*), quiescence (*śama*), are closely related to the ideal of absolute detachment and are greatly emphasized in the concept of a liberated man. Non-violence is another important virtue. The ideal of non-violence seems to have been directly borrowed from the heterodox sects of Buddhism and Jainism, along with their creed of world-renunciation. That is why, it was first accepted as a virtue that characterizes the renunciants and was only gradually acknowledged as a universal virtue. It is one of the most cherished virtues (or values) of later Hinduism, and we shall discuss it in greater detail later. Some other virtues that are closely related to the ideal of non-violence, such as forbearance, forgiveness and equanimity, also constitute the ideal of a man of renunciation,[56] or a liberated man. They are seen as expressions of complete detachment towards, or transcendence of, all mundane interests and concerns which necessarily characterize an ideal man in this tradition.

(iii) As we have seen (vide chapter I, section III *supra*), these two traditional moralities and their respective ideals of human perfection were probably developed in independent circles; but there was constant interaction between them from the beginning. As a result of this interaction, both traditions have been modified to a certain extent, and have come closer to each other. Several attempts have been made to synthesize these two traditional moralities. Of all such attempted syntheses, that of the *Bhagavadgītā* is the most meaningful and convincing. Though in some passages the *Bhagavadgītā* seems to advocate extreme detachment, on the whole, it favours the ideal of desireless performance of all one's duties. This ideal seeks to synthesize the previous two concepts, emphasizing the performance of all one's socio-moral duties and absolute detachment and equanimity towards all things and beings respectively. The *Gītā* believes that detachment and equanimity are a matter of mental attitude and have nothing to do with man's outer mode of life. It contends that in order to achieve this state of detachment and mental transcendence, one need not give up a life of action-in-the world. No one can survive without action, and the only choice consists in whether one confines oneself to actions aimed at the maintenance of one's body, or performs other duties also.[57] The *Gītā* assures us that the world order, including the division of society into different classes, is ordained by the will of God; and it is the Lord's will that man should do his allotted work, so that the wheel of creation is kept rotating and the social order is not disturbed.[58] Having argued for the inevitability and advisability of a life of action, the *Gītā* further assures us that the performance of one's duties, undertaken in the right frame of mind, does not result in one's involvement in the world:

"Satisfied with what comes to him by chance, rising above

the pairs of opposites, free from envy, equanimous in success and failure, though acting, he is not bound."[59]

And,

"He who is equipped with yoga, whose mind is quite pure, by whom the self has been conquered, whose senses have been subdued, whose self has become the self of all beings, though doing, he is not tainted."[60]

The *Bhagavadgītā's* option of desireless action seems to be the perfect answer to the common fear of involvement in the transmigratory existence. Also, the detachment that the *Gītā* generally upholds, excepting a few passages, is neither as extreme, nor as negative, as that of the later Advaita works. Vidyāraṇya rightly points out that the *Bhagavadgītā* uses the term 'like a detached person (*udāsīnavat*)' which means that absolute detachment is not required by it.[61] Its ideal of equanimity or desirelessness refers mainly to the mental attitude of the agent and does not mean disowning one's duties and social obligations. The theism of the *Bhagavadgītā* further transforms the dry and negative ideal of world-renunciation and absolute detachment towards one's fellow beings into a much more positive ideal of performance of all one's duties in a spirit of total self-surrender to the Lord.[62] It seems that while the ideal of absolute detachment and world-renunciation is closely related with a monistic or transcendentalist approach to world and life, the ideal of a full life-in-the world is more easily reconciled with a polytheistic world view. In contrast, the ideal of doing one's duty desirelessly seems to be more in conformity with a theistic approach to life, at least in the Indian context.

The *Mahābhārata* presents the same ideal independently. According to it, renunciation of the world is easy, but not desirable; and an ideal renunciant (*saṁnyāsin*) is one who lives in the world, performing all his actions in a spirit of detachment and equanimity. It is useless for an intemperate man to go to the forest, and it is equally useless for a man of tranquillity and self-restraint to go there, as wherever the latter lives, his life is as austere and meritorious, as that of a forest-dweller.[63]

According to Manu, an ideal householder has complete control over his senses and mind, as well as his desires and passions. He is also very quiet, forbearing, forgiving and equable towards all beings.[64] And of course, he performs all his socio-moral and ritualistic duties without any selfish motive. Some of the virtues that constitute the ideal of a householder in Manu are common in his concept of an ideal renunciant. Thus, Manu's concept of an ideal householder seeks to comprehend and synthesize the first two ideals.

But in spite of all these attempts at synthesis, the two ideals of an active life-in-the world (*pravṛtti*) and its renunciation (*nivṛtti*) could never be fully integrated. As we have seen above, certain passages of the *Bhagavadgītā* itself give a rather extreme version of the ideal of detachment. The Advaitins could argue for a life of inaction and absolute detachment on the basis of such passages. In a way, this ideal of desireless action was never developed at a philosophical level till the modern times, when B.G. Tilak and Sri Aurobindo presented it in a forceful manner.[65]

(iv) At the same time, there was a continuous interaction between the two religio-moral traditions which naturally resulted in an intermixing of the two valuational approaches, resulting in the general acceptance of certain cardinal virtues by all Hindu thinkers. The Vedic-Dharmaśāstric tradition, being the more receptive of the two, absorbed most of the virtues and values of the second tradition. Gradually certain virtues were accepted as having more intrinsic worth than others and came to be included in all the descriptions of an ideal or perfect man. The cardinal virtues which constitute this vaguely formulated synthetic ideal are truth, magnanimity, self-control, non-violence and compassion.

Truth, perhaps, is the most important cardinal virtue of Hinduism. It is unanimously recognized and cherished in all the traditions of Hinduism. Both the *Manusmṛti* and the *Mahābhārata* sing homilies of truth as the highest *dharma* and the source or basis of all other virtues. According to Manu, being guided by truth in one's actions is the greatest virtue, while acting in disregard to it is the greatest sin. Tempering truth or justice finally leads to the destruction of the sinner.[66] To be truthful means never to indulge in any kind of lies or slanderous and malicious talk and to adhere to the highest measure of rectitude in one's conduct. It also means knowing the metaphysical nature of reality (*satya*) and acting in harmony with it.

Charity (*dāna*) is the second cardinal virtue which has been unanimously recognized in Hinduism. Like truth, it originated in the Vedic tradition, but has been whole-heartedly accepted in subsequent Hinduism. Epics and Purāṇas praise the virtue of charity endlessly. It is definitely an inter-personal virtue which emphasizes man's obligation towards his fellow beings, though it falls much short of the ideal of love and service of others.

Self-control (*dama* or *indriya-nigraha*) is the third most important virtue of this composite ideal. It is more or less a class name for a group of related virtues like control of mind and senses, detachment towards sense objects or quiescence, forbearance, egolessness and absence of evil passions like anger, avarice etc. All these qualities are included in almost every description of an ideal man in later Sanskrit literature. Though self-control was originally conceived in the context of self-culture, it gradually came to be conceived in a markedly social or inter-personal context. Thus, an ideal man, whether he is a recluse or a householder, is expected to be immensely patient, forbearing and completely free from any negative feelings like anger, enmity and ill-will towards other beings.[67]

Ahiṁsā (non-violence) is the fourth cardinal virtue of Hinduism. Non-violence, along with truth, forms the basis of the entire super-structure of Hindu 'religio-culture'. It seems to be fairly certain that the value of non-violence was introduced into Hinduism as a result of the direct influence of the heterodox sects of Buddhism and Jainism. At first the value of non-violence was only conditionally accepted as a virtue which characterizes a certain class of persons, viz. the renunciants. Gradually non-violence came to be accepted as the guiding principle of life or the supreme universal virtue—*ahiṁsā paramo dharmaḥ*.[68] The acceptance of non-violence resulted in the rejection of Vedic sacrifices involving violence.[69]

At first glance the ideal of *ahiṁsā* seems to be a limited and negative concept. Probably it was so in the beginning. But gradually it acquired a richer and profounder meaning. *Ahiṁsā* is an all-encompassing ideal, both in its conception and scope. Mahatma Gandhi's interpretation of *ahiṁsā*, as never hurting another in any way and harbouring positive feelings of friendliness and good-will towards all, including one's enemies, is not something new, but is rather a true interpretation of the concept of *ahiṁsā*. The ideal of *ahiṁsā* means that a man must not ever hurt others physically or mentally, or cause fear in them, and must never indulge in feelings of animosity or ill-will towards others. *Ahiṁsā* or non-violence is also giving the gift of fearlessness (*abhaya-dāna*) to all, which means that one should behave so as not to cause fear in any creature. The ideal man is repeatedly described as one who is not afraid of others and who is not a source of fear to anyone else.[70] Not only must one not cause physical injury to another, one must desist from causing any mental agony or anxiety in another person. Absolute harmlessness and friendliness towards all beings are expected from a man of non-violence.

Ahiṁsā and its allied virtues are further integrated with the religious quest for one's liberation by the theistic-devotional tradition and popular Hindu texts. Thus, the *Mahābhārata* contends that a man, who causes no harm to others through body, mind and speech and who never thinks ill of others, reaches the supreme *Brahman*.[71]

The real worth of the ideal of *ahiṁsā* lies in its exceptionally broad application. All living beings, from gods and men to smallest creatures, are *jīvas*. The term *jīva* is generally used for the individual soul, but basically it means one who has got life breath (*prāṇa*). The ideal of *ahiṁsā* is applicable to all and in all circumstances of life. Nowhere in the history of human thought has the animal kingdom been treated as deserving equal consideration and kindness as human beings, as in the concept of non-violence. The Aryans were enthusiastic meat eaters. But once the ideal of non-violence was accepted, they strove hard to give up meat eating on the sole consideration that animals who are killed for meat have the same life as humans.[72] Not only must the animals not be killed, they must also not be beaten or treated cruelly in any way.[73]

Closely associated with the ideal of *ahiṁsā* is the virtue of compassion or kindness to all beings (*bhūtadayā*). Universal kindness may be regarded as the fifth cardinal virtue of Hinduism. According to the *Mahābhārata*, kindness is the highest duty, the highest norm of morality that must govern our entire conduct.

The *Mahābhārata* hails the character which is governed by kindness. Such a character necessarily expresses itself in actions which aim at the good of all. It adds that ideal persons are those who are self-restrained, kind towards all and ever ready to sacrifice their lives for the good of others.[74] The *Bhagavadgitā* describes an ideal devotee as one who is kind and friendly towards all.[75] The *Manusmṛti* describes an ideal forest-dweller as one who is non-violent and kind towards all beings.[76] Desisting from any activity which may cause some injury to any living being and desiring the good of all beings[77] are the necessary ingredients of the ideal of human perfection, as conceived in Dharmaśāstras and other religious texts. A knower of *dharma* (a righteous person) or an ideal man (*sādhu*) is consistently defined in the Epics and Purāṇas as one who is ever busy in doing good to others through body, mind and speech, who has no complaint against anybody, no ill-will or jealousy towards others, and who sees and treats all beings equally.[78]

Unlike the Yoga version of compassion, kindness, as conceived in popular religious texts, is not a mere passive feeling to be nurtured, but a positive virtue to be practised by all in day-to-day life. In an interesting narrative, the *Mahābhārata* describes the original character of *asuras*, before it degenerated, as an ideal one.[79] These *asuras* of old practised all the ideal moral virtues, such as self-restraint and truthfulness, and were very kind towards the poor, the destitute, the distressed, the orphans, the weak, the old and the unprotected women. They actively helped them by giving them food and clothes and were always ready to offer solace and succour to the suffering and the oppressed. Of course, the virtue of compassion or kindness is not always presented in this positive manner; but it is an integral part of every Hindu description of a perfect man.

Even Śaṁkara has affirmed that kindness or magnanimity motivates the great souls to work for the good of the ignorant, suffering human beings.[80] It is difficult to say what exactly is meant by doing good to others (*paropakāra*). It definitely includes magnanimity and philanthropic works, as digging wells, planting trees etc., though perhaps active physical service is not intended. Often it means only instructing or guiding the ignorant human beings, since according to the Hindu point of view, helping a man to obtain his freedom from transmigratory existence is the best help one can offer to anyone. Swami Vivekananda has given a new dimension to the old ideal of compassion by emphasizing the need of providing for the physical needs of the masses before offering them religion.[81] though at the same time, he concurs with the Hindu idea of spiritual help as the best help that one can give. We think that the motive of compassion is present in Hinduism; only it is to be given the right direction by modern Hindu thinkers.

IV. The Philosophic Basis for an Altruistic Morality

Though the Vedāntic vision of one Self in all could not by itself inspire a morality of love and active service of one's fellow beings, the Aryans were not insensitive to the practical implications of this vision, as is evident from the following passages of the *Bhagavadgītā*:

"The Self abiding in all beings and all beings abiding in the Self sees he, whose self has been made steadfast by Yoga and who everywhere sees the same....

"He, O Arjuna! who sees with equality everything in the image of his own self, whether in pleasure or in pain, he is considered a perfect yogin."[82]

The phrase, '*ātmopamyena sarvatra samaṁ paśyati*', that is, 'one sees all in the image of oneself', expresses the quintessence of all morality and is the basis of all inter-personal moral virtues. This idea is repeated in all the Hindu texts. According to Manu, being equal towards all beings or seeing the same Self in all characterizes a knower of *Brahman.*[83] *Mahābhārata* repeatedly exhorts man to treat others as oneself. This advice of the Epic is based not on any esoteric philosophic vision, but on the common-sense perception of the essential sameness of all living beings:

"Don't treat others in a way in which you would not want to be treated by others.

"A man who is guilty himself has no right to point to the guilt of others....

"How can a man who wants to live himself kill another? Therefore, you should wish for others whatever you want for yourselves....

"We should treat others in a way which is desirable for ourselves. And we should not act towards others in a way which is undesirable or unplesant for us.

"That upright conduct is *dharma* which is determined by kindness."[84]

The gift of fearlessness, as we have seen, is regarded as the greatest gift, and the reason given is that we should always remember that all beings love their life (*prāṇa*), just as we do. Therefore, one is exhorted to understand and treat all beings like oneself. *Mahābhārata* does not bother about metaphysical consistency. The words life (*prāṇa*) and self (*ātman*) are used indiscriminately to express the essential similarity of all beings.[85] 'Self' or 'life' (*prāṇa*) here refers to the individual self which is similar, but not identical, in all beings. Without going into metaphysical details, the Epic simply asks man to seek the same Self in all, even as he instinctively recognizes the self (*ātman*) in himself.[86]

This vision of the essential affinity of all living beings is the most basic vision of Hinduism, and it permeates the entire Hindu 'religio-culture'. The *Tirukkurāḷ* advocates a morality of universal kindness, and justifies its moral ideal on the basis of the basic affinity of all beings:

"If a person does not protect other beings from injury, realizing that their pain is his own pain, then what use is his knowledge...?"[87]

A man who perceives the sameness of all selves transcends the dualities and conflicts arising out of the distinction between himself and others. According to the *Yoga Vāsiṣṭha*, such ideas, as 'this man is a friend and that other is a foe', or, 'this object is mine, and that other is another's', or, 'this self is mine and that one is another', are all false projections of the mind, and must be wiped off from it. In fact, such ideas are cherished by the low-minded only, the minds of the noble-hearted men are not clouded by such distinctions. According to another reading, the entire world is like a family to the noble-minded.[88]

The advice to treat others as one wants to be treated by others is an advice found in other religions also. There is one difference though. Hinduism has made it more convincing by basing it on the metaphysical vision of one Self in all. In an oft-quoted passage, Paul Deussen has said the same thing:

"The Gospels quite correctly establish as the highest law of morality, 'Love your neighbour as yourselves'. But why should I do so, since by the order of nature I feel pain and pleasure only in myself, not in my neighbour? The answer is not in the Bible. But it is in the Vedas, in the great formula, 'That art thou', which gives in three words the combined sum of metaphysics and morals: 'you shall love your neighbour as yourselves, because you are your neighbour.'"[89]

The Hindu thinkers could not always succeed in deriving a morality of love and kindness to all from their grand vision of the identity of all selves with the one universal Self; but they were always conscious that this vision becomes meaningful only when one habitually sees all in the image of one's self and acts accordingly. This vision and its related moral virtues have very well compensated for certain soul-centric tendencies of Hindu moral philosophy. Any future reconstruction of a Hindu philosophy of morals must first of all try to develop the Vedāntic vision at a philosophical level, and then make it the basis of a positive morality of universal love and compassion.

Notes

1. *Bṛhad. Up.* I. 4.14.
2. *M.S.* IV. 155, 161.
3. Ibid IV. 175.
4. *Tirukkuraḷ* IV. 33.
5. *M.S.* VIII. 84-85, 91.
6. Ibid IV. 172-174.
7. Ibid IV. 238-243; VIII. 17; XII. 7-11.
8. Ibid IV. 155-158, 172-174, 242; XI. 232; XII. 23; *Mbh. Āraṇ. P.* XXXII. 19 ff., 29.
9. *The Ethics of the Hindus* (1963), pp. 3, 17.
10. *Mbh. Āraṇ. P.* CLXXVII. 16 ff.; CCVI. 11-13.
11. Ibid, *Śān. P.* XIV. 14-16; XXII. 4; XXIII. 8-12.
12. Ibid, *Āraṇ. P.* ch. CIC, especially 1-3.
13. *B.G.* II. 31-33; XVIII. 47-48; cf. *M.S.* X. 97.
14. *M.S.* I. 91; VIII. 413-414; X. 100, 123.
15. *M.S.* V. 151 ff; IX. 29.
16. *Chān. Up.* IV. 4.1-5.
17. *Taittirīya Up.* I. 11.1.
18. *Chān. Up.* III. 17. 1-4.

19. *Bṛhad. Up.* V. 2. 1-3.
20. *M.S.* VI. 92.
21. Ibid X. 63.
22. Ibid IV. 132.
23. Ibid IV. 176.
24. Ibid V. 58.
25. *Gaut. D.S.* VIII. 22-24.
26. *Yājñ. S.* I. 122.
27. Ibid III. 65-66.
28. Quoted in Cromwell Crawford, *Evolution of Hindu Ethical Ideals* (1974), p. 141.
29. S.K. Maitra, op. cit. (1963), pp. 206 ff.; Cromwell Crawford, op. cit., pp. 135 ff.
30. *Nyāya Sūtra Bhāṣya* I. 1.2.
31. *Yoga Sūtra* II. 30-45.
32. Ibid I. 33.
33. *B.G.* XVI. 1-3.
34. *Mbh. Śān. P.* CLIV. 14 ff.; CLVI. 8 ff.
35. Ibid, *Śān. P.* CLII. 21 ff.
36. Ibid, *Śān. P.* CLII. 2 ff.; CLVII. 1 ff.; CLXII 6 ff.
37. *Bhāg. P.*, bk. I, ch. 16, (1973, vol. I, p. 67).
38. *Tirukkuraḷ* III. 30; XXV. 250; XXVII. 261; XXXII. 312; 316; XXXIII. 322.
39. *Mbh. Śān. P.* CLIV. 24; CCLXII. 27; *Bhāg. P.*, bk. VII, ch. 11, (vol. I, p. 672); bk. XI. ch. 17, (vol. II., p. 427).
40. *Mbh. Śān. P.* CCLXII. 37-38.
41. *Bhāg. P.*, bk. IV, ch. 31, (vol. I, p. 430); bk. VII, ch. 6, (vol. I, p. 640).
42. Ibid, bk. III, ch. 28, (vol. I. pp. 264-265); bk. VII, ch. 7, (vol. I, p. 647); *B.G.* VI 29-32; XII. 13-14.
43. *Mbh. Śān. P.* XXI. 11; LX. 7; *Āraṇ. P.* II. 51-53; *Bhāg. P.*, bk. VII, chs. 11 and 15, (vol. I, pp. 672, 688).
44. *Bhāg. P.*, bk. VII, ch. 14, (vol. I, p. 684).
45. *Mbh. Anuś. P.* CXXIX. 16-19; *Śān. P.* CCLI. 22.
46. *Mbh. Śān. P.* CXIV. 64-65.
47. W.M. Urban, *Valuation, Its Nature and Laws* (1909), pp. 254, 269-270, 284 ff., 295 ff.
48. *Mbh. Āraṇ. P.*, ch. CCXCIV; *Udyoga Parva*, ch. s CXXXVIII ff.
49. Ibid, *Aśvamedha Parva*, chs. 92-93.
50. *B.G.* II. 55-57; cf. ibid IV. 19-21.
51. Ibid XIV. 25.
52. *Mbh. Śān. P.* IX. 14 ff.; XVII. 16 ff.
53. *Ś.B.*, *Br. S.*, introd.; I. 1.4; *Ś.B.*, *Bṛhad. Up.* II. 1.20; *Ś. B.*, *Chān. Up.* II. 23.1.
54. *B.G.* V. 8-9.
55. *Bhāg. P.*, bk. V, ch.s IX-X; (vol. I, pp. 460 ff.).
56. *M.S.* VI. 8ff; VI. 40 ff..
57. *B.G.* III. 5, 8; XVIII. 11.

58. Ibid III. 10 ff., 25; V. 25; XVIII. 41-45.
59. Ibid IV. 22; cf. ibid II. 38, 47-50.
60. Ibid V.7.
61. *Pañcadaśī* VI. 269-270; ref. to *B.G.* XIV. 23.
62. *B.G.* IX. 2?, 26-28, 34; XII. 6.
63. *Mbh. Śān. P.* CLIV. 36.; cf. XII. 13 ff.; XVIII. 29 ff.; XXXVII. 28.
64. *M.S.* IV. 138 ff.; 171 ff.; 238, 246.
65. Sri Aurobindo, *Essays on the Gītā* (1972), pp. 27 ff., 126 ff., 168 ff., 236 ff.; *Selections From Swami Vivekananda* (1957), pp. 41 ff.; *Karma Yoga* (1956), pp. 24 ff., 40 ff.
66. *M.S.* VIII. 81 ff.
67. Ibid IV. 179 ff., VI. 45 ff., *Mbh. Śān.P.* CLII. 21 ff.; CLIV. 6 ff.; CLVI. 8 ff.; CCXIII. 8 ff.
68. *Mbh. Anuś.P.* CXVII. 13, 37-38.
69. Ibid, *Śān.P.* CCLV. 6, 24 ff.; CCLVII. 4 ff.; CCLX. 6 ff.
70. Ibid, *Śān.P.* CLIV. 26-28; CCLIV. 9. 16, 25 ff.; *Anuś.P.* CXVI. 20-21; CXVII. 25-26.
71. Ibid, *Śān.P.* CCXLIII. 5-7; CCLXII. 36 ff.
72. Ibid, *Anuś.P.* CXVI. 12 ff., 20 ff., 59; CXVII. 13, 18 ff., 31 ff., *M.S.* V. 51 ff.
73. Ibid, *Śān.P.* CCLIV. 43.
74. Ibid, *Śān.P.* CLII. 24, CCLI. 17; CCLIV. 9; *Anuś.P.* CXVII. 18 ff.
75. *B.G.* XII. 13-14; cf. "He must always promote the good of others and do evil unto none, for the best virtue of a brāhmaṇa is universal benevolence". *Viṣṇu Purāṇa*, bk. III, ch. 8, (1972, p. 235).
76. *M.S.* VI. 8.
77. Ibid V. 46-47.
78. *B.G.* V. 25; *Bhāg.P.*, bk. XI, ch.s 11 and 17, (vol. II, pp. 409, 427); *Mbh. Śān.P.* CLII. 21 ff.; CCXXXI. 23; CCLIV. 9-11; *Āraṇ.P.* CXCVIII. 38 ff.
79. *Śān.P.* CCXXI. 30 ff., especially 39-40.
80. *Viveka-cūḍāmaṇi* 37-38, 82.
81. *Lectures From Colombo to Almora* (1956), pp. 446 ff.
82. *B.G.* VI. 29, 32.
83. *M.S.* XII. 118.
84. *Mbh. Śān.P.* CCLI. 19-21, 24-25.
85. Ibid, *Anuś.P.* CXVI. 20-22; CXVII. 18 ff.
86. Ibid, *Śān.P.* CCCVIII. 126.
87. *Tirukkuraḷ* XXXII. 315.
88. *Yoga Vāsiṣṭha, Upaśama Prakaraṇa*, ch. XVIII, (1978, vol. II, pp. 776-777).
89. Quoted in S. Radhakrishnan, *Eastern Religions and Western Thought* (1958), pp. 101-102.

CHAPTER VII

SOME CONCLUDING OBSERVATIONS

I. Recapitulation and Looking Forward

The preceding chapters prove our two basic contentions: First, that Hindu religio-philosophy and morality are so integrally related that it is impossible to understand the latter without a proper understanding of the former; and second, that Hindu Dharma, i.e. the entire Hindu 'religio-culture' is a very complex and multi-faceted one, being constituted of several, rather divergent, religio-philosophical traditions. This diversity of metaphysical beliefs and valuational attitudes is strongly reflected in Hindu morality which is as diverse and multi-faceted as the rest of Hindu 'religio-culture'. We must, however, dispel here any impression created in the minds of our readers that there is neither any specific world-view or ethos, nor any definite moral code which can be called Hindu as such. Though Hinduism has been excessively receptive to new ideas and values, it has also been quite discerning in its choice of ideas to be incorporated in its religio-moral thought. It welcomed the transcendentalism and world-and-life-negation of the Sāṁkhyas and Buddhists, the ideal of non-violence of the latter, and the strict monotheism of Islam, because all these ideas found a receptive soil in its own Vedāntic philosophy, or appealed to the intuitive perceptions of its people. On the other hand, Hinduism has persistently refused to accept various beliefs of the Christian creed, such as predetermination and atonement of all our sins by the sacrifice of Christ, as they go against its own law of karma.

(i) It means that there is a definite philosophy or world-view which permeates the entire Hindu 'religio-culture' and which has determined the development of Hinduism through the ages. Admittedly, it is not well-defined and is somewhat in the form of a nebulous vision or faith. Ever since the time of Upaniṣads, a vaguely conceived monism has been the constant background or framework of entire Hindu Dharma. (See chapter I, section V; chapter IV, section II; chapter VI, section IV *supra.*) It signifies that the Divine Absolute is the Creator, as well as the essence, of the entire creation and the Self of all beings. Not only the Upaniṣads, all popular religious texts, from the *Bhagavadgītā* to the *Manusmṛti* and Purāṇas, affirm the Vedāntic monism in their own way. The same vision is also proclaimed by the teachers (ācāryas) of theistic Vedānta and innumerable *bhakta* saints. True the masses do not read the Upaniṣads and the *Bhagavadgītā*, but they all hear Purāṇas and sing the devotional songs of various *bhakta* saints in their own languages. As a result, the Hindu masses are very much at home with the idea of the Divine Being indwelling all hearts.

The second most important article of the Hindu faith concerns the moral order of the world. The idea of the world being governed by moral laws is very much compatible with the faith in the Divine immanence in the world, but is not derived therefrom. Instead, it is directly traceable to the Vedic concept of *ṛta*. It is also related to the beliefs in the law of karma and transmigratory existence. As we have observed earlier (vide chapter I, section V, *supra*), the law of karma, being a thoroughly individualistic hypothesis, is contrary to the spirit of Vedāntic monism. And yet, the two assertions, regarding the Divine Reality being both the Creator of the world and the inner Self of all living beings and the world being a moral order, understood largely in terms of the law of karma, form the nucleus of the entire creed or religio-philosophy of Hinduism. At the same time, these have never been fully synthesized.

(ii) We would also like to make three observations here. First, Hinduism is an extremely dynamic and ever changing 'religio-culture'. The adaptability of Hinduism to changing times, so far without any conscious guidance from its intellectuals, gives us hope that Hinduism can adapt itself to modern values and the needs of modern times even more easily, if it is given some directive guidance by its philosophers. In order to be able to provide the right direction to the ever-changing Hindu socio-moral norms and attitudes, Hindu thinkers would have to reconstruct the Hindu philosophy of morals, so that it can offer a rationale to Hindus for a meaningful moral life in the present-day society.

Secondly, Hinduism has long accepted the fact that man's *dharma*, comprising all his duties and virtues, changes with the changing times. This contention provides us with a traditional basis for our attempt at the reconstruction of Hindu philosophy of morals, that is, it gives us hope that any worthwhile changes in Hindu moral values and norms, suggested by our philosophers, would be acceptable to the Hindus. And thirdly, due to the very composite nature of the Hindu 'religio-culture', it contains certain inner tensions which must not be brushed aside, but should be frankly recognized. Not only would it help us in a better understanding of Hindu religion and morality, it would also help us in choosing those aspects of Hindu 'religio-culture' which are most in harmony with our modern values, and rejecting others.

II. The Flexibility and Adaptability of Hinduism

(i) Hinduism is an extremely dynamic and ever-changing 'religio-culture' which adapts itself very readily to changing times and their needs. (See chapter I, section II and III *supra.*) It has changed sometimes due to its own inner dialectic, at other times due to the impact of new ideas which it absorbed from other sources.

Hinduism has generally been changing due to its own inner dialectic. We have had occasion to discuss the development of Hinduism through the ages. (See chapter I, section III *supra.*) Without repeating our earlier observations, we would just recall here that each phase of Hinduism is best understood in contradistinction to its previous one(s). Thus, while the Upaniṣadic philosophy was developed as a reaction to the Vedic ritualism; the Dharmaśāstras were the expressions of the dissatisfaction of the then Aryans with the esoteric and transcendentalist philosophy of Vedānta. The theistic-devotional tradition, in its turn, was a revolt against both the externalistic ritualism of the Vedas and the transcendentalist and esoteric approach of the Vedānta. In Hinduism a new tradition never destroys the old, but definitely and unmistakably modifies it, and is gradually itself modified through long centuries of interaction with the rival traditions. Slowly and steadily Hinduism has been changing due to the constant interaction between its various component traditions.

Hinduism has often changed under the impact of new ideas also. We can discern two very major upheavals in the Hindu thought which can be directly traced to foreign sources. The first such upheaval was brought about due to the overwhelming influence of Buddhism and Jainism. Hinduism borrowed from them the ideal of non-violence (*ahiṁsā*) and the world-and-life-negation implied in their creed of renunciation. Both the ideas or values transformed Hinduism. Not only did Hinduism reject the violent Vedic sacrifices, once it accepted the ideal of non-violence, it also changed its entire conception of human perfection and ideal morality to accommodate non-violence and its allied virtues, such as forgiveness, fortitude and equanimity. Similarly, the entire Hindu religio-moral thought became profounder and also more pessimistic and negative towards the world and life under the influence of these heterodox philosophies.

The second most all-encompassing change was brought about in Hinduism by the impact of modern Western thought. The positivist, liberal and humanitarian ideas of Renaissance reached India late, but once they became known, they created an unprecedented upheaval in the Hindu society. For the first time in its history, Hindu thinkers became conscious of the gross injustice of the Hindu social organization and its discriminatory practices against the so-called lower classes and the weaker sex. They also became acutely conscious of the discrepancy between Hindu ideals and social practices, and set about the Herculean task of questioning and even rejecting those practices which were against both, Hindu ideals and modern values. It is due to the missionary zeal and untiring efforts of the thinkers and reformers of the Hindu renaissance that most of the extreme evils of the Hindu society, such as ill-treatment and even burning of the widows and the practice of untouchability, have either been eradicated, or are at least fast on the decline. (See chapter I, section III *supra.*)

Conditions have changed tremendously in the last few decades, especially in the urban Hindu society. Though caste distinctions are still widely practised, because they serve the vested socio-economic interests of certain caste groups, they have lost all their religious (ritualistic) relevance, due to the conditions created by industrialization and urbanization of the Indian society. Revolutionary changes have been brought about in the conditions and social rights of women. The Hindu Code Bill, passed in the early fifties, gives equal rights to women in every respect. They are given the right to divorce, remarry and inherit ancestral property. And more and more women are availing of the rights given to them under modern laws.

(ii) We can appreciate the liberality of modern Hindu legislation only if we compare it with: (i) the highly conservative and reactionary stance of ancient legislators, and (ii) the refusal of other religious communities to accept such reforms. Take the women's right to divorce and remarry for instance. Most ancient Law-givers, especially Manu, are strongly against it. Manu has declared categorically that the second husband of a woman is never heard of.[1] All Hindu texts give excessive importance to a wife's ideal of extreme loyalty to her husband (*pativrata dharma*) which excludes any possibility of divorce or remarriage for Hindu women. In fact, they are just unthinkable in the traditional context. Similarly, most Hindus, the literate and the illiterate alike, are opting for planned families. And they do so in direct defiance of their sacred tradition. Procreation has been regarded as most sacred in Hindu religion. The Upaniṣads, in spite of their transcendantalist philosophy, glorify the act of procreation as a sacrifice.[2] Procreation or proliferation of the race was so important for the Aryans that it was stipulated that a girl should be married early, so as not to waste a single productive year of her life.[3] Furthermore, a son is very important in Hindu religion. A man is supposed to be born with various debts, including the one to his parents. He can repay his debt to his parents by procreating and continuing the family line. Above all, as we know (*vide* chapter II, section I *supra*), the funeral rites performed by son(s) are a must for ensuring the eschatological destiny of the deceased,[4] in the absence of which a man's soul is said to become a ghost (*preta*). And it is just not a casual belief; Hindus actually take their funeral rites very seriously. The acceptance of the principle of planned family by the Hindus implies a rejection of this very vital article of Hindu faith, and expresses the extreme adaptability of Hindu Dharma. To give one more example, Hindu women have entered every field of public life, from medicine to police and administration. Hindu society has accepted the public role of women, even though Manu and others have repeatedly affirmed that there should be no independence for women at any stage of their lives.[5]

We can appreciate the adaptability of the Hindu society even more when we compare the ease with which the Hindu society has allowed itself to be transformed by the forces of modernisation with the resistance offered to new liberal ideas by the Christian Church during the Renaissance. For example, Hindus have accepted all modern scientific theories, without ever feeling that their religion is threatened by them, while each new scientific doctrine was opposed vehemently by the Catholic Church in the West. The latter is still not ready to give its formal sanction to family planning and divorce. Till recently the Church in Kerala refused the right to inherit the family property to women. Both Muslims and Catholic Christians have persistently refused to adopt the idea of planned families on the plea that procreation or proliferation is commanded in their respective religious texts, and curtailing the size of the family goes against that command. But, as we have seen, a son is far more important for a Hindu than for a member of any other religious community. And yet, the Hindus are adopting family planning on a large scale, while other Indian religious groups are still reluctant to do so. Similarly, the Muslim society has persistently refused to accept any reforms in its personal law. While polygamy is strictly prohibited under the modern Hindu law, it is both practised and defended by modern Muslims in the name of religion. The immense opposition to the liberal court judgment in the Shah Bano case (granting a pittance to her by way of alimony) from all sections of the Muslim society expresses the unwillingness of the latter to adapt itself to the changing times.

(ii) It is usually argued here that Hinduism does not have either a central Church or a definite Book (religious text). Therefore, Hindus can adapt themselves to changing times, whereas the followers of prophetic religions are bound to obey their respective Churches and Books or creeds. True, Hinduism does not have a single religious text; but the Dharmaśāstras, especially the *Manusmṛti*, are unanimously regarded as authoritative in matters of *dharma* (socio-moral duties). The Lawgivers and the Hindu society in general have always expected strict adherence to the norms of conduct, as enunciated in the Dharmaśāstras and the traditions or customs of the society. Till recently one had to face social ostracism if one failed to adhere to all the taboos and customs of the society. And yet, despite the powerful religio-social sanction for old values and norms of conduct, the Hindu society has managed to welcome and assimilate new ways and values, some of which are quite contradictory to the traditional ones. The fact that new ways, laws and values have not invited any strong opposition from the more conservative elements of the Hindu society certainly proves the immense catholicity and adaptability of Hinduism.

III. The Concept of the Relativity of Dharma and the Possibility of Change

(i) Hinduism's immense adaptability stems from its faith in the relativity of man's *dharma* (duty) to place (*deśa*), time (*yuga*) and other relevant factors.[6] (See chapter III section I *supra.*) The *Mahābhārata* presents a strong case for the relativity of morals to place, time and the circumstances. It argues against accepting either Vedas or Smṛtis as unconditional authority for determining one's *dharma* (duty). It observes that Vedas or their injunctions and prohibitions have a rather limited scope and they cannot possibly cover all the eventualities of life. It then rightly points out that with the changing times, circumstances in peoples' lives also change, so that whatever was morally right in the earlier times may not be so in modern times. It goes so far as to say that there is no conduct or custom which is conducive to the good of all equally.[7] Therefore, onc's duty or *dharma* must be decided not on the basis of religious injunctions only, but on pragmatic considerations, after taking into account all the relevant factors of a given situation.

The *Smṛtikāras* (Law-givers) discuss the sources of *dharma* and cite the Vedas, Smṛtis and the conduct of righteous persons as the chief sources or criteria for determining men's duties, both religious and socio-moral. Manu asserts in the very beginning of his work that it deals with the sacred laws of Vedas and Smṛtis, as well as the norms of conduct (*ācāra*) followed by the four classes (*varṇas*). What is more, Manu seems to equate the three as the sources or authorities for determining the right mode of conduct.[8] Out of the three most important sources or criteria of *dharma* (duty), the Vedas are theoretically the supreme authority, then come the Smṛtis, and last of all the conduct of good people. But generally all the three are cited together as the sources or criteria of *dharma*.

Manu even seems to think that the conduct of the wise and good men of the society is the most important criterion for determining a man's duty or right course of conduct in life. Manu asserts quite early in his work:

"Learn that sacred law which is followed by men learned (in Vedas) and assented to in their hearts by the virtuous, who are ever exempt from hatred and inordinate affection."[9]

He repeats the same advice later on:

"Let him, untired, follow the conduct of the virtuous men, connected with his occupation, which has been declared in Vedas and Smṛtis and is the root of *dharma* (or is rooted in *dharma*)." And,

"Let him walk on that path of holy men which his fathers and grandfathers followed. While he walks on that he suffers no harm."[10]

The conduct of the wise men of society (*sadācāra*) is agreed to be a very important criterion to determine one's *dharma* (duty). According to Āpastamba:

"That is *dharma* (duty and virtue) the practice of which is praised by the wise men of the three upper classes; what they blame is sin.

"He shall regulate his course of action according to the conduct which in all countries is unanimously approved by men of the three twice-born classes, who are obedient, aged, of subdued senses, neither given to avarice, nor hypocrites."[11]

Hārīta explains the term *sadācāra* as derived from the root *sat*, and understands *sat* as meaning good. Good men (*sādhu*) are those who are devoid of any evil (moral defect); and the conduct of such good men is called *sadācāra*.[12] Thus, though theoretically the authority of Vedas and Smṛtis was supreme, the conduct and agreed opinions of the learned and righteous men of the society were given more importance in practical matters. Viśvarūpa even says that the Smṛtis should be followed only in those cases wherein they are in accordance with the agreed mode of ideal conduct of the good people (*śiṣṭa*) of the Aryan society.[13] Medhātithi goes a step further and says that since Dharmaśāstra is that which gives the knowledge of *dharma*, the conduct of the righteous persons (*śiṣṭācāra*) is also a kind of Dharmaśāstra or Smṛti.[14] Medhātithi further says that practices or norms of conduct which are approved by Smṛtis, but which are criticized by the good people of the community, or offend the moral sense of the people, such as the practice of *niyoga*, should not be regarded as authoritative.[15]

Theoretically, the standard or criterion of man's socio-moral conduct consists of the conduct followed by the morally upright persons (*sadācāra*). But mostly the prefix *sat* (good or right) was dropped, so that a man was simply advised to follow the customs (*ācāra*) of his community. Generally, the ancient Law-givers did not make any distinction between the two criteria, the conduct of good men (*sadācāra*) and custom (*ācāra*), probably because the latter was expected to be based on the former. Sometimes the relation was even reversed, and the conduct of good men was explained in terms of the customs of a given community.[16]

Āpastamba starts his work by distinguishing between two *dharmas* (duties), the ritualistic duties for which Vedas are the sole authority, and the social duties which have to be determined on the basis of the agreement (*samaya*) of learned men.[17] This agreement is expressed in the customs of a given country at a given time.

What are these customs which are to serve as the criterion for men's socio-moral conduct? Generally any usages or practices that are in vogue in a particular community and are old, that is, are handed down to the people by their forefathers, are accepted as standard for determining men's duties.[18] These customs are relative to various factors, such as place (*deśa*), time (*yuga*) and community. All Hindu Law-books point out that customs differ from one society or community to another. The difference in the conduct and customs of the peoples of the North and the South are often cited as an example of the relativity of customs to place (*deśa*).[19]

Generally, it is agreed among the Law-givers that whereas the Vedic injunctions regarding various Vedic rituals are universally authoritative, in other matters people should be left free to follow their respective customs. It is frankly recognized that Vedas cannot possibly cover all real life situations. Therefore, the injunctions of Vedas and the laws of Smṛtis should be supplemented by local customs. These customs should have authority in the absence of Vedic instructions in a particular case. A king is constantly advised to take into consideration the various customs of his people, while deciding legal matters. The customs which should be followed by the people and the king alike include those of the countries, classes (*varṇas*) and communities (*jātis*), as well as families (*kulas*).[20] The Law-books instruct a king that he should respect the customs (*ācāra* or *paraṁparā*) of the vanquished people and must not impose those of his people on them.[21] Yājñavalkya even says that the varying usages or conventions of guilds, traders and various associations or professional groups should be respected by a king in the same manner, as he respects the usages of brāhmaṇas.[22]

Two stipulations are added to this general rule. First, the *dharma* (here custom) of countries, castes or families has authority only if it is not opposed to the Vedas.[23] Secondly, such customs should be followed only by the people of that community in which they are in vogue; but if they are followed by people of other communities, then their practice becomes sinful.[24]

These customs or ideal modes of conduct are not only relative to place, but also to time. Hindu thinkers were very much aware of the power of time and the changes it brings in men and society, especially in the values and ways of a given people. Manu has specifically stated that the ideal conduct of men changes in the four legendary ages (*yugas*) of *Satya*, *Tretā*, *Dvāpara* and *Kali*.[25] It is asserted by the Law-givers that a conduct which may be alright for the people of early ages, such as *niyoga*, cannot be permitted in the present *Kali* age. (This perception led to innumerable ritualistic and often amoral prohibitions or taboos, called *kali-varjya*).[26]

In addition to the customs and ideal modes of conduct of good people which are expected to change according to place (*deśa*) and time (*yuga*), reason is also accepted as a criterion for determining the right course of action. A king is not only advised to respect the different customs of his subjects, he is also advised to use his discrimination or reason in deciding legal disputes, since an exclusive reliance on religious texts can defeat its own purpose and harm the interests of *dharma* (justice).[27] Significantly, Manu has added the satisfaction of one's heart (conscience) among the sources or criteria of *dharma*. He even asserts that in case of a conflict between the views of these different authorities, a man should take recourse to his reason to decide his course of conduct.[28] He adds that the pronouncements of good brāhmaṇs (*śiṣṭas*) should be accepted as authoritative in cases in which no definite rule from religious texts is available for guidance.[29] Of course, Manu was not able to consistently maintain his liberal position. But such passages do suggest that reason or conscience was acceptable to ancient thinkers as an authority in judging moral matters.

(ii) The above discussion must have proved that Hindu socio-moral thought acknowledges both the possibility and even the advisability of change in the mores (customs) of a society. The customs or concepts of the ideal mode of conduct and the values of a particular society change with changing times. And such changes can be easily accepted by the Hindu society, since some sort of sanction to that effect already exists in Hindu thought. Alternatively, when the elders or leaders of a community (*mahājana*) agree that the customs prevailing in their community should change, then the king (or the society) should recognize the changed customs and values. We have seen that Manu and other Law-givers have accepted the right of the elders or learned men of good conduct (*śiṣṭa*) to provide guidance to the society through new norms of conduct in two kinds of situations: first, in which no specific guidance is available in the ancient sacred laws, and second, in which the changed times and circumstances make it necessary that old norms should be rejected or modified, as in the case of the ancient sanction for the practice of *niyoga*. The present-day life is full of both kinds of situations in which old rules are either inapplicable or offend the moral sense of the modern man. All these situations require the modification or rejection of old norms of conduct and formulation of new ones. Hinduism seems to demand only that the new norms should come from men who are *śiṣṭas*, that is, are both learned and morally upright persons. Then only can we be sure that the new norms and values are worthy ones from a religio-moral point of view.

For Manu *et al* their age (about two millenniums ago) was the age of degeneration (*Kali-yuga*) which demanded stricter restrictions on man's socio-moral conduct and rejection of many of old practices. We in the present age may think the same, that is, may find our times as a period of moral crisis and may feel that the rules and regulations, put down by Manu and other Law-givers about two thousand years ago, are to be rejected (*varjya*) in our present age. And if we decide to do so, we would be strictly in accordance with the spirit, if not the letter, of Dharmaśāstras.

It may be that Manu and other Law-givers, who were highly conservative men from our standards, would not have approved the changes in old customs and values that a modern Hindu philosopher may propose. But their ancestors would have, in their turn, disapproved the drastic changes brought about by them in old values and customs. For example, we know that the ancient Hindus effected a revolutionary change in the Vedic rituals when they substituted the bloody Vedic sacrifices by new vegetarian sacrifices in which butter and grains were poured into fire.[30] Seeing that the Vedic *yajñas* enjoyed the highest prestige in the ancient society, and were clearly defined and determined by the Brāhmaṇas (texts), the substitution of the sacrifice of animals by simple oblations into fire in the Epic period was as revolutionary a change in Hindu Dharma, as has ever been attempted by any people in the world. If such a fundamental change in the very core of Hindu religion was accepted both by Hindu thinkers and priests, there is no reason to doubt that any changes suggested by modern Hindu thinkers would be unacceptable to the Hindu society, provided of course, they have intrinsic worth.

As we have seen in our previous section, Hindu society has accepted far-reaching social reforms through secular legislation. A major part of this civil legislation (Hindu Code Bill and the Bill against untouchability) goes against the grain of ancient Hindu laws and values. Their acceptance by the Hindu society expresses the basic Hindu perception that the socio-moral norms change with the times. To a Western observer the acceptance of civic reforms by the Hindu society may not seem extraordinary, since socio-moral matters are quite separate from religious concerns, and at least theoretically independent of religious authority, in Western thought. The tradition of distinguishing religious concerns from secular ones goes as far back as Christ himself.[31] But things are entirely different for Hindu Dharma. (See chapter I, section I and VI *supra.*) As we know, there is no separate word for religion in the Sanskrit language. Religion in the Western sense is called *mārga* (way) or *saṁpradāya* (sect). It is vaguely distinguished from, but integrally related to, the more comprehensive concept of *dharma.* And *dharma* comprehends or has authority over the entire life of a man. Dharmaśāstras are mainly concerned with regulating the life and conduct of men, but they also have supreme religious authority. It means that the acceptance of liberal reforms by the Hindu society is not due to the fact that secular concerns are independent of religious authority in the Hindu 'religio-culture'; but is rather due to the inherent catholicity of Hinduism that makes allowance for necessary changes in socio-moral norms and customs with the change in times and circumstances.

IV. Some Inner Tensions in the Hindu Thought

There is no doubt that Hindu Dharma is a very complex and unsystematic whole which comprehends and unifies, even though in a very general way, several religio-philosophical and valuational approaches. (See chapter I, section I *supra.*) There was a continuous interaction between these different religio-philosophical traditions. Hinduism is a product of that interaction and contains ideas and values which originated in quite different cultural milieus, and hence are not always mutually compatible. At the same time, though some of the inconsistencies of Hinduism can be traced to divergent religio-philosophical traditions, many have their origin in one and the same Vedic tradition. Thus, the Vedāntic philosophy, though a creation of the Vedic Aryans, goes against several very important contentions of its parent tradition.

(i) The Vedāntic vision of one 'Divine' indwelling all living beings is contrary to the insistence on innate differences between, and basic inequality of, all men in the Vedic-Dharmaśāstric tradition. At the philosophical level, the assumption of the inequality of men is sought to be justified on the basis of the law of karma which traces these inequalities of the present life to the actions of different selves in their past lives. (See chapter III, section II *supra*.) There is nothing wrong in the recognition of differences between man and man, but the assertion of basic inequality of all men is another matter. This assertion seems natural in the context of such ancient civilizations, as the Greek and the Roman, which frankly advocated the essential inequality of all men and practised slavery. But it is very incongruous in the Indian context, because it totally contradicts the Vedāntic vision of the Divine Self indwelling all beings. The stratification of the society into innumerable castes and sub-castes is very much in harmony with the Vedic-Dharmaśāstric ethos, but entirely inconsistent with the Vedāntic vision. The tension between the two sets of beliefs is all the more remarkable in view of the fact that both of them belong to the Vedic tradition.

As we have seen (vide chapter IV, section VIII *supra*), Śaṁkara has declared the universal Self to be beyond all caste distinctions and other empirical qualifications. He has further asserted that since all individual selves are identical with the supreme Self, there is no metaphysical basis for distinguishing one self from another.[32] And yet, the same Śaṁkara not only denies the right to practise the Vedic Dharma to śūdras, he also recommends cruelest punishment to that unfortunate man who dares to overstep his limitations.[33] Śaṁkara's views are the best example of the self-inconsistency of the Hindu approach.

(ii) Even though the Vedānta originated in Vedas, both its metaphysics and moral approach are essentially different from the Vedic-Dharmaśāstric tradition. Above all, the Vedāntic approach is at variance with the Vedic polytheism and ritualism. All Vedāntic schools, whether belonging to the tradition of liberation or devotion, affirm the immanence of the 'Divine' in all hearts, as well as the importance of the inner spirit, as against the outer acts, in both religion and morality. The Vedic Polytheism and ritualism are entirely contrary to the above approach. It is the properly performed ritual that brings the reward, and both righteousness (*dharma*) and evil or sin (*adharma*) mainly refer to external ritualistic acts. Moral qualifications or the purity of the heart are not much relevant in one's religion which largely consists in the performance of various rituals. Now, Hindus have accepted both the traditions. They believe in the Divine Self indwelling all beings, and then go and worship innumerable gods in temples and under trees! They also believe in the worth of the inner spirit, and then very carefully perform various rituals, or take baths in the holy rivers to wash off their sins, without ever bothering about the essential contradiction between the two beliefs.

(iii) At least one important inconsistency of Hinduism can be explained on the basis of the fact that Hinduism has absorbed the ethoses of two opposing religio-philosophical traditions, without seeking to synthesize them. The reference here, of course, is to the polytheistic, ritualistic, world-and-life-affirming and relatively more socio-centric Vedic-Dharmaśāstric tradition and the transcendentalist, world-and-life-negating and liberation-centric tradition of the schools of philosophy. As a result, almost every aspect of Hindu Dharma (its religion, philosophy and morality) is bi-polar, that is, consists of two almost divergent view-points and valuational approaches. (See chapter I, sections II and III *supra.*) That is why we find that on the one hand, Hindus desire and cherish worldly goods and prosperity; on the other, they constantly talk of the transience of all worldly objects and futility of all mundane pursuits. On the one hand, they affirm and actually try to fulfil their socio-moral responsibilities, especially towards their families; on the other, they venerate the renunciant most who has abandoned all his worldly tics and socio-moral responsibilities. Similarly, the virtues of magnanimity and manliness, cherished in the first tradition, are in sharp contrast to the more saintly virtues like self-control and equanimity of the second tradition. And Hindus cherish both sets of virtues.

(iv) Another related tension within Hinduism is between its socio-centric and self-centric tendencies. We have assumed that the Vedic-Dharmaśāstric tradition is socio-centric, while the tradition of liberation is self-centric. To a certain extent this assumption is true. The law of karma is one single factor, most responsible for the self-centric tendency of the Hindu ethos.

(See chapter I, section V and chapter IV, section III *supra.*) The theory of karma and transmigratory existence engenders extreme individualism. In all probability, the theory was initially developed in heterodox circles. At the same time, the tension between the socio-centric and self-centric tendencies within Hinduism goes much deeper than the simple polarity suggested by us. Though the Dharmaśāstric morality is definitely socio-centric, the polytheism and ritualism of this tradition, especially of Vedas and popular Hinduism, is quite self-centric. V.M. Apte has pointed out that all Vedic sacrifices were performed at the individual level, and there were no temples or public places of worship in the Vedic times.[34] Popular Hindu religion is positively self-centric in the simple sense that most persons following popular religion are solely motivated by the selfish desire for personal gain. Now, this self-centric tendency of Vedic and popular ploytheism goes against the definite socio-centric stance of the Dharmaśāstras. A certain tension between the two valuational approaches is present throughout Hinduism.

(v) The law of karma is very basic to the entire Hindu religio-moral thought. It is also responsible for two inner contradictions of Hindu thought and practice. First, the hypothesis of karma and transmigratory existence presupposes plurality and isolated existence of individual souls who are entirely unrelated to one another. This view goes directly against the Vedāntic monism which is very basic to the Hindu faith. The latter categorically affirms the Divine Absolute (*Ātman-Brahman*) to be the Self of all beings, and implicity denies the separate or independent existence of individual souls.

The law of karma which emphasizes the aloneness of individual souls also goes against the spirit of the Vedic tradition which believes in the solidarity of all men. Above all, a very special bond is supposed to exist between parents and progeny in the Vedic-Dharmaśāstric tradition. Manu expresses this idea by saying that a father is born again in the son.[35] The funeral rites (*śrāddha*), as we know (vide chapter II, section I *supra*), are an essential part of the Vedic-Dharmaśāstric religion, and presuppose this solidarity or continuity between parents and progeny. The entire group of funeral rites, even though it is a later innovation, is harmoniously related to the Vedic ethos. The

Vedic ritualistic tradition emphasizes the correct performance of the external act more than the inner spirit, and believes that the fruits of rituals performed by the priests can be reaped by the host (*yajamāna*). Similarly, the belief in and the practice of funeral rites means that the rites performed by a man's son(s) can help him in the other world and secure a long stay in heaven for him.

On the other hand, the theory of karma judges the moral worth of an action on the basis of inner spirit or motive. It also emphasizes the moral accountability of the individual for all his actions (*karmas*) and asserts that a man cannot escape the results of his actions. No amount of rituals can alter his lot which is determined by the moral quality of his own actions. The law of karma is an extremely individualistic hypothesis which asserts that no man can ever help another and that every man has to work out his destiny alone.[36] This belief thus completely denies the possibility of the ancestors benefiting from the funeral rites performed by their son(s). Moreover, while the practice of funeral rites presupposes that the ancestors keep on waiting in the other world to be benefited by the rites performed by their son(s) and grandson(s),[37] the theory of karma and transmigratory existence asserts that the soul immediately relates itself to another body here on earth itself.[38] The ontology and moral approach of the law of karma are so diametrically opposed to those implied in the practice of funeral rites,[39] that it is a wonder that Hindus have been able to cling to both beliefs-cum-practices for so long.

(vi) There is a definite ambivalence in the Hindu thinkers' attitude towards women. (See chapter III, section V *supra.*) We find passages condemning and adulating women in all Hindu religious texts. Sometimes completely opposite views are given in one and the same text. Take the *Manusmṛti* for example. It contains the famous passages declaring the mother to be the supreme object of reverence and hailing the positive role of women in ensuring the welfare of the family.[40] Manu is also the author of those infamous passages which denounce women as lustful and degenerate creatures.[41] There are even more glaring inconsistencies. While Manu admits the practice of *niyoga* in some passages,[42] he declares such a practice as unthinkable, immoral and highly objectionable in others.[43] Manu has affirmed at one place that the murder of a woman is as grave an offence as that of a *brāhmaṇa* or a child.[44] But on another occasion he has included the murder of an (adulterous) woman of any class under minor sins.[45] Now, it is reasonable to suppose that some of these views might be interpolations. But the fact that none of the learned commentators of the *Manusmṛti* during the middle ages noted these contradictions is significant. The attempt to explain the inconsistencies in the Hindu approach towards women by assigning the conflicting views to different writers or different times would not help us, as all the conflicting views are found in each of the numerous religious texts! For example, the *Yājñavalkya Smṛti* contains all the usual cliches about the purity of women, the immense respectability of mother, as well as the advice to guard all women, since they are lustful, frivolous creatures![46]

V. Some Suggestions For A Reconstruction of the Hindu Philosophy of Morals

We have observed above: i. that Hinduism is an immensely dynamic and adaptable 'religio-culture'; ii. that it has a strong tradition which sanctions changes in the socio-moral norms in accordance with the needs of changed times or circumstances; and iii. that it contains several pairs of beliefs and practices which are mutually inconsistent. The first two observations give us hope that any desirable changes in the ancient values and norms, suggested by modern Hindu thinkers, would not be rejected by the Hindu society. They also put a great responsibility upon our philosophers who can, if they so choose, give a right direction to the ever-changing Hindu Dharma. The last, i.e. the presence of several inconsistencies within Hindu thought, suggests the possibility and scope for a reconstruction of the Hindu philosophy of morals.

In order to attempt a critical reconstruction of Hindu thought, the modern philosopher would have to reaffirm or emphasize those perceptions or values of Hinduism which are more in harmony with our modern values and sensibilities, and oppose or reject others which are incompatible with our modern ones. There need not be any misgiving that such a reconstruction would result in a total transformation or loss of identity of Hindu

Dharma. Hinduism does not give a *carte blanche* for change in its philosophy or morality. It has a vision or philosophy which must form the nucleus of any future reconstruction of Hindu philosophy of morals.

The proposed reconstruction of the Hindu philosophy of morals would consist of several related steps or tasks. It would include a reassertion of certain basic Hindu beliefs and values, a rejection of those beliefs, values and practices which go against these basic beliefs, an attempt at synthesizing those beliefs and values which are found to be worth-while, but mutually inconsistent, and development of some other ideas which have been only vaguely suggested in Hindu thought, but can be useful for a philosophy of morals. A philosopher attempting to reconstruct such a philosophy may either start by first selecting and rationally presenting those basic ideas of Hinduism which have intrinsic worth, or he may take up various beliefs and values of Hinduism and notice the inconsistencies or tensions between them, compare and contrast them, and then select those ideas which have intrinsic value and are basic to the Hindu ethos. We have opted for the second kind of approach, while suggesting below some tasks for our philosopher.

(i) The first step towards a reconstruction of the Hindu philosophy of morals would be to challenge the organization of the society on the basis of hereditary castes and the practice of untouchability. Both have so far enjoyed strong religious sanction, but are at the same time contrary to the basic Vedāntic vision of one universal Self in all beings. Any modern philosopher can legitimately question the practice of untouchability and caste discriminations by reasserting the basic Vedāntic faith and pointing out the glaring contradiction involved in the Hindu faith and practice. Not only the Upaniṣads, all other religious texts have unanimously and emphatically affirmed the metaphysical unity of all living beings. (See chapter VI, section IV *supra.*) The *Bhagavadgītā* proclaims that the real yogin or devotee is the one who sees one Self or the Lord in all living beings and looks upon all in the image of oneself.[47] The *Mahābhārata* repeatedly points out that the self or life (*prāṇa*) is the same in all living beings.[48] All the *bhakta* saints insist on the 'Divine' indwelling all beings, which makes all beings equally divine or sacred.[49]

Moreover, all Hindu philosophic systems believe in the duality of self and body, and assert the transcendent nature of the self. If so, class distinctions cannot pertain to the inner self, as they are supposed to pertain to the body. But they cannot belong to the body either. The thinkers of the tradition of liberation have given very vivid descriptions of the loathsome constituents of the body, such as blood, bone, urine etc. It is also agreed that the bodies of all living beings consist of the same five basic elements (*pañcatattva*); and nowhere is there any suggestion for any basic biological difference between man and man. Kabīr concludes that all men are born same and the differences between them are man-made and artificial.[50]

There is no philosophic justification in Hinduism for discrimination against large sections of the society. Mostly the law of karma is implicitly accepted as providing a pseudo-justification for such unjust practices. The law of karma is very basic to Hindu thought, and cannot be rejected, or even questioned in its totality. The future philosopher of Hinduism, therefore, would have to seek to understand and present this belief in its original moral context, as implying: first, the moral responsibility of the individual, and second, the moral order of the world which ensures that every evil is punished and every suffering is compensated in the end. It was only gradually that the law of karma became an ally of the practice of class discriminations. The two should be delinked now, so that no semblance of justification remains for the above social evils.

(ii) The second task of our moral philosopher would be to challenge the strong alliance between polytheism and ritualism at the popular level. Both go back to the Vedas and are the major ingredients, or rather constitute the whole, of popular Hinduism. So we can hardly hope that the writings of a few philosophers would break their hold over the masses. Yet we think that the two beliefs-cum-practices have very unhealthy ramifications for morality, and every effort should be made to emancipate Hinduism from their overwhelming influence. First, both polytheism and ritualism, implying the faith in the self-efficacy of rituals, are highly irrational and dogmatic, and definitely undermine a rational approach to life and morality. We feel that genuine morality can exist only at the rational level, and hence both polytheism and ritualism are detrimental to morality. Secondly, both beliefs are equally detrimental to human effort (*puruṣārtha*). Faith in the availability of gods' help and the efficacy of rituals kills all incentive for effort for achieving one's goals, sometimes with disastrous effects. (To give just one example, children used to die for want of medical care in cases of the disease of pox which is even now supposed to be the result of the wrath of some goddess.) Thirdly, since the one term *dharma* means both ritualistic and moral duties in Hinduism, the prevalence of a very strong ritualistic tradition has confused the moral perspective of Hindus. It has also resulted in a tendency to be satisfied with the performance of some ritualistic acts as a substitute for genuine socio-moral duties (such as throwing some food on the ground to feed all living beings in the daily sacrifice of *Balivaiśvadeva*). Such ritualistic substitutes permanently undermine genuine moral consciousness of one's responsibilities towards one's fellow beings. Fourthly, both, belief in various gods and the practice of various rituals, are undertaken in a spirit of business transaction, i.e. with an express motive to get some specific personal desire fulfilled thereby. Since there is no marked difference between ritualistic and moral duties in Hinduism, the attitude associated with ritualism is usually transferred to socio-moral matters, thus undermining the very basis of morality. Fifthly, and possibly most importantly, both polytheism and ritualistic practices directly undermine a moral approach to life and religion, in that no moral qualification is required for the worship of gods or the practice of rituals. A man can expect to receive a boon from a god if he carries out a ritual or a ritualistic vow (*vrata*) in the specified manner; and this is ensured irrespective of whether the man deserves the boon or not. (See chapter II, section I and IV *supra*.) Therefore every effort must be made to emancipate the Hindu society from the overwhelming and amoral influence of polytheism and ritualism.

A Hindu thinker can seriously challenge Hindu polytheism by a reassertion of the Vedāntic theism, as enunciated in the devotional sects. The theism of the devotional sects is rooted in the Vedāntic monism, and is highly respected among the Hindu masses. True religion, for the *Bhakti* sects, consists in one-pointed devotion to the supreme God. This devotion is at the same time integrally related to the practice of highest moral virtues. Vedāntic theism, thus, both contradicts and undermines Hindu polytheism and provides a very convincing justification for a profound morality. We are here not oblivious of the possible negative socio-moral ramifications of common theism, such as intolerance, fanaticism and fundamentalism. But Vedāntic theism does not generally lend itself to fanatical tendencies.

(iii) There are certain beliefs and valuational attitudes in Hinduism, none of which can be rejected, even though they seem to be mutually contradictory, since both of them have intrinsic worth. Thus, the third task of our ethical philosopher would be not to choose out of, but to reconcile, the world-and-life-affirmation of the Vedic-Dharmaśāstric tradition with the devaluation of the world and life in the tradtion of liberation. At first glance it would appear that we must altogether reject the perceptions and values of the tradition of liberation, as they seem to go against both, the interests of social morality and modern perceptions or ways. And by the same argument we must adopt the philosophy and values of the Vedic-Dharmaśāstric tradition which are much more in consonance with modern values and ways. But such a choice would not only be false to the synthetic Hindu ethos, it would also be harmful to the interests of morality. A certain amount of world-and-life-negation gives depth and profundity to the world-view and approach of a society. This is especially needed in the modern times as a corrective to the extreme materialism of the West. Large sections of the Hindu society have unconditionally accepted Western materialism and whatever else goes with it, e.g. selfish, individualistic pursuit of one's interests, violence and rejection of one's socio-moral obligations and all traditional Hindu values. This has given rise to a strange hybrid culture in Indian cities which misses the good points of both ethoses, Indian and Western. Hence there is the need to develop a more rational and milder version of Hindu world-and-life-negation and synthesize it with the positive or affirmative ethos of its original Vedic tradition.

(iv) A similar synthetic approach must be adopted towards the socio-centric and the self-centric tendencies within Hinduism. The choice here seems to be even more obvious in favour of the socio-centric stance of the Vedic-Dharmaśāstric tradition, as against the apparent self-centric tendencies of the tradition of liberation. But again, this would be a wrong choice for two reasons: first, because the Vedic-Dharmaśāstric polytheism and ritualism also have a strong self-centric tendency, and secondly, because they emphasize the external act more than the inner spirit, and hence cannot provide us with a worthy moral code. On the other hand, the tradition of liberation advocates a profounder moral approach. It emphasizes the value of purity of heart and such virtues as self-control, fortitude, forgiveness and non-violence. These virtues form a very important part of any comprehensive moral ideal, and are even more important in the present-day Hindu society which seems to have forgotten even the meaning of self-control and non-violence. Now, we cannot accept the virtues advocated in the tradition of liberation without imbibing a certain amount of world-and-life-negation of this tradition.

A modern Hindu ethical philosophy would definitely include the world-and-life-affirmation of, and the emphasis on the discharge of one's socio-moral obligations in, the Dharmaśāstric tradition. It would, at the same time, seek to reconcile the above with the perceptions and values of the second tradition. A certain synthesis of the two valuational approaches is already achieved in the *Bhagavadgītā's* ideal of desireless performance of one's duties and the Dharmaśāstric concept of an ideal householder who performs all his socio-moral duties with immense self-control and equanimity.[51]

The task before our philosopher, therefore, is not the simple one of choosing one of the two ethoses, but of synthesizing them. While reformulating a Hindu philosophy of morals, our philosopher would be required to emphasize those values and moral perceptions which are in accordance with the more liberal values of modern times, and reject the others. At the same time, he would have to judge the modern Western values in the context of the basic Hindu philosophy and valuational approach. This would require him to affirm some of those values which may not be fully in tune with the modern Western ones, but which are basic to the Hindu vision and approach, such as contentment, detachment and equanimity. These virtues or values would understandably be presented in a milder form in our modern synthetic Hindu philosophy of morals.

(v) Another task of our philosopher of Hindu morality would be to develop or clearly formulate certain vaguely presented ideas of Hindu social thought. The Dharmaśāstras contain some valuable ideas in seed form which should be properly developed in the context of modern conditions. First such idea is the ancient concept of man's owing debts to various sections of the society which can be repaid only by discharging various socio-moral obligations towards others. The concept is an extremely valuable one and should be emphasized in modern times, when the individual's rights have become the basis of all socio-moral thought and practice.

Another such morally relevant idea is the accountability of the individual for his moral conduct to the society. We know that this concept has often been misused to exploit the poor masses in the Hindu society. Admittedly, there is always the possibility of its misuse in the hands of powerful, but unscrupulous, men in any society. Still, the idea in itself is a worthy one and must be developed with proper safeguards. This idea of the individual's answerability to the society for his moral conduct goes directly against the modern principle of individual's life and conduct being his own personal concern. We do not agree with this latter view, that is, we believe that the individual's life and conduct necessarily affect the happiness or otherwise of other persons around him. To give an example, marriage and divorce are regarded in modern thought as the exclusive concern of the individual partners. But they do influence the happiness and the life or lot of other members of the family, especially the children. And they indirectly influence the entire society through those persons who are thus affected. A casual glance at the insecurity, unrest and frustration felt by the members of broken homes would prove the wisdom of Hindu perceptions. None of the ancient ideas need be accepted as such. Rather, they have to be carefully modified in accordance with the modern emphasis on the individual's right to lead one's own life. As we see it, a reasonable synthesis of the above two points of view, the Hindu and the modern Western, is both possible and desirable.

Though the Dharmaśāstric idea of man's indebtedness

towards other members of the society is an invaluable asset for any philosophy of morals, the Hindu concept of society is very vague and narrow, and must be suitably modified. It mostly refers to the limited community in the immediate neighbourhood of the individual, largely organized on the basis of caste, community or region, which has resulted in the division of society into innumerable segmented groups. This suggests the failure of Hindu thinkers in developing a wider and morally more relevant concept of society. We must reject all these limiting divisions and affirm the concept of nation-society. The individual's loyalties and responsibilities should no more be limited to his immediate community, but must be directed to the society as a whole. The very survival of the highly segmented Indian society depends on the rejection of these narrow loyalties by its members in favour of a direct and sole loyalty towards the society as a whole.

(vi) Our moral philosopher would be further required to reconcile the contradictory attitudes of Hindu society towards women, one idealizing them as mothers and partners in life, the other denouncing them as frivolous and lustful. (See chapter III, section V *supra.*) It seems to us that the forces of change have been too strong for the Hindu society, rendering both the traditional attitudes irrelevant in modern times. Our liberated women would not only scoff at the ancient depreciation of women, but also at the idea of being idealized and protected as mothers or masters of hearth and home.

The image of woman as mother is a deep-rooted archetype in the Hindu psyche and represents the deepest sentiments and values of the original Hindu (Vedic) ethos. Any new role of woman which seeks to question this image or role would be unacceptable to the Hindus. As we have seen (vide chapter III, section VI *supra*), family is the pivot round which a man's entire life revolves in the Hindu society. It is also the training ground for a comparatively high standard of inter-personal morality. Women are traditionally given a central role in the family life. If women's role in the family is disturbed due to the forces of modernization, it would result in the de-stabilization of the family structure and eventually of the society as a whole. It means that the role of woman in the family has to be duly acknowledged in modern Hindu social thought. All other atavistic values or ideas concerning women, their nature and place in the society are to be rejected outright; and we are sure that this rejection would be acceptable to the Hindu masses. Thus, the task of a modern philosopher would not be so much to reconcile the opposing views regarding women in ancient thought, most of which have to be rejected, as to seek to reconcile the traditional role of women with the role of the modern 'liberated' women in the society.

(vii) The above process of comparing, contrasting and rejecting various ideas of Hindu religio-moral thought would lead our thinker to certain ideas and values which are basic to the entire Hindu Dharma. More importantly, these ideas and values have immense intrinsic worth and must be incorporated into, or form the basis of, a reconstructed Hindu philosophy of morals. It would, therefore, be the final task of our philosopher to select, develop and emphasize these basic principles. The first such idea is the old Vedic vision regarding the ultimate Truth being one, even though it is called by many names.[52] It recognizes the transcendence and infinity of the ultimate Reality and contends that no human account, insofar as it seeks to put determinate labels on the 'Infinite' and the 'Indeterminable', can exhaust the mystery of the 'Transcendent'. At the same time, every religion possesses some glimpse of Him (It) and should be respected as such. Hinduism thus teaches mankind universal tolerance, a tolerance which does not express the ego of being the chosen people of God, and which means respect for, and being receptive to, all other religious faiths. Since of all world religions, it is Hinduism (along with other religions of Indian origin) which alone possesses this tradition of universal tolerance, it is Hinduism alone that can convincingly argue for it before mankind. The Hindu faith that one Reality can be apprehended in many ways, implying the intrinsic worth of various religions, is not appreciated by Western critics. Their lack of appreciation stems from their conviction that their own religion is the supreme and cannot thus be equated with other 'degenerate' religions. The naivety of the entire approach is too obvious to need any rejoinder.

Unfortunately, the modern Indian society is being torn apart by communal conflicts. Hindu fanaticism, which sometimes goes under the curious name of Hindu nationalism, is rather a recent development. Of course, it cannot be understood in isolation, that is, it is to be understood in the context of similar fanatical activities of other religious communities. But while the fanaticism of other religious communities may lessen the guilt of Hindu masses indulging in aggresively chauvinistic activities, it increases the responsibility of Hindu thinkers who can very well see the inconsistency in the Hindu approach. We cannot see how any fanaticism can breed in a 'religio-culture' for which tolerance or respect for all faiths is mandatory. It seems to us that a Hindu society which affirms the oneness of the ultimate Truth and then allows aggressive activities against other religious communities is a contradiction in terms. Hinduism cannot preserve its identity by merely projecting Vedic and other rituals and forsaking its basic vision. Only when the Hindu society is convinced of this vision can it convince other religious communities. It is now the responsibility of Hindu thinkers to present the Hindu vision of all religions being different ways of arriving at one ultimate Truth in a rational and convincing manner to the Indian people. Once it is consciously accepted by them, it would provide a rationale and a motive for the practice of universal tolerance and good will.

The Vedāntic vision of the Divine Absolute being the source and essence or Self of the entire creation and all living beings is the second most important Hindu idea that must be rationally presented and emphasized by a modern Hindu thinker. It is closely related to the Vedic vision of oneness of ultimate Truth. In the context of a Hindu philosophy of morals, there would be no need to go into the metaphysical details of the Vedāntic monism; a simple affirmation of the 'Divine' indwelling all beings is all that is required. Such an assertion may sound dogmatic and mystical to a modern philosopher. It may also be contended here that ethics need not depend on dogmatic metaphysical assertions for its justification. But we think that some kind of ontological beliefs, whether asserted explicitly or accepted implicitly, are always presupposed by a philosophy of morals. (See chapter I, section I *supra.*) It should also be remembered that we are attempting here the Hindu philosophy of morals, and not a philosophy of morals. The Vedāntic assertion of the

Divine immanence in all living beings, implying the essential unity or even identity of all selves, is the most basic assumption of such a philosophy. And as pointed out by Paul Deussen (*vide* chapter VI, section IV *supra*), this assertion of all selves being essentially the same gives the most convincing justification for an inter-personal morality of the highest order. In a beautiful passage of *Viṣṇu Purāṇa* (*vide* chapter V, section III *supra*), it is stated that since the same Divine Being is the essence or Self of all living beings, He is the object of all our inter-personal dealings. That is to say, if a man loves another, he loves the universal Self; and if he perpetrates violence against another, it is the Self who is the real object of that violence.[53] If we compare it with the saying of Christ, that a man who helps and serves his fellow beings serves Christ, and he who rejects another man in need of help and succour rejects Him,[54] we would be able to appreciate that a vision of the metaphysical affinity of all living beings can alone provide a genuine basis for a morality of love and compassion for all living beings.

The ideal of non-violence (*ahiṁsā*) is another fundamental principle of Hinduism (and all religions of Indian origin). It is closely related to the above vision. Even the Buddhists, who do not believe in a substantial self, appeal to the principle of the essential affinity of all living beings for a rational justification of the ideal of universal non-violence and compassion. As we know (*vide* chapter VI, section III *supra*), non-violence is not a negative virtue, rather it implies a positive attitude of compassion and concern for others, and a perception of all beings in the image of one's self. Only recently, Mahatma Gandhi adopted non-violence, along with truth, as his central creed and guiding principle in his socio-political crusades. He even succeeded in persuading the entire nation to adopt the principle of non-violence in its struggle for freedom.

Violence erupted on an unprecedented mass scale in Mahatma's lifetime itself, and his violent death may be a symbol of the victory of violence over non-violence and all traditional values in modern India. Violence is on the increase in the Indian sub-continent, as elsewhere in the world. It seems to have become the creed of large sections of Indian society. It is evident everywhere, whether in the form of communal riots, caste conflicts, terrorist activities, or aggressive violent campaigns for chauvinistic demands on the part of some regional, linguist or other such group(s). If this increasing tendency to adopt violence as a means to achieve one's socio-political goals is not checked immediately, it would engulf and destroy the entire society. The onus of presenting the ideal of non-violence in such a way that it becomes a strong intellectual force which can counter the creed of violence rests with the Hindu thinkers. The ideal of non-violence would be much more convincing, if it is presented in the right context of the perception of the metaphysical affinity of all human beings.

Perhaps a few thinkers alone cannot either mitigate the frenzy of violence that has gripped the Indian society in recent times, or eradicate various other evils of the Hindu society. The causes of these evils or a general rejection of moral norms by large sections of the Hindu society are very complex, and most of them have nothing to do with the influence of Hinduism. At the same time, ideas have tremendous potential power. If presented correctly, they can become powerful forces which can determine the course of events or transform the face of a society. We believe that if certain basic ideas and values of Hindu Dharma are presented to the Hindu society in a rational and convincing manner, they would definitely sooner or later have a positive influence on the socio-moral values and conduct of the people. It is now the responsibility of the Hindu thinkers to give right direction and guidance to the Indian people (including Hindus). The task, though difficult, is not an impossible one.

Notes

1. *M.S.* V. 155-162.
2. *Bṛhad. Up.* VI. 2. 13; VI. 4. 1-6.
3. *M.S.* IX. 4, 88-90; *Gaut. D.S.* XVIII. 21-23.
4. *M.S.* III. 274; IX. 137-138.
5. Ibid V. 147-149; IX. 2-3.
6. The writer is indebted to P.V. Kane for the following discussion. See *History* (1973), vol. III, pp. 856 ff.
7. *Mbh. Śān.P.* CCLII. 7-19.
8. *M.S.* I. 107-108; II. 6-8.
9. Ibid II. 1.

10. Ibid IV. 155, 178.
11. *Āpast. D.S.* I. 7. 20. 7-8.
12. *Hārīta Saṁhitā*, quoted in History , vol. III, p. 856.
13. Commentary on *Yājñ.S.* III. 250, quoted in ibid, vol. III, p. 874.
14. Commentary on *M.S.* II. 10, quoted in ibid, vol. III, p. 874.
15. Commentary on *M.S.* IV. 176, quoted in ibid, vol. III, p. 874.
16. *M.S.* II. 18.
17. *Āpast. D.S.* I. 1. 1. 1-2.
18. *Kātyāyana Smṛti*, quoted in op. cit., vol. III, p. 862; *M.S.* II. 18.
19. *Baudhāyana Dharma Sūtra* I. 1. 19-26, quoted in op. cit., vol. III, p. 858.
20. *Gaut. D.S.* XI. 20-22, cf. *Vasiṣṭha Dharma Sūtra* I. 17, quoted in op. cit., vol. III, p. 857.
21. *M.S.* VII. 203; *Yājñ.S.* I. 343.
22. *Yājñ.S.* II. 192.
23. *Gaut. D.S.* XI. 20.
24. *Baudhāyana Dharma Sūtra* I. 1. 24-26, quoted in op. cit., vol. III, p. 858.
25. *M.S.* I. 84-86.
26. See *History*, vol. III, pp. 874, 885 ff.
27. *Bṛhaspati Smṛti*, quoted in ibid, vol. III, p. 867; cf. *Gaut. D.S.*XI.23.
28. *M.S.* II. 8; XII. 106.
29. Ibid XII. 108.
30. *Mbh. Śān.P.* CCLV. 6; CCLVII. 4 ff.
31. *Matthew* 22: 21.
32. *Ś.B., Br.S.*, introd.; I. 1-4; *Ś.B., Bṛhad. Up.* II.1.20.
33. *Ś.B., Br.S.* I. 3. 34-38.
34. *The Cultural Heritage of India* (1975), vol. I, p. 245.
35. *M.S.* IX. 8.
36. Ibid IV. 239 ff.
37. Ibid II. 274-275; IX. 137-138.
38. *Bṛhad. Up.* IV. 3. 35-36; *B.G.* II. 13, 22.
39. See *History* (1974), vol. IV, p. 335.
40. *M.S.* II. 145; III. 55 ff.; IX. 95 ff.
41. Ibid IX. 13 ff.
42. Ibid IX. 59-63.
43. Ibid IX. 64-68.
44. Ibid XI. 191.
45. Ibid XI. 139.
46. *Yājñ.S.* I. 71-72; I. 85.
47. *B.G.* VI. 29-32.
48. *Mbh. Śān.P.*, CCLI. 19 ff.; CCLIV. 25 ff.; CCCVIII. 126; *Anuś.P.* CXVI. 20-22; CXVII. 18 ff.
49. *Bhāg.P.*, bk. III, ch. 29, (1973, vol. I, pp. 264-265); bk. VII, ch. 7, (p. 647); bk. XI, ch. 29, (vol. II, pp. 475-476).
50. *The Bījak* of *Kabīr* (1986), pp. 55, 67, 69-70.
51. *B.G.* II. 47 ff.; III. 5 ff.; IV. 18 ff.; V. 3 ff.; *M.S.* IV. 138 ff., IV. 171 ff.
52. *Ṛg Veda* I. 164.
53. *Viṣṇu Purāṇa*, bk. III, ch.8, (1972, p. 264).
54. *Matthew* 25: 36 ff.

BIBLIOGRAPHY

Original Works Cited

Āpastamba Dharmasūtra
tr. by George Bühler
The Sacred Books of the East, vol. II,
The Sacred Laws of the Aryans, part I,
Delhi: Motilal Banarsidass, 1975

Aṣṭāvakra Saṁhitā
tr. by Swami Nityaswarupananda,
Calcutta: Advaita Ashrama, 1969

The Bhagavadgītā
ed. and tr. by S. Radhakrishnan,
New Delhi: Blackie & Son, 1977

Bhāgavata Purāṇa or The Śrīmad Bhāgavatam (two vols.)
tr. by J.M. Sanyal
Delhi: Munshiram Manoharlal, 1973

Gautama Dharmasūtra
tr. by George Bühler,
The Sacred Books of the East, vol. II,
The Sacred Laws of the Āryans, Part I,
Delhi: Motilal Banarsidass: 1975

Kauṭilya,
Arthaśāstra
tr. by R. Shamasastry,
Mysore: Mysore Printing and Publishing House, 1967

Kabīr,
The Bijak of Kabir,
tr. by Linda Hess and Sukhdev Singh,
Delhi: Motilal Banarsidass, 1986
One Hundred Poems of Kabīr,
tr. by Rabindra Nath Tagore and Evelyn Underhill,
Delhi: Macmillan India, 1985

Laghu Yoga Vāsiṣṭha
tr. by K. Narayanaswami Aiyer,
Madras: The Adyar Library and Research Centre, 1980

Madhusūdana Sarasvatī on the Bhagavadgītā (*Gītā-bhāṣya*)
tr. by Sisir Kumar Gupta,
Delhi: Motilal Banarsidass, 1977

Mahābhārata
Hindi transl., ed. by Damodar Satvalekar, (15 vols.) based on the original Sanskrit text, edited and published by Bhandarkar Oriental Research Institute, Poona.
Paradi: Svādhyāya Maṇḍal, 1968

Mahānārāyaṇopaniṣad
ed. and tr. by Swami Vimalananda,
Madras: Sri Ramakrishna Math, 1979

Manusmṛti—The Laws of Manu,
ed. and tr. by G. Bühler,
The Sacred Books of the East, vol. XXV,
Delhi: Motilal Banarsidass, 1982

Mīmāṁsā Sūtra, Śabara Bhāṣya, (2 vols)
Hindi transl. by Yudhisthira,
Bahalgarh, 1977

Nārada Bhakti Sūtras
ed. and tr. by Swami Tyagisananda,
Madras: Sri Ramakrishna Math, 1978

Nyāya Sūtras of Gautama, with Bhāṣya of Vātsyāyana
tr. by Ganganath Jha,
Delhi: Motilal Banarsidass, 1984

Rāmānuja,
Śrī Bhāṣya of Rāmānuja (*on Vedānta Sūtra*), (3 vols.)
ed. and tr. by R.D. Karamkar,
Poona: University of Poona Sanskrit and Prakrit Series, 1959

Vedānta-sāra of Bhagavad Rāmānuja,
ed. and tr. by V. Krishnamacharya and M.B. Narasimha Ayyangar,
Madras: The Adyar Library and Research Centre, 1979

Vedārtha-Saṁgraha of Śrī Rāmānujācārya
tr. by S.S. Raghavachar,
Mysore: Sri Ramakrishna Ashrama, 1978

The Ramayana of Valmiki (*Rāmāyaṇa*)
tr. by Makhan Lal Sen,
Delhi: Munshiram Manoharlal, 1978

Śaṁkara,
Ātmabodha—Self Knowledge of Śrī Śaṁkarācārya
tr. by Swami Nikhilananda,
Madras: Sri Ramakrishna Math, 1967
Bhāṣya on the Aitareya Upaniṣad,
Hindi transl.
Gorakhpur: Gita Press.
The Bhagavadgītā With the Commentary (*Bhāṣya*) of *Śrī Śaṁkarācārya*
tr. by A. Mahadeva Sastri,
Madras:V.R. Shastrulu & Sons, 1961
The Bṛhadāraṇyaka Upaniṣad with the Commentary (*Bhāṣya*) of *Śaṁkarācārya,*
tr. by Swami Madhvananda,
Calcutta: Advaita Ashrama, 1965
Brahma Sūtra Bhāṣya of Śrī Śaṁkarācārya
tr. by Swami Gambhirananda
Calcutta: Advaita Ashrama, 1965
Bhāṣya on Chāndogya Upaniṣad
Hindi transl.,
Gorakhpur: Gita Press
Bhāṣya on Taittirīya Upaniṣad
Hindi transl.,
Gorakhpur: Gita Press
Upadeshasāhasri of Śrī Śaṁkarācārya
tr. by Swami Jagadananda,
Madras: Sri Ramakrishna Math, 1961
Vivekachūḍāmaṇi of Śrī Śaṁkarācārya
tr. by Swami Madhavananda,
Calcutta: Advaita Ashrama, 1966
Sāṁkhya Kārikā
Hindi transl.,
Varanasi: Chawkhamba Vidya Bhavan, 1975
Śatapatha Brāhmaṇa
tr. by Julius Eggling,
Sacred Books of the East, vol. XII,
Delhi: Motilal Banarsidass, 1963

Sureśvara,
Naiṣkarmya Siddhi
tr. by S.S. Raghavachar,
Mysore: University of Mysore, 1965
Thirty Minor Upaniṣads
tr. by K. Narayanaswami Aiyar,
Delhi: Akay Book Corporation, 1979
Tirukkuraḷ
tr. by A. Chakravarti,
Madras: Diocean Press, 1953
Tulasidāsa,
Rama-carita-mānasa
Gorakhpur: Gita Press
The Upaniṣads
tr. by Swami Nikhilananda,
London: George Allen & Unwin, 1963
Vedāntasāra of Sadānanda,
tr. by Swami Nikhilananda,
Calcutta: Advaita Ashrama, 1978
Vidyāraṇya,
Pañcadaśī of Śrī Vidyāraṇya Swāmi
tr. by Swami Swahananda,
Madras: Sri Ramkrishna Math, 1967
Jīvanmuktiviveka of Vidyāraṇya
ed. and tr. by S. Subrahmanya Sastri & T.R. Srinivasa Ayyangar,
Madras: The Adyar Library and Research Centre, 1978
Viṣṇu Purāṇa
tr. by H.H. Wilson,
Calcutta: Punthi Pustak, 1972
Yājñavalkya Smṛti
Hindi transl. with *Mitākṣara Ṭikā* (two vols.),
tr. by Umesha Chandra Pandeya,
Varanasi: Chawkhamba Sanskrit Sansthan, 1983
Yoga Sūtras (of Patañjali)
tr. by Swami Vivekananda in *Raja Yoga*,
Calcutta: Advaita Ashrama, 1959

Yoga Vāsiṣṭha—Mahā Rāmāyaṇa of Vālmīki
tr. by Viharilal Mitra (4 vols.),
Delhi: Bharatiya Publishing House, 1976

Some Works on Hindu Philosophy and Ethics

Apte, V.M.
Social and Religious Life in the Gṛhya Sūtras
Bombay: The Popular Book Depot, 1954

Aurobindo, Śrī
Essays on the Gītā
Pondicherry: Sri Aurobindo Ashram, 1976
The Foundations of Indian Culture
Pondicherry: Sri Aurobindo Ashram, 1968

Banerjee, Nikunja Vihari
The Spirit of Indian Philosophy
New Delhi: Arnold Heinemann, 1974
Studies in the Dharmaśāstra of Manu
Delhi: Munshiram Manoharlal, 1980

Bhandarkar, R.G.
Vaiṣṇavism, Śaivism and Minor Religious Systems
Varanasi: Indological Book House, 1965

Bowes, Pratima
The Hindu Religious Tradition
New Delhi: Allied Publishers, 1976
Hindu Intellectual Tradition
New Delhi: Allied Publishers, 1977

Crawford, S. Cromwell
Evolution of Hindu Ethical Ideals
Calcutta: Fa. K.L. Mukhopadhyaya, 1974

The Cultural Heritage of India (4 vols.)
Calcutta: Ramkrishna Mission Institute of Culture, 1975

Chatterjee, Satishchandra
The Fundamentals of Hinduism
Calcutta: University of Calcutta, 1970

Chennakesavan, Sarasvati
A Critical Study of Hinduism
Delhi: Motilal Banarsidass, 1980

Dasgupta, Surendranath,
A History of Indian Philosophy (5 vols.)
Delhi: Motilal Banarsidass, 1975

Dasgupta, Surama
Development of Moral Philosophy in India
Bombay: Orient Longmans, 1961

Devaraja, N.K.
The Mind and Spirit of India
Delhi: Motilal Banarsidass, 1967
Hinduism and Modern Age
New Delhi: Jamia Nagar, 1975
Philosophy, Religion and Culture
Delhi: Motilal Banarsidass, 1974

Hindery, Roderick
Comparative Ethics in Hindu and Buddhist Traditions
Delhi: Motilal Banarsidass, 1978

Hiriyanna, M.
Outlines of Indian Philosophy
London: George Allen & Unwin, 1956
The Quest After Perfection
Mysore: Kavyalaya Publishers, 1952
Indian Conception of Values
Mysore, op. cit., 1975

Jhingran, Saral
The Roots of World Religions
New Delhi: Books and Books, 1982

Kane, Pandurang Vamana
History of Dharmaśāstra (5 vols.)
Poona: Bhandarkar Oriental Research Institute, 1973-75

Maitra, Sushila Kumar
The Ethics of the Hindus
Calcutta: University of Calcutta, 1963

Mckenzie, John
Hindu Ethics
Delhi: Munshiram Manoharlal, 1971

Moore, Charles A, ed.
The Indian Mind
Honolulu: Hawaii University Press, 1967

Motwani, Kewal
Manu Dharma Sastra
Madras: Ganesh & Co., 1958

Murty, K. Satchidananda
The Indian Spirit
Waltair: Andhra University Press, 1967

Pande, G.C.
Foundation of Indian Culture (2 vols.)
(vol. I *Spiritual Vision and Symbolic Forms in India*;
vol. II *Dimensions of Ancient Social History*)
New Delhi: Books and Books, 1984

Patel, Satyavrata
Hinduism: Religion and Way of Life
New Delhi: Associated Publishing House, 1980

Phillips, Maurice
The Teaching of the Vedas
New Delhi: Seema Publications, 1976

Potter, Karl H.
Presuppositions of Indian Philosophy
New Delhi: Princeton Hall of India, 1965

Radhakrishnan, S.
Indian Philosophy (2 vols.)
New York: The Macmillan Company,
London: George Allan & Unwin, 1956
Eastern Religions and Western Thought
London: Oxford University Press, 1958
The Hindu View of Life
London: Unwin Books, 1960

Ranade, R.D.
Mysticism in Maharashtra: Indian Mysticism
Delhi: Motilal Banarsidass, 1982

Singh, Balbir
The Conceptual Framework of Indian Philosophy
Delhi: The Macmillon Co. of India, 1976
Foundations of Indian Thought
New Delhi: Orient Longmans, 1975

Schweitzer, Albert
Indian Thought and Its Development
Bombay: Wilco Publishing House, 1980

Shakuntala Rao Shastry
Women in the Vedic Age
Bombay: Bharatiya Vidya Bhavan, 1951

Sharma, I.C.
Ethical Philosophies of India
London: George Allen & Unwin, 1964

Shrirama,
Social Structure and Values in Later Smṛtis
Calcutta: Indian Publications, 1972

Smart, Ninian
Doctrine and Argument in Indian Philosophy
London: George Allen & Unwin, 1964

Srinivasachari, P.N.
The Philosophy of Viśiṣṭādvaita
Madras: Adyar Library and Research Centre, 1965

Vivekananda, Swami
Selections From Swami Vivekananda
Calcutta: Advaita Ashrama, 1957
Lectures From Colombo to Almora
Calcutta: op. cit., 1956
Karma Yoga
Calcutta: op. cit., 1957

Vora, Dhairyabala Prabha
Evolution of Morals in the Epics
Bombay: Popular Book Depot., 1959

Williams, M. Monier
Hinduism
Delhi: Rare Books, 1971

Wilson, H.H.
Religions of the Hindus
Bombay: Asian Publications, 1977
Analysis of the Purāṇas
Delhi: Nag Publishers, 1979

Zaehner, R.C.
Hinduism
London: Oxford University Press, 1972
Mysticism: Sacred and Profane
London: New York: Oxford University Press, 1973

Zimmer, Heinrich
Philosophies of India
ed. by Joseph Campbell
New Jersey: Princeton University Press, 1969

Other Works Cited

Encyclopaedia of Religion and Ethics
Ed. by James Hastings
New York: Charles Scribner & Sons, Edinburgh: T & T Clark, 1954

Urban, W.M.
Valuation, Its Nature and Laws
New York: Macmillan Co., 1909

INDEX

ācāra 74-75, 205ff.; *sadācāra* 206-207
adhikāra bheda 24, 29
Advaita Vedānta 15-16, 118, 122, 126, 128, 130, 132, 141, 155
Āgamas 148
adharma (evil or sin) 37, 87, 212
ahiṁsā 9, 18, 39, 90, 172, 174, 176, 190-191, 202, 226
ālwār (s) 20, 148, 154
Āpastamba, *Dharmasūtra* 38, 50, 63, 65, 74, 77, 85, 86, 88-89, 97, 207
apūrva 33
Arthaśāstra, Kautilya 75, 86, 90, 96-97
Aryans, Aryan 5ff, 9ff, 16, 34, 38, 45-46, 74-75, 80ff, 193, 201, 203, 211
āśramas 17; *āśrama dharma* 76ff:
brahmacarya 17, 76-77;
gṛhastha 17, 76, 78ff; ideal householder 102ff, 181ff;
vānaprastha 17, 76-78;
saṁnyāsa 17, 76-78, 115
asuras 5-6, 67, 153, 154, 192
Aṣṭāvakra Saṁhitā 122, 140
Ātman (Self) 35, 116ff, 119ff, 122ff, 128, 131, 139, 193ff.
Ātman-Brahman 15, 32, 116, 119, 152, 214
avidyā 126, 128, 130, 132

Bhagavadgītā 11, 15, 19, 28, 29, 32, 35, 38-39, 114, 118, 130, 140-141, 148, 158-159, 172, 178, 180, 185ff, 187ff, 200
desireless performance of duty 38, 158-159, 187-188, 221
human perfection 178, 185-186, 192, 193
polytheism 31, 67
rituals as duty 59
sva-dharma (duty according to class) 39, 80-81, 172
theism and devotion 32-33, 150, 152, 158-159
Bhāgavata Purāṇa 64, 68, 148, 151, 160-161, 166, 180
devotion (*bhakti*) 151, 160-161, 180
Divine indwelling all 154-155,
morality 156, 158, 159, 180, 182
bhakti, the ideal nature of, 20, 151-152, 154ff., 160ff.
ekāntika 20
dāsya 162
kārpaṇya 152
Nirguṇa 162ff.
parā 151
prapatti 152
Saguṇa 162ff.
mārga 21, 29, 160
morality 152ff., 155ff.
philosophy 149ff., 152ff., 158ff.
rituals 164ff.
saints 148, 151, 162-163
sects (cults) 31, 148ff., 150, 158-159
Sūtras 33, 148
texts 25, 148-149
tradition or movement (Theistic-devotional) 20, 25, 147ff., 150ff., 153ff., 155, 159-160, 167
Brahma Sūtra 114
Brahman 9, 32, 116-117, 119ff., 122, 126, 129-130, 131, 133, 135, 151, 152, 173
knower of *Brahman* 129ff., 135ff., 142-143
Brāhmaṇas (texts) 13, 45, 46ff, 60 62; 66, 79, 91
Aitareya 48, 92
Śatapatha 83, 91
brāhmaṇas 6, 9, 60, 64, 76, 79, 82, 89, 101, 104, 154, 171-172, 182
exaltation of 82ff.
Brāhmaṇic, Brāhmanism 7, 9, 13, 14, 70, 182
Buddhism, Buddhist 2, 9, 14, 15, 122, 129, 202

cāṇḍāla (lowest caste) 85, 104, 153
caste 80ff., 85ff., 153-154, 212, 217
dāna 13, 79, 99, 103ff., 181-182
daṇḍa 11-12, 88, 172
dāsa, dasyu 6
devas, devatā (gods) 5, 31, 67-68
Dayananda Saraswati 21
Dharma 2, 10, 17, 33, 37ff., 55ff., 58ff., 74ff, 98, 99, 106, 113, 169ff., 181ff, 204, 205ff
as entire morality 37ff., 55, 70, 169ff., 175ff., 204, 205ff.
as duty or righteousness 2, 75, 101, 103-104, 105-106, 108, 114, 170, 175, 181ff., 205ff., 212